P9-DMT-048
Edward L. Dooley

THE FUTURE OF CATHOLIC CHRISTIANITY

THE FUTURE OF CATHOLIC CHRISTIANITY

Yvonne Lubbock
Bernardine Bishop
Magdalen Goffin
John Todd
T. L. Westow
Andrew Boyle
Ronald Brech
Daniel Callahan
Archbishop Thomas Roberts, S. J.
E. I. Watkin

Edited with an Introduction by
Michael de la Bedoyere

J. B. LIPPINCOTT COMPANY
Philadelphia & New York

Printed in the United States of America
Library of Congress Catalog Card No.: 66-23144

CONTENTS

Introduction

MICHAEL DE LA BEDOYERE

EIGHTEEN months ago, *Objections to Roman Catholicism* was published. Very much to my surprise, the book became a best-seller not only in Britain but in a number of other countries. I felt that this success did not depend so much on the contents of the book, or even its title, as on something quite new in serious religious publications. These had seemed to belong almost exclusively to the world of theologians and the more intelligent traditional and committed Christians. They went round and round in circles. Then something happened. An Anglican bishop, as much to his own surprise as to the surprise of the rest of us, wrote *Honest to God*. And he might have added 'Honest to Myself'. It immediately became a best-seller. Within my own Communion, something not so very dissimilar also happened. A new Pope, with few pretensions to the higher flights of theological erudition, became almost a father-figure to the world itself. I do not, of course, wish to embarrass the Bishop of Woolwich by comparing him to Pope John, except perhaps in one respect. They both broke through the barrier of precedent, the done thing, the top men. And in doing so, they enabled you and me to think for ourselves about our relations with God and our loving duties to our fellow-men. This, of course, does not mean that we are free to make our own religion; but it does mean that we are called upon to make religion our own, i.e. that we worship, pray, love our neighbour, study, not from any mere sense of compulsion, but because it is our desire to serve God, the Father of all, and get to know Him better. In so far as we do this, we achieve the freedom of the sons of God.

This, as I understand it, has been the purpose and the meaning of the four sessions of the Vatican Council, a Council which hardly could have been convened but for the faith and courage of Pope John. So immense and unwieldy an assembly of prelates could not have been able, one would have thought, to reach practical conclusions with the whole world watching and reporting the cumbersome, but partially democratic, system of discussion and voting. Yet it succeeded and, in succeeding, it indirectly fathered, first *Objections*, and now *The Future of Catholic Christianity*.

May I be honest and say that, in my view, *The Future of Catholic Christianity* is an infinitely better and more serious book than *Objections*. It is made up of ten essays, six of which may be called critical, in greater or less degree, of the traditions and present customs of the Church in its day-to-day work. It is, of course, obvious that the spirit and teaching of the Council cannot 're-form' the Church from one day to the next. It is, for example, a fact that even in European countries and in America, the vast majority of Catholics know very little of the work of the Council. Indeed, the only means of communication has so far been through the press, religious or secular. And this has only touched the highlights. It will take a great deal of time before the 'man in the pew' can understand and learn what the Council Fathers have decided, put forward and implemented. This will come about through the slow work of the bishops and priests. Nor will it be readily accepted, for religious traditions and customs die hard. The sense of freedom which derives, however vaguely and superficially, from the spirit and acts of the Council, is by no means to the taste of the millions accustomed from the earliest years to live their religious life according to long laid-down commandments and 'black and white' precisions. I doubt whether any of us, however well educated, can entirely escape a sense of uncertainty and bewilderment. Yet this is precisely the challenge which the Council puts to us all. Having lived so long in swaddling clothes, we fear the challenge of the 'Light immortal, light divine, visit thou these hearts of thine, and our inmost being fill'. Never were those words more needed than today when uncertainties, changes, new vistas, new worlds pour over mankind for good or evil.

The Future of Catholic Christianity seeks to suggest and describe ideas and pointers towards the way ahead. The essays, however, do not derive from any concerted plan. I have tried, rather, to invite a number of writers, nearly all of whom are friends of mine, to put on paper their hopes, their fears, their ideas. Their views are very various. The order in which they appear is roughly based on the length of their essays—the shorter ones set between the longer ones, for ease of reading. I feel particularly honoured by having been able to include the last and the longest of the essays, Mr E. I. Watkin's *The Wisdom of the Spirit*. I have known and admired his writings for many, many years, and I have always believed that he is the deepest Catholic thinker writing in the English tongue. In this collection of essays Mr Watkin stands alone in that his views challenge the views of all the other contributors. He looks back, seeking truth, beauty, and goodness, in a word, God, in the mystical approach and the baroque beauty and richness of the past. Very different indeed is *The Broken Pitcher: An Essay on the Present Christian Crisis,* by Magdalen Goffin, the daughter of Mr Watkin. Her summing up might be the Church's 'infallibility of vital direction'. One of the shorter essays which I found to be especially helpful was Mr Westow's *The Heart of Unity*, the best and clearest practical explanation of genuine 'Unity' that I have read. Andrew Boyle and John M. Todd, both closely connected with *Search* which I founded and edit, stress the importance of love and freedom, and Bernardine Bishop writes with great understanding and common sense on the feminine role in the Church. This leaves three essays that might be called 'specialist'. The first (and technically the most important of all) is Mr Ronald Brech's *Economic Planning for the Church*. This is a 'must' for the administrators of any church organisation, whether lay or clerical. Next I note Mr Daniel Callahan's *Liberal Catholicism in America*, a subject-matter steadily increasing in importance about which we in this country know far too little. Here perhaps is the spear-head of the future. I need hardly say how happy I am to have persuaded Archbishop Roberts to contribute once again, and this time with a 'Dialogue between Conscience and Coercion', entitled *Quaker Marriage*. As always, the Archbishop takes the largest and the deepest view, not least on the contraception question. And I want specially to commend to your attention the first of the essays, and for me the most important, Yvonne Lubbock's. Her last lines are a quotation from the Anglican divine William Law: "Begin to search and dig in thine own field for this pearl of eternity that lies hidden in it; it cannot cost thee too much, nor canst thou buy it too dear, for it is *all*; and when thou hast found it thou wilt know that all which thou hast sold or given away for it is as mere a nothing as a bubble upon the water."

The future of Catholic Christianity? It is clear that the Vatican Council has created a fresh Catholic Christian situation. To a person like myself, who for some thirty years edited the *Catholic Herald*, the change which the Council has made is greater than may appear to the majority of Catholics. One sought, even in those years, to gain areas of greater Catholic Christian freedom. For example, it seemed to me obvious that there should be a close relation between the separated Communions who sought to serve God in their different ways, and I think I was the first person in Britain to publicise in a big way the annual Church Unity Octave. Each year, by pictures and articles, I tried to bring to the readers of the *Catholic Herald* a sense of the closeness between Roman Catholics, Anglicans and the Free Churches in their common service of God. Today, all this is taken for granted and indeed goes a good deal further than was possible in the thirties and forties. The point I want to make is: why was this an original idea? Why did it not strike everyone else? We know today that the Council has promoted ecumenism, and promoted it in a way that goes far beyond what could be suggested in those days in a Roman Catholic journal. Doubtless, the time factor is important, but it is only important because of something fundamentally wrong in the outlook of the Church, the bishops, the clergy. If it is right today that there exists this close relation between Christian Communions, why was it wrong or at least frowned upon only a few years ago? One could, of course, multiply examples of this fear of change, whether in Roman Catholic or other Communions. Had it not been for the saintly Pope John we should still find ourselves today in much the same position as I was when I tried to do what I could to bring Communions closer together in the love and service of Our Lord.

The Vatican Council has made changes infinitely greater than the changes I was able to suggest as a Catholic journalist, always likely to be called up by a bishop for my extravagant and dangerous views, petty though they seem in retrospect. The obvious danger today is that the work of the Council should become petrified, just as the post-Reformation Catholicity became petrified. One recalls the Modernist era when the deeper Catholic thinkers found themselves face to face with this religious petrification. Tragically, a number of them, like Loisy and even the deeply Catholic Tyrrell, turned away from the Faith itself or were condemned out of hand.

I refer to all this because it is quite certain that the great work of the Vatican Council will not be the last word in Catholic life and thought. We are not at the end of a chapter, but at the beginning of a new chapter. And this is even more the case than it ever was in the past. The future of Catholic Christianity will see changes probably greater than any in the past. It must be so because this twentieth-century world is changing more rapidly than anything the world has known in the past. The eternal, revealed truths of the Church will not change, but they will need to fit themselves to stupendous changes which the coming decades will see. If we study the history of the Church, not only in its truth and beauty, but in its errors, cruelties, its outdated narrow-mindedness, we shall take it for granted that the Vatican Council and any subsequent Council will undo as much as it will create for the human race of tomorrow. How little, for example, do most of us know about the spiritual side of those we glibly think of as pagans? How little do we know today of the mental and psychological problems born of our present human relationships? One could multiply indefinitely the examples of the spiritual and moral dilemmas with which the world—and the Church—of tomorrow will be concerned if they face the realities of human life. It is hard not to think that, so far, and taking into account the great efforts of the Vatican Council, the Church is still a very long way from the anguish and suffering which is still the lot of the greater part of mankind today.

In a sense, the work of the Council was not difficult, though it necessarily fell short of much that might have been studied and brought to our world's attention. The next phase is surely clear. It is to maintain the impetus of Catholic and Christian reform, from Rome, from the Bishops, from the clergy, from the people, with an eye not only on Catholic Christianity in its 'sacristy' outlook, but even more on the men and women of the world, our brothers and sisters in God. We could do with a great deal less triumphalism and juridicism and a great deal more study of mankind and its problems from both the spiritual and the temporal angle.

These pages of *The Future of Catholic Christianity* are at most 'Chapter One'—a very small beginning, hardly as yet in grips with the world's future. May they, however, prove to be a stepping stone to a more Christian future.

MICHAEL DE LA BEDOYERE
Edenbridge, January 1966

Belief is Being

Thoughts on the Survival of Christian Belief

YVONNE LUBBOCK

IT is an interesting fact that in a world which is generally acknowledged to be growing always less religious, a really provocative book on Christianity, or even on Roman Catholicism with its less wide appeal, can become a best-seller. It may be said that works like *Honest to God* and *Objections to Roman Catholicism* would have a considerable appeal for critics of Christianity and Roman Catholicism respectively who positively enjoy seeing the weaknesses of one or other exposed in forthright terms. But do people buy books for the malicious kick they can get out of them when this pleasure can be had without cost from any public library? It is far more likely that the sale of these two particular works is due to the great interest in religion which, despite a widespread increase of unbelief, still persists in a large number of people who are deeply concerned to find one that will satisfy their souls without doing too much violence to their intellects.

But what is wrong with Christianity—especially with Roman Catholicism with which I am here chiefly concerned—that these religiously inclined people cannot accept it as it is presented to them by the Churches? We are reminded of the remark of Matthew Arnold: 'At the present moment two things about the Christian religion must surely be clear to anybody with eyes in his head. One is, that men cannot do without it; the other that they cannot do with it as it is.' The latter half of this statement is even truer now than it was in his day. But before we can begin to discover reasons for this we should start with fundamentals and decide what we mean by religion *per se*. Although the word is seldom defined in all the religious discussions which are so common today, many 'believers' assume that whatever it may be it is inevitably 'a good thing'. But if we reflect at all we realise that it is never something which goes floating about by itself detached from the subjective element in men; and that it is therefore bound to issue in good or bad thoughts according to a man's character and the stage of spiritual and intellectual development he has reached. We have only to consider the history of Christianity with its frequent bloodshed, its massacres, tortures and persecutions to understand that any religion is at the mercy of its adherents and that also 'When religion is in the hands of the mere natural man, he is always the worse for it; it adds a bad heat to his own dark fires and helps to inflame his four elements of selfishness, envy, pride and wrath'.[1]

It is clear that when we identify our own dark fires with religion we are caught up in a vicious circle. We drag

[1] William Law, *Christian Regeneration.*

down religion and are in turn dragged down by the conception we have of it. But what do we mean by religion? We have to distinguish between religion *per se* and systems of religion with their beliefs and practices, and to find a statement as to the nature of religion in itself that would be accepted by the majority of men and women. I suggest as a definition that 'Religion is belief in an unseen power superior to man, an invisible and different order of being to which he must adjust himself if he wishes to attain to the supreme good; with this belief there is also a desire to enter into communication with this "power" '.[1]

It is the individual relationship between man and this unseen power which Jews, Christians and Muslims call God that is the essence of religion proper. And according to the conception that the creature has of his Creator so will a man's religion tend either to nurture and bring out all that is best in him, to raise him up, or to foster and give expression to the darker sides of his nature, to drag him down. Thus, totally unworthy conceptions of God can move a man to strange beliefs—beliefs so utterly incompatible with anything other than the sub-human that it is not surprising to hear the humanist say that only the best and wisest of mankind can be trusted with religion, and that a great number of men, satisfied that they are serving God when they are virtually denying him, are blinded to the harm that they do in his name. There can be little doubt that it is the unworthy conception of God that has been allowed to persist in much Christian teaching that has done most to bring Christianity into disrepute. Other contributory factors will emerge in the course of this chapter.

[1] A composite definition taken from William James and from A. C. Haddon. See J. D. Unwin, *Sex and Culture*, p. 436, O.U.P., 1934.

But provided that a man is aware of all the dangers of religion and that he seeks primarily his own regeneration through the action of the Holy Spirit—that 'Holy Ghost (who) moveth ne'er a thing against charity, for if he did he would be contrary to his own self, for he is all charity' —it is in this individual relationship with God that the human soul will find the means to transcend the perils arising from its own dark fires. This communication between the 'I' and the 'Thou' is as necessary to a man's spiritual growth as the air he breathes and the food he eats are to his body. It is unmediated in the sense that no Church or priesthood intervenes in the relationship, although in another sense mediated since knowledge of God must always reach a man through his human limitations. This is the most real and fundamental factor in a man's life and can therefore be the most transforming and enduring of ties, stronger than any other, and this could continue if every organised system of religion, every ecclesiastical building with every form of ritual enacted therein were to be swept away. *Religare* means to bind, and this binding tie is the root of all real religion, and persists as a kind of heavenly umbilical cord between the Author of all being and every one of his praying creatures.

The actual basis, then, of religion is something 'infinitely simple', as Rilke said, 'an orientation of the heart'. How could it not have this fundamental essence since religion must be for all men and the vast majority are unsophisticated, artless beings? It is a constant and just reproach against the Church that she has endlessly complicated something that should be essentially simple. Yet we must recognise that religion cannot be confined to its essence, to an individual relationship between the human and the divine. For the Christian, with whom I am here concerned, will be faced with the fact of Christianity as a revealed religion: with the contents of the Bible and the whole corpus of Christian belief. Granted perception and honesty, he will discover that a religion of the Spirit cannot provide an invariably valid authority in matters of belief and in the interpretation of the Scriptures, not indeed because the Spirit is not to be trusted, but because of the human tendency to self-deception which can always lead to a man's seeing only his own face at the bottom of the well.[1] The Christian *ipso facto* has to hold fast to revelation.

But much depends upon our understanding of revelation, and two different views will have to be considered later. For the moment it suffices to say that although it is in one sense something which is imposed upon a man from outside himself, yet at the same time if he is spiritually alive and seeks for his regeneration by the Christian truth, he knows that in order to be possessed by this truth he has to bring to it a contribution of his own, that what is only notional may thereby be transmuted into something real, that it may become revelation for him. There has to be a personal participation of the knower in all acts of understanding. 'Into every act of knowing,' writes Professor Michael Polanyi, 'there must enter a contribution of the person himself, and this co-efficient is a vital component of his knowledge.'[2] It is only belief based on this act of unification between himself and the truth which has the power to change a man. And in this sense belief is being.

It is the exact nature of belief in religious truth which

[1] See G. Tyrell, *Christianity at the Crossroads*, p. 49, Allen & Unwin, 1963.

[2] *Personal Knowledge*, Preface, Routledge & Kegan Paul, 1958.

presents the greatest problem for the world today. 'We must make allowances,' writes T. S. Eliot, 'for differences in the emotional quality of believing not only between persons of different occupation, such as the philosopher and the poet, but different periods of time.'[1] Furthermore if, as is generally accepted, no two people looking at the most ordinary commodities of life see them identically, how much truer it must be that, even within the bounds of orthodoxy, each religious doctrine is inevitably assimilated differently by each individual. How could it be otherwise when we know that 'Truth must endue each individual on the basis of his own thought'?[2] All religious truth has two aspects. There will always be the primary meeting of a religious proposition by the individual soul when it asks, 'What does this mean for me?' and the ultimate question, 'What does this mean in itself?' which no man can fully answer. It is true, as Blondel remarks:

> '... Modern thought ... considers the notion of immanence as the very condition of philosophising ... the idea, which is at bottom perfectly true, that nothing can enter into a man's mind which does not come out of him and correspond in some way to a need for development, and that there is nothing in the nature of historical or traditional teaching or obligation imposed from without which counts for him ... unless it is in some sort autonomous and autochthonous.[3] On the other hand, nothing is Christian or Catholic unless it is ... strictly supernatural, i.e., beyond the power of

[1] 'Shakespeare and the Stoicism of Seneca', from *Selected Essays*, Faber, 1932.

[2] St Severus of Antioch.

[3] We are to understand that Blondel does not commit himself without reserve to the 'notion of immanence'.

man to discover for himself and yet imposed on his thought and on his will.'[1]

A full, living religion demands a prudent recognition of these two aspects. On the one hand, a religion of immanence alone tends to sink to the level of a merely ethical philosophy, to become secularised to the point of ceasing to be a religion. Religious truth then no longer makes any demands upon a man; it does not require him to 'suffer the divine', to believe in order to understand. On the other hand, a religion of strict supernaturalism divorced from the element of immanence results in a petrifaction of dogma in a system so transcendental and alien to men that it fails to impinge on their minds and hearts, thus discouraging interest in the truth and giving rise to an apathy which may lead to the rejection of the whole system.

Difficulties beset the individual not only when he seeks to discover Christian truths for himself but also when he finds them in institutional Christianity. He knows that but for the Church he would have no framework in which to pursue his search, and that no Christian can lightly dismiss what has been the constant Christian experience for well-nigh two millennia. Yet he sees too that the Church demands only a passive acceptance of her doctrines, although, as Blondel points out, 'unless each believer brought his own little contribution to the common life, the organism would not be fully alive'.[2] It must certainly be asked whether we have been encouraged by the *magisterium* to work our passage in the ark of salvation by transmuting for ourselves the merely

[1] Blondel, *Letter on Apologetics, and History and Dogma*, Texts presented by Alexander Dru and Illtyd Trethowan, pp. 151–52, Harvill Press, 1964.

[2] *Ibid.*, p. 277.

notional into the real. 'From the point of view of notional knowledge on which the "system" (Thomism) takes its stand,' writes Blondel to Laberthonnière, 'that passivism (i.e., a purely receptive idea of knowledge) is false and fatal.' Yet he continues, '... What is false and bad about the notional knowledge ... does not alter the fact that where real knowledge is concerned there is an essential moral and supernatural truth in the idea of the *pati divina et omnia*'.[1] Here we are brought to what should be the two inalienable functions of the Christian believer; the continual search for a greater individual understanding of Christian truth whilst suffering those things divine which lie beyond human reason.

The lack of encouragement by the Church and our own failure to bring more vital contributions to the common life of belief have indeed resulted in the organism's being less alive and spiritual than it might otherwise be. But these deficiencies themselves have their source in a view of the *depositum fidei* as a kind of sacred stone thrown from heaven into an alien land. 'How strange,' writes Blondel, 'to find the acme of orthodoxy in assertions such as these: "The Church does not search for the truth; she has nothing to learn; a Church which still has something to discover is not the Church to which Jesus Christ has taught all that he learnt from his Father". So the sacred deposit of faith is simply an aerolith to be preserved in a glass case from a sacrilegious curiosity.'[2]

[1] *Op. cit.*, p. 65. This is to be understood as 'To experience in passivity the operation of God and whatever he communicates'.

[2] *Ibid.*, p. 278. This quotation resembles the remarks of Tillich when rejecting the supranaturalistic method of correlation between doctrine and the believer: 'The supranaturalistic ... takes the Christian message to be a sum of revealed truths which have fallen into the human situation like strange bodies from a strange world. No mediation to the human situation is possible....' (*Systematic Theology*, vol. I, p. 72, Nisbet, 1960 edition.)

It is this 'sacred stone' quality attaching itself to so much of the Church's teaching which has been largely responsible not only for the widespread rejection of Christianity generally but for the particular revolt against the idea of the supernatural so common today and which has resulted in an exclusive emphasis on immanence throughout the world outside Catholic orthodoxy (whether Roman or Anglican). We appear now to be faced with the alternatives of either a sacred stone which retains the transcendent essence of Christian truth but which fails to impinge on the modern mentality; or of a liberal thought which does so impinge but at the cost of voiding the Christian religion of its inalienable essence of transcendence. The power of Christian truth, already attenuated, will melt away once it is severed in men's minds from its transcendent source; and it is unrealistic to suppose that this deprivation can lead to anything but the ultimate extinction of the Christian religion however numerous the pseudo-Christian philosophies to which such a dispossession may give rise. For when we deny the transcendent character of Christian truth it is the existence of the Unconditional that we are rejecting; and without this the whole web of our belief becomes unravelled like a textile with insecurely fastened threads. It is perfectly true that religious formulations which no longer have any meaning for us have in fact ceased to exist as far as we are concerned. But that does not prove that supernatural truths have no meaning in themselves, but simply that they have not become truly incarnate, have not assumed the flesh of human ideas which a man can understand, nor been related to real human needs but only to a world of piety where faith is demanded in the unintelligible. It seems that petrifaction is virtually as sure a means of destroying the power of Christian truth as is deliquescence; and the sacred stone quality of Catholic dogma provides an illustration of the parable of the talents. The Church has wrapped up truths in a concealing, swaddling napkin, preserving as something static, unproductive and lifeless that which invested with meaning would bring to men a more abundant life. For true belief is being.

That man is an inhabitant of two worlds is at once his glory and his anguish, the source of his *grandeur* and his *misère*. He cannot attain the truths of one world by employing the criteria of the other; for the spiritual world which surrounds him transcends his natural understanding, and he is part of the physical world where the test of truth is correspondence with established fact and where probability has a major influence in more doubtful cases. But this test and this probability are powerless in the verification of supernatural truth. 'Since supernatural reality (if there is any),' remarks Professor Barrows Dunham, 'never gets directly perceived, and since thus comparison fails, tradition or authority or general consent tend to replace correspondence as the test of truth. Accordingly, Vincent's [St Vincent of Lerin's] criteria' [that which has been believed everywhere, always and by all] 'suit the supernatural order as aptly as scientific method suits the natural order.'[1]

But it is obvious that no one outside the Church would accept St Vincent's criteria of truth, as it could well be said that in the Church belief in man's origin from a single pair, the cosmogony of Genesis and in a pre-Copernican system continued long after science had proved her teaching upon these matters wrong. And I think that even by those inside the Church, these criteria cannot be held as being rigidly exact, for there never was a time since the coming of Christ when there was

[1] *Heroes and Heretics*, p. 166, Knopf, New York, 1964.

entire unity of belief. We know that the disciples themselves often failed to understand his teaching, and that there was disagreement amongst the Apostles even before the manifold heresies arose.

But in spite of all this there has been, broadly speaking, a general *consensus fidelium* which formed a basis of unity of belief and which, through the decisions of the Councils, ensured the stability of the Church. It is interesting, however, to note that during the Arian controversies, it was the laity, according to Newman, who, rather than the episcopate, preserved the doctrine of the Incarnation.

> '... In that time of immense confusion the divine dogma of our Lord's divinity was proclaimed, enforced, maintained, and (humanly speaking) preserved far more by the *Ecclesia docta* than by the *Ecclesia docens* [the Church taught and the Church teaching]; that the body of the episcopate was unfaithful to its commission, while the body of the laity was faithful to its baptism; that at one time the Pope, at other times the patriarchal, metropolitan, and other great sees, at other times general councils, said what they should not have said, or did what obscured and compromised revealed truth; while, on the other hand, it was the Christian people who, under Providence, were the ecclesiastical strength of Athanasius, Hilary, Eusebius of Vercelli, and other great solitary confessors who would have failed without them.'[1]

Indeed, Dom Paul Grammont, O.S.B., and Dom Philibert Zobel, O.S.B., tell us that in the Orthodox Church 'the decisions of Councils are only authoritative in so far as they are received by the whole body of the

[1] *On Consulting the Faithful in Matters of Doctrine.*

Church'.[1] But although this is confirmed by writers on the Orthodox Church, there is no information as to what machinery exists by which the faithful might make known their dissent. However that may be, it would seem that in the *consensus fidelium* in both Roman and Orthodox Churches, *Viribus unitis docet discendo et discit docendo semper.*[2]

Before any more can be said about belief, two views of revelation must be mentioned. Until the coming of Vatican Council II, the idea of revelation which appeared to be dominant in the Church was of some mysterious factor working in an incomprehensible unilateral manner, divorced from men's thought and being, much as if the heavens were suddenly rent asunder and through a gap in the clouds God spoke by means of a golden megaphone to his chosen recorders. Plonk! the revelation has dropped from the skies. The appointed scribes scribble it upon the sacred stone. The clouds draw together again and God withdraws his mighty megaphone until such time as he wishes to make another proclamation.

It is this idea of revelation which the world today sees as a story which people might one day have believed but which is now outmoded and incredible. The unbeliever suspects that a one-sided revelation working so incomprehensibly without human co-operation—apart from the actual recording of a mysterious voice—is merely an archaic and esoteric invention of the Church

[1] *Problems of Authority*, ed. John Todd, p. 91, Darton, Longmans & Todd, 1962.

[2] Blondel, *op. cit.*, p. 278. Blondel himself believed that 'divine assistance ensures the normal indefectible exercise of this essential function'. The Latin quotation can be translated as 'With combined strength it [the *consensus fidelium*] always teaches by learning and learns by teaching'.

by which she can foist on the credulous beliefs which cannot be substantiated and which are designed to suit her own ends. That this superficial dismissal of revelation is the result more of a psychological reaction than dispassionate thought is obvious. But hasn't the Church herself been largely responsible for this psychological block? And, if a more realistic account were given of revelation would it be so widely rejected?

We know that God makes himself known to the world through man, however inadequate as his instrument. There is no unmediated divine word; and throughout history from time to time there have been prophets the best of whom were men open to God's word and with a deeper wisdom and more penetrating vision than that of their fellow-men, and who have claimed to speak in God's name. But revelation is never merely man's discovery although he must participate in it. This is borne out in the history of the Jewish people where we see how progressive that revelation was; how the anthropomorphic tribal Deity was at first all that they could understand, and how through a succession of great prophets God was gradually revealed as a God who desired mercy and the sacrifice of a contrite heart.

The Church hitherto has been reluctant to afford man his true nature as a child of God. She allows that man co-operates with God in the making of a family; indeed it suits her purpose to use this fact as an argument against the practice of contraception; but the *magisterium* has never explicitly taught that man co-operates with God also in the matter of revelation by the exercise of a responsible human judgment. With the coming of Vatican Council II, however, we find that Cardinals Meyer and Jaeger conceive of revelation as divine inspiration making use of human instruments, as God's self-disclosure through human beings and human history; and that Cardinal Döpfner dismisses the idea that revelation is a mere collection of propositions delivered by Christ to the Apostles and handed down to us through the apostolic succession and the teaching of the Church.

Karl Barth teaches that the Christian revelation is to be treated as a revelation that must continually occur afresh in relation to men, in order that it may indeed be revelation to them. It must never become a 'revealed state' which men can seize and control as they please. It is always an event by which they learn to see . . . and not something given to them once for all; it becomes God's Word for them whenever it becomes revelation for them through the workings of the Holy Spirit in them according to God's pleasure.[1]

Although its two-fold character explains why revelation will always be partial and incomplete in a world of human instruments, it might be thought that with the coming of Christ we should have received more decisive words. But we are not to expect 'lucid declarations addressed to the intelligence', for that would be 'to ignore the fact that what Jesus desired and obtained was not elucidated like a theological theme, but to be loved above all things'.[2] His primary mission, as Fr Gabriel Moran, F.S.C., reminds us, 'was not the bringing of a doctrine but who was himself the Way, the Truth and the Life'.[3]

The culmination of the progressive self-revelation of God having occurred with the appearance of the God-man Jesus, revelation comes to a close. Yet in another

[1] See *Church Dogmatics,* I, 1, p. 132; and IV, 2, p. 313, and H. Hartwell, *The Theology of Karl Barth*, p. 34, Duckworth, 1964. (It must be added, however, that Barth denies any co-operation by men in revelation. It is therefore hard to understand how the Holy Spirit can work in men's hearts and minds.)

[2] Blondel, *op. cit.*, p. 278.

[3] *Continuum*, Autumn, 1963.

sense it must and will continue till the end of the world, for the journey of a man towards God is a history of God's revelation to the individual soul. As Père Bouillard, S.J., tells us,

> 'God reveals himself to each of us at the heart of the act of faith which he himself determines.... Our awareness of this revelation has the character of a direct and personal apprehension ... of a supernatural perception analogous to mystical knowledge. Many theologians admit today that it is this experience of God on which the certainty of our faith is founded.'[1]

It is this experience which has the deepest, most compelling authority for men, and is the true basis of faith for them as it was for St Peter on whose living experience the Church was founded.

This personal apprehension is, however, in direct conflict with the idea of a static 'revealed state' which is the ever present danger not only in our attitude to religious formulations but in the formulations themselves. The Church has tried to provide that stability which all men crave by presenting Christian truths in the same language for hundreds of years. But this is not the kind of stability that men need. For the words in which Christian truth is formulated tend with time to obscure the living quality of the Christian experience they sought to contain. Every doctrine bears the mark of the age of its definition, the slant against the heresies which necessitated its statement in particular categories and tendentious terms. Admittedly, the Church has to 'preserve' doctrine (though the very word suggests the pickling of something from which life has departed); but her mission is also to impart the truth to men and thereby bring them to eternal life. Men when they cry for bread which

[1] *Logique de la Foi*, quoted in *Downside Review*, July 1964.

will nourish them cannot be content with a stone, however sacred. Formulations of truth which use language, categories and terms that have lost their life and meaning have themselves *ipso facto* lost their power and usefulness as a vehicle of truth to the world today. They present a stumbling-block to a faith seeking understanding and lead a man to suppose that they can have no power to affect his life and thought, and that he therefore loses nothing by remaining content with a passive, notional belief. Yet if it be true that truth is not something which we possess as if it were altogether separate from our experience but rather something by which we have to be possessed, it is clear that the measure of such a possession will depend upon the degree of meaning this truth has for us.

But we read in *The Constitution on the Church of Vatican Council II* that 'definitions . . . are justly styled irreformable'.[1] The argument for this opinion, which he shares, is given by Fr George Tavard:

> 'The Church has canonised dogmas because it has appeared at various periods of the faith that a certain formulation would preserve the reality of the Christian experience in its totality, whilst another formulation would be, if not incorrect or false, at least dangerous for our understanding of Christian realities. To clothe the invisible in visible words, the ineffable in human phrases, the eternal in languages that are born, live and die, is the glory and the inherent limitation of dogma. Because this is the task of the Church, which is ultimately guided by the Holy Spirit, *dogmatic formulations, once adopted by the Church, lie beyond reform*; the languages used can become dead, the categories borrowed can lose their

[1] p. 113.

living meaning, whereas the substance intended by the Church when the definition was formulated remains ever the same, immutable like the rock on which the Church is built.'[1]

The substance appears, in Fr Tavard's view, to be for ever wedded to its formulation even though this partner in the marriage may long since have become a corpse. This not only flatly contradicts Pope John's opinion that 'the substance of doctrine is one thing, the way in which it is expressed is another', but suggests that Christian experience is something static that took place once and for all and is never to be enriched, enlarged, enlightened.

We know that in a world preponderantly humanistic, men have to be changed in order to be able to accept truth which lies beyond their human nature fully to understand; but we know also that it is only the truth itself which has the power to effect this conversion. There is here a virtuous circle into which it is hard for a man to penetrate, and he needs every help which can be given him by the Church in her selection of language, categories and terms in which she endeavours to communicate eternal truth in transient form. No selection can have permanency. The definitions—the words themselves—which have in some cases been with us for some 1,500 years—no longer convey the living substance; but even should a better way of presentation be found and adopted, there is no reason to suppose that its greater adequacy would survive any longer than did the original definitions. Our Christian experience is a continual revelation and the language in which it is expressed must be constantly reflecting this progression whilst still preserving continuity with the past. Only so can truth be a living reality for the world of today.

[1] *Continuum*, vol. 1, no. 3, Autumn 1963. (Italics mine.)

All true Christian belief depends upon the incarnational character of Christian doctrine. It is, generally speaking, by providing an answer to the question 'What is the meaning of this truth for men of the present day?' —an answer in which the questioner can himself participate—that theology can best encourage a love of the great Christian truths. The doctrine of the Trinity we know once exercised an immense attraction just because men saw in it something of inestimable value to themselves, some living quality in its truth. Of this, the Reverend H. A. Williams writes:

> 'I suspect that the doctrine of the Trinity was felt to meet two threats to which every human being is subject . . . each of which, if fully implemented, would destroy us . . . [that it] was felt as something like a promise or guarantee that these two threats would be finally overcome. So that the cry of the heart, "I am not made for destruction", was felt to be symbolised or schematised in the doctrine of the Three in One. The two threats are the threat of isolation, on the one hand, and of absorption, on the other. Each is a potential murderer . . . Extermination, the triumph of non-being over being . . .
>
> '. . . The threat of isolation is overcome because the One God is described as being eternally in relation . . . Where there is relatedness there can be no aloneness. At the same time the opposite threat of absorption is met and vanquished. The persons of the Godhead are for ever distinct and unconfused. The Son and the Spirit cannot be absorbed into the Father . . . The overcoming of this threat of destruction, of non-being in its two forms, is something after which men hunger and thirst, as their behaviour clearly shows . . . This surely, is the compelling attraction of Trinitarian doc-

trine, which makes it a matter of living faith and ultimate concern.'[1]

Here, it seems that transcendent truth has become incarnate as a living reality for men by its fundamental relation to their being. What has arisen from truths implicit in the gospels is now seen to be indeed good news and not just an incomprehensible mathematical conundrum above human understanding.

But it is not only the doctrine of the Trinity which in its bare statement leaves the believer in a condition of purely notional belief. The greatest Christian truth of all, that of the Incarnation, is more obscured than any other by the categories, terms and language used in its definition. We know that the object of the definition was to place signposts at all the roads which are barred to faith seeking understanding. 'No Entry', 'No Through Road' signs warn us from the heretical paths which the *consensus fidelium* has rejected as leading to barren deserts. But what is thus safeguarded and never to be invalidated as a basis of further Christian experience gives us a Christology which is not only insufficient but which itself creates insuperable problems. A serious attempt to provide one that would reach the world today has been made by Tillich; and it is in an endeavour to bring this more into line with Catholic teaching that Fr George Tavard has occasion to describe the way in which a post-Chalcedonian Christology could be developed which, although by-passing the philosophical and psychological problems raised by the Chalcedonian definition, would yet not be unorthodox but scriptural and grounded in the patristic tradition. The urgent need for a new Christology will, I hope, excuse the

[1] *The True Wilderness*, pp. 124, 126 and 127, Constable, 1965.

length of my quotation. 'Oscar Cullmann,' writes Fr Tavard,

'shows that . . . Jesus claimed the title of *the Man* more definitely than any other . . . St Paul developed the idea of *the Man* and identified "the heavenly Man", "the second Adam", "the second Man" with the concrete Jesus. *The Man* is "from heaven". He is spiritual as contrasted with the first Adam who was earthy. He appeared on earth as Jesus of Nazareth.

'These and other texts of the New Testament impose the following conclusion: The early Church initiated a Christology in which Jesus was considered to be the incarnation of a pre-existing celestial Man. In spite of its scriptural basis (or perhaps largely because of its biblical categories), this Christology gradually disappeared in Greek territory. Yet Cullmann believes that the Christology of St Ireneaus of Lyons is a direct offshoot: "His entire Christology," says Cullmann, "is dominated by the contrast between Adam and Christ, and he makes the only attempt in the whole history of doctrine to build a Christology on the concept *Man*."[1]

'*The Man*, the "celestial Man" is equal with God (Phil. ii. 6). A post-Nicaean Christology that would take this as a scriptural basis would have to describe the Three Persons as the Father, the Man, and the Spirit. In examining the meaning of "the Man", it might follow the patristic line of thought according to which man's essence is to be the image, the *eikon*, of God. The second Person, the Man-God, is the perfect image of the Father, of whom he is eternally born. It is precisely that which makes him the pre-

[1] Oscar Cullmann, *The Christology of the New Testament*, p. 189.

existent Man. To be a man on earth consists in being destined to imitate this Man, in being created an image of God. All men are types of this eternal archetype, of the Image of the Father, of *the Man*. Mankind is thought out in God neither as a collection of individual creatures, nor even as creaturely in the first place. *The Man* is God himself, the Son. Mankind is *man*kind only by participation in the divine likeness, in the divine Man.

'A post-Chalcedonian Christology can be developed along these lines. What the Council of Chalcedon, using a Greek vocabulary, called the two natures, divine and human, of Christ, we should call the two humanities of Jesus: the divine humanity, which is God himself, the eternal Exemplar of all images of God; and the creaturely humanity, in whose shape the divine Humanity appeared on earth at a given moment of history. These two are one . . . by way of exemplarity; the creaturely humanity of Jesus is the perfect created likeness of the divine Man. In order to avoid Nestorian implications, we should not speak of Jesus as two men, but as two humanities—divine and human—in one man, the pre-existent divine Man. In order to avoid Monophysite misunderstandings, we should insist on the integrity of the creaturely humanity assumed by the eternal Man, "in all things like his brethren" (Heb. ii. 17). The philosophical difficulty of explaining the co-existence of two natures in Christ, and the psychological problem raised by the co-existence of a human psyche with a divine knowledge might both be by-passed; the Exemplar itself is, eternally so, divine and yet human, the divine Man. This could conceivably open the door to a solution of the ever-recurrent problem of the knowledge of Christ.'

In a footnote quoted from Cullmann we read:

'It [this Christology] would have the advantage of putting the logically insoluble problem of the two natures of Christ on a level where a solution becomes visible; the pre-existent Son of Man, who is with God already at the very beginning and exists with him as his image, is *by his very nature* divine Man. From this point of view the whole toilsome discussion which dominated the earlier Christological controversies actually becomes superfluous.'[1]

Fr Tavard concludes by saying,

'Such a Christology would be scriptural. It would be seriously grounded in the patristic tradition. By respecting the relation of the divine and the human in Christ, which the Council of Chalcedon defined, it would be in keeping with Catholic orthodoxy.'[2]

It was Irenaeus who gave a positive value of its own to Christ's full manhood by developing a doctrine of the celestial Man: the Christ who not only expresses God in time, but sums up humanity in himself. As Athanasius was later to say, 'He was made what we are that he might make us what he is himself'.

'If we want to be understood when we speak of the Christ,' says Fr Tavard, 'we should use another problematic than that of the fifth century.' But whether the Christian truth of the Incarnation can be expressed in categories other than those of nature and person 'canonised by the Council of Chalcedon' is a matter upon which an ordinary layman without theological training is not competent to judge. To many, I think, the great

[1] Cullmann, *op. cit.*, p. 192.

[2] George Tavard, *Paul Tillich and the Christian Message*, pp. 170–72, Burns & Oates, 1961.

virtue of this Christology will lie in the emphasis placed upon Christ's humanity—an emphasis which will make far readier appeal to the non-Christian than the repellent cardboard humanity given him by Catholic manuals of piety. For although the Church tells us in so many words that Christ was indeed a man, much of her presentation of him obscures his true humanity. The faithful are not allowed to observe that the sacrifices which have to be made by all men dedicated to a great mission, included for Christ too the rejection of any strong family ties that would necessarily come between him and complete dedication to his divine vocation. It is clear from the gospels that, although our Lady 'kept all these things, and pondered them in her heart', generally speaking his family understood little or nothing of his nature or of his purpose during his lifetime, and that at one period his brethren feared that he was insane. Yet piety dictates that, through an ostrich-like argument from congruity and a false sense of reverence, we should read into the gospels evidence of a perfect relationship, in the human sense, between Christ and his Mother which in fact is not there.[1] And in ignoring all such evidences of his human nature which, like any other, required for complete dedication an utterly undivided heart, we make of Christ something incompletely human. It is only by presenting him in the fullness of his manhood that the non-Christian can be brought in the first place to see him as the great Exemplar, and then through struggling to follow him, perhaps to understand something of the truth of the divine Incarnation.

But even as I write, I have little hope that the Church will reformulate any of her doctrines. Pope John's words

[1] One voice at the second session of Vatican Council II was brave enough to declare this truth.

will be silently ignored and we shall remain burdened with the old language that is doing so much to convince men and women that organised religion with its doctrine has nothing to offer them today. It is difficult sometimes not to wonder if, after all her claims to infallibility in matters of faith and morals, the Church really does believe that in her decisions she will be led by the Holy Spirit, today and tomorrow just as yesterday;[1] difficult too to feel sure that she always searches for the truth when she appears to consider herself in possession of most of it already, and her task primarily that of preserving it in the static rigidity of a corpse. She dare not alter one word of any definition lest, she says, the faithful may think that something of the immutable substance is being surrendered. But, as it has frequently been pointed out, the Church has for too long made the little ones an excuse for her immobility. And to keep the old language means that their present contentment is assured at the cost of the belief of future generations.

The problem which the Church hitherto has had to face has been that of combining conservation of unity with a search for truth. Unity was essential for her survival. But now her old unity is largely gone, replaced by a unity of charity in diversity. Although some semblance of uniformity of belief may be restored, too much has been reported and written about the debates in Council for it to be possible to believe that authority can do more than silence opinions that are unwelcome to it. It is extremely doubtful whether some of the opinions themselves can be abandoned; for they are

[1] If she genuinely so believed, why were the debates on contraception and on the celibacy of the clergy not allowed to take place at the Council which would be the gathering where, above all others, his presence could be expected? Why, one wonders, is secrecy deemed to be more important than his guidance?

rooted in the human conscience which must always be the final arbiter.

Since the volume of which this chapter forms a part concerns the future of Catholic Christianity, it is necessary to consider here the present ecumenical position. In the face of a world in which unbelief is steadily growing, it is clear that an eventual reunion of all Christian Churches—however difficult this may prove—is essential if the power of Christianity is not to be attenuated still further. Christianity must be seen to be Christian if it is to be a real force in the world which, knowing nothing of the intricacies of doctrine, finds only a crying scandal in the absence of intercommunion in the Churches. The problem, however, to their various members who do understand something of the doctrinal matters involved, is not quite so simple. Broadly speaking, two main and fundamental divergences between Protestants and Catholics concern their respective beliefs on the nature of the Church and on the sacraments. More specifically, the most formidable stumbling-blocks to reunion are the Catholic doctrines of Infallibility and of Transubstantiation.

Many people of all religious persuasions will have been much heartened by the recent reinstatement of the rights of conscience during the last session of the Council, seeing in these declarations the greatest contribution it has made to an essential factor in true belief. Hopes might have been raised that the Church would free herself from the fear which could lead her to prefer any proposition considered vital for the preservation of the system to an attempt to endue truth with meaning for men of today. But the encyclical, *Mysterium Fidei* has made such hopes impossible. Without questioning the duty of the Pope as mouthpiece of the Church to correct doctrinal error, many cannot avoid the suspicion that, since the doctrine of Transubstantiation is said to be essential to Catholicism, the reaffirmation of the doctrine was designed more to preserve the system than to meet the new theories of the Eucharist on a basis which would be convincing to their protagonists and advocates (none of whom as far as I know denies the Real Presence). Not only does the encyclical increase the obduracy of one stumbling-block to reunion, but it sweeps aside the dissatisfaction with the doctrine of many Catholics themselves. The very fact that there has been so much speculation about other ways of expressing the mystery of the Eucharist demonstrates that this dissatisfaction is not something to be driven underground as was Modernism by *Pascendi* in 1907, but a matter which should be made, as Modernism should have been, the subject of open discussion with the protagonists on intellectual as well as spiritual grounds. The desirability of this is further enhanced when we consider the question of re-union; for there is no denying that, in the terms as stated, the doctrine of Transubstantiation appears to the vast majority of Protestants as a crude literalism signifying an anthropophagy which would always deter them from having any connection with the Roman Church.

Although the need for authority in every institution is undeniable, the ecumenical movement raises the question of how the doctrine of infallibility is viewed by Christians outside the Roman Catholic Church. We know that in the Orthodox Church, 'Infallibility belongs to the whole Church, not just to the episcopate in isolation'; and that 'The infallibility of the Church must not be "exteriorised", nor understood in too "material" a sense'.[1] Khomiakov writes that 'The Pope [Pius IX] is

[1] V. Lossky, *The Mystical Theology of the Eastern Church*, p. 188.

greatly mistaken in supposing that we consider the ecclesiastical hierarchy to be the guardian of dogma... It is guarded by the totality, the whole people of the Church...'[1] For other non-Catholic Christians generally, papal infallibility is seen not only as another stumbling-block to reunion of the Churches but also as a potential for harm. They consider that the preclusion of any Church from ever admitting that she may have erred in her teaching on faith or morals, must have grave consequences for herself, her members and above all for the truth itself which should be her prime concern. To Protestants it seems that for the Roman Church herself, this doctrine leads to an absence of all humility and a tendency towards stagnation. They see that the doctrine makes it very difficult for the Church to revise any of her teaching on faith or morals, however imperative this might be; and that when she is confronted by beliefs in her own ranks which are more in accordance with a worthier conception of God than is found in some doctrines (hell and limbo for example) as she has taught them, she cannot directly repudiate those ideas which are compatible only with a grievously shrunken and distorted God. She remains tied to her errors by her own claim to inerrancy. This gives rise to a certain evasiveness or even a specious shuffling by writers loyal to the Church, and, as repeatedly seen on television, to a terpsichorean skill with which orthodox speakers in a tight corner side-step the real issues. There must be something wrong with a doctrine, according to Protestants, that could oblige any Church to give precedence to her own effigy even when a worthier conception of God is at stake. It is admitted that all organisations have

[1] Letter in W. J. Birkbeck, *Russia and the English Church*, p. 94. Quoted by Timothy Ware, *The Orthodox Church*, p. 255, Pelican.

to consider the guise in which they present themselves to their members, but it is also recognised that any confusion of priorities which leads the Church to compromise on a matter of truth must ultimately destroy the very thing she seeks to preserve.

The influence of the doctrine of infallibility is seen by Protestants as inclining the masses of the faithful towards a divinisation of the Church and their regarding her as the exclusive repository of all truth[1]—an attitude which often seems to confuse priorities. Indeed, we remember the outcry there was when, by speaking of the 'imagery' used in reference to hell, an enlightened theologian sought to correct the concept of God implicit in the conventional teaching. It certainly appeared as if some of the faithful were gladly sacrificing a worthier idea of him to the belief in an infallible Church which had never erred in her teachings.[2] Critics of this infallibility see it as resulting in an unquestioning obedience in belief and practice without reference to the individual conscience—an obedience which becomes the prime virtue and leads to religion by automation, with infallibility as a sort of Maginot line behind which souls can shelter.

[1] Certainly we have read in Catholic newspapers of the dismay attending the suggestion—albeit made by a prominent Jesuit—that other Churches besides the R.C. Church also contain a great measure of truth.

[2] The allusion to 'imagery' provoked protest in the correspondence columns of a Catholic newspaper, and a firm restatement of the doctrine in its crudest form by another Catholic priest. In fairness to the faithful it must be said that they have been taught that Christ himself believed in eternal physical torment of the damned with its unavoidable implication that God resurrects some bodies solely in order to torture them for ever; and that the Church has never recognised that the Christ who spoke in parables and metaphors, used in reference to hell as final separation from God—the greatest disaster that could happen to a man—language which would stab his hearers broad awake.

Security is all. But this kind of security, Protestants maintain, rests contentedly on the claims of the Church rather than on the only true basis of the Christ who is the same today as yesterday and for ever.

It is difficult even for Catholics to deny that, in spite of Pope Pius IX's saying that 'The Church is made for man and not man for the Church', it has been increasingly the besetting sin of Catholicism that the Church has become an end in herself instead of a means to salvation. This has resulted in a Churchianity within her ranks which atrophies the human conscience and confuses priorities. We have, however, always to bear in mind that the vast majority of the faithful are, and always to some extent will be, peasants, since the numbers in this category exceed those of other groups in most Catholic countries. We have too to distinguish between two kinds of simple souls: those who have the priceless gift of penetrating to the core of a truth without all the sweating and swinking suffered by their more intellectual but less happily endowed brethren, and those who are not interested in the truth for itself. All that the latter require is the safety and comfort of a maternal lap and to be fed with a clerical spoon. Yet, however right and necessary it is to make such provision, the policy of the Church hitherto has been geared too exclusively to the satisfaction of the simple wants of the masses, ignoring the claims and needs of those who require something more. Clearly, the Church has not wished for an educated laity, and she has been content to demand from the whole body of the faithful no more than a *fides implicita* in her word which has resulted, as Newman said it would, in indifference in the educated classes and in the poorer, superstition. Our non-Catholic friends are quick to remind us that the doctrine of infallibility fosters such a *simpliste* response, and that

Newman himself saw the definition as 'inopportune'. They themselves see it as a disaster. As one Protestant has written, 'Close corporations are proverbially inaccessible to new ideas, and blind to new facts; they are averse to any enlargement of mind from without, and their natural tendency is to be the whole world to themselves'.[1]

All these objections to infallibility, however, deal with the harmful effects of the doctrine and do not attack its roots. What, in fact, is advanced by Protestants against the truth of the dogma? Leaving aside even the most succinct arguments, from biblical texts, Church history and so forth—for which exposition I have neither the space nor the qualifications, and which are already well known—I give another argument which, although not so commonly voiced, appears to me to be fundamental to the Protestant attitude to truth. It goes something like this:

The promise of the Holy Spirit to lead men into the truth could never have meant an automatic directive regardless of whether his voice were being listened for, prepared for by prayer and fasting or not. And often it has seemed that unlike the architects of Plato's republic, the Roman Church has neglected to raise her eyes continually to the heavenly pattern. A promise, moreover, that was interpreted as confining itself to the exclusion of error from *ex cathedra* pronouncements concerning doctrinal propositions and moral prohibitions smacks of human manipulation and limitation rather than of divine outpouring of the Holy Spirit. To be 'led into the truth' means far more than the reception of a set of dogmas and prohibitions, however important these may

[1] J. B. Mozley, quoted by Alec Vidler, *The Church in an Age of Revolution,* p. 150, Pelican.

be. It cannot possibly be understood as excluding that truth which is the basis of all true religion: the gradual progression towards knowledge of God and what is pleasing to him. Christian experience continually contradicts any narrowing or limiting of the interpretation of the text. Is it not an expedient casuistry that discriminates between the *ex cathedra* and the private decisions of the Vicars of Christ—decisions which were bound just as much to affect the belief and policy of the Church? Were Popes who betrayed the spirit of Christ not rendered less pervious to the action of the Holy Spirit? Some Protestants assuredly think that they were, and that where the question of inerrancy is concerned these decisions, whether private or *ex cathedra,* must stand or fall together.

Amongst these decisions, Protestants versed in ecclesiastical history recall Pope Gregory IX sanctioning the death by fire of the convicted heretic; Innocent IV commanding the use of judicial torture in inquisitorial procedure; Clement V ordering, as tool of Philip IV of France, the Templars to be tortured; John XXII decreeing that the Spirituals should be burned at the stake; Urban VI reciting his office as he walked up and down outside the building where, by his decree and amongst other heretics, the elderly Cardinal of Venice was being tortured; Leo X pronouncing the burning of heretics not to be against the will of God (contrary to Luther who thought that it was); Gregory XIII having a *Te Deum* sung in gratitude for the massacre of Protestants in Paris during the night of St Bartholomew; and so on. That such cruelties were never explicitly part of an *ex cathedra* pronouncement is not to a Protestant of the slightest importance since they formed part of the implicit teaching of the Church that torture was a legitimate means of securing a confession of heresy, and that the massacres and burnings of heretics were not displeasing to God.

Protestants confess their own guilt for similar tortures and burnings at the stake and admit that such atrocities were the general practice in barbarous times that knew no better. But those who argue that if her holiness[1] had been genuine, the Roman Church should have known better, forget that what is sauce for the goose is sauce for the gander; and that no Church formed as a body separated from Rome has ever repudiated its own holiness. The judgment implied in 'By their fruits ye shall know them' cannot fairly be reserved for Rome alone. A more common objection to the doctrine of infallibility is now that an institution which cannot ever admit to the slightest error in her teaching on faith and morals must carry within it the seeds of its own decay.

But what, it must now be asked, does the Catholic himself understand by 'infallibility'? An interesting and important article by Fr Gregory Baum, O.S.A., in *The Ecumenist*[2] on 'The Teaching Authority of Vatican II' shows that the question is not quite as straightforward as some Christians think. I cannot here do more than quote a few of Fr Baum's conclusions; but the article should be read by all who are interested in the subject. Briefly, we are told that 'Vatican Council II insists that its teaching, while of the greatest authority in the

[1] The Abbot of Downside has recently told us that the words 'one, holy, catholic and apostolic' with reference to the Church may be interpreted as meaning that the Church must be *believed*, even against appearances, to be one, etc., and that 'one' does not mean 'visibly united' but 'unique'; and that 'holy' may mean 'set apart for God' and not 'morally and visibly holy'. (*Tablet*, September 11, 1965.)

[2] Sept./Oct., 1965, New York.

Church, is non-infallible'. It is 'authoritative for Catholics' but 'it is well known that nothing has been defined infallibly by Vatican Council II'. And he quotes from the Theological Commission (the episcopal drafting committee responsible for the *Constitution on the Church*), '... matters which this holy synod proposes as the teaching of the highest magisterium of the Church must be accepted ... by each and every one of the faithful ...'. This means that Catholics are to accept teaching which is not infallible and which may therefore prove to be erroneous.

Fr Baum points out that there is here an 'important distinction between infallible teaching and authoritative teaching (though fallible)'. He remarks that 'Few doctrines are proposed by the magisterium as infallible teaching. Most of the teaching proposed by the Church is offered simply as authoritative teaching.' Further, he tells us that 'The assent due to this authoritative teaching is expressed as "religious assent" or "obedience of the mind"' and is 'not an act of faith'. 'Authoritative fallible teaching is received simply with assent of the mind, which differs from the unconditional surrender of the mind in faith.'

An interesting point is raised when Fr Baum speaks of extraordinary cases where a Catholic may be unable to integrate some teaching 'into the total understanding of God's revelation as announced by the Church. In this case, the particular teaching will remain barren in his mind', and after every possible endeavour to accept it has failed the Catholic 'may responsibly reveal his convictions and work towards a revision of the official position'. It is clear that Fr Baum attaches immense importance to the power of any teaching to 'produce life' in the individual soul. For he concludes his article by declaring that 'The authority of the conciliar teaching will depend on its actual power in producing life among the faithful!' Some of its teaching will possess our minds and prove to be creative, whilst other parts although accepted will 'rest in a corner of the mind' and 'will not make much difference in the real life of the Church. . . . We simply do not know beforehand the real authority of conciliar teaching! . . . The life of the Church, guided by the Spirit, will tell us the power of conciliar teaching.'

What are we to understand from these quotations? The first thing to emerge is seemingly that we are being exhorted to buy a pig in a poke, or to back a horse which may eventually fail to run. But this is not really so although the implication is that we should place a little money on it whilst not staking our whole fortune. However, this 'religious assent'—words which Fr Baum admits are hardly ever explained—appears to me, at any rate in this context, as a dim half-belief which amounts to little more than an absence of disbelief. Genuine belief is a part of one's very being, something that has the power to affect life. And for this reason I see this 'religious assent' more as a refusal to reject anything proposed by the Council. This is a point which I have tried to make concerning the *consensus fidelium* in the earlier part of this chapter and to which I should like to return later. All I will say here is that Fr Baum's emphasis on the actual power of a teaching to produce life amongst the faithful appears to me as immensely important. And that his frank admission that we do not know beforehand the real authority of conciliar teaching betokens a humble agnosticism which has often been absent from the tutelage of a legalistic Church. It explains too the reason why it has proved impossible to ascertain which of the pronouncements of the Church in the past are to be considered infallible. We have been told that in the whole history of the Church these number about twenty;[1] but the rest is silence. Now, however, when we see that the spirit of Gamaliel is indeed working in the Church the silence becomes understandable.

At this point it might be useful to ask if any agreement can be reached between Protestants and Catholics as to where authority is to be found. 'From the Protestant view,' it is said, 'God . . . works within history where the conditions are finite freedom. God has annulled neither man's finitude nor his freedom. In the workings of the eternal in time, of the infallible God among fallible men and Churches, the tension remains. For the Protestant, any absolutising of historical structures, by Protestants or Catholics, bears the mark not of divine sovereignty so much as human idolatry.'[2] Yet there is still much common ground upon which we might agree. The first seat of authority must be in the experience of the human soul, as described by Père Bouillard. We have, too the *consensus fidelium*, the constant teaching of the Church, of which the *ecclesia docta* forms just as important a part as the *ecclesia docens* because of the truth, *viribus unitis docet discendo et discit docendo semper*. Although the Protestant will not believe in a literal inerrancy, many will agree that the constant teaching of the Church has served them well throughout the years and may be trusted to bring them to safe harbourage in the end. Every truth, however, must be constantly placed in the light of a man's own confrontation with Christ in the gospels, and also in that of his

[1] Advertisement for the Catholic Enquiry Centre.

[2] The Rev. Raymond E. Gibson, Minister of the Central Congregational Church, Providence, R. I., writing in *The Ecumenist*, Sept./Oct., 1965.

own conscience. Nothing which conflicts with either is to be believed, or, for that matter, *can* be believed.[1]

To believe in order to understand is to adopt the attitude of Coleridge rather than that of Bentham. Of these John Stuart Mill has written:

> 'By Bentham, beyond all others, men have been led to ask themselves, in regard to any ancient or received opinion, Is it true? and by Coleridge, What is the meaning of it? The one took his stand *outside* the received opinion, and surveyed it as an entire stranger to it; the other looked at it from within, and endeavoured to see it with the eyes of a believer in it; to discover... [how] it has seemed, to a succession of persons, to be a faithful interpretation of their experience. Bentham judged a proposition true or false as it accorded or not with the result of his own inquiries; and did not search very curiously into what might be meant by the proposition, when it obviously did not mean what he thought true. With Coleridge... the very fact that any doctrine had been believed by thoughtful men, and received by whole nations or generations of mankind, was... one of the phenomena to be accounted for...'[2]

A certain empathy in our approach to all religious

[1] In 'The Day of the Periti' (*The Tablet*, November 27, 1965), Douglas Woodruff warns against the disadvantages of the obverse side of Protestant virtues now incorporated into the Church. With a new emphasis on scripture, conscience and encouragement of every Christian to bring his own contribution, we must expect diverse interpretations of the New Testament by men confident in their own judgment, which in the history of Protestantism led to fragmentation and division. Mr Woodruff's caution is timely for those who have learned nothing from the lessons of the Reformation.

[2] *Essay on Coleridge.*

truth is as necessary as it is in all human relationships. For, as Laberthonnière wrote, 'We only believe sincerely in that which we love'. The Christian truths behind the rigid dogmas should be shown in all their beauty and desirability and not administered to us as so much physic that must be swallowed on pain of being put out of the Church. Also, since it is repeatedly being said that it is primarily the laity who must come to grips with modern unbelief in the world around them, that it is they who must shoulder the burden of presenting the great Christian truths as being meaningful for our time, one wonders how well equipped are the rank and file Catholics to speak with the unbeliever in a language that he can understand. How many can give an account of the beliefs of Christians that is not virtually in the language of the Catechism? It is certain that few unbelievers are likely to be impressed by second-hand arguments for belief by those who believe solely on an authority which has absolved them from any personal responsibility in making Christian truths their own. Of course there must always be many for whom Christian truths will 'rest in a corner of the mind', and their 'religious assent' is not to be undervalued. But there are also numbers of others who could find a source of more abundant life in making belief a greater part of their being if only they were encouraged to do so. There will always be the widest possible difference between a belief which remains only an acceptance on authority, and one which transcends its basis by a personal response which effects a unifying act between the belief and the believer. Only such belief is being. And if the Christian is to have the remotest likelihood of having any impact on an unbeliever, it can only be through a believer who is thus possessed by the truth.

But who can hope that all Christian truths will spring

into life for him with equal vividness? Lao Tzu said that muddy water allowed to stand, slowly becomes limpid. The important thing is never, in a frenzied spring-cleaning and general tidying up of the mind, to throw it despairingly away. For many of us faith will be for great stretches of time little more than a patient waiting, assured that part of the purpose of life is that we may learn to *see*. It is largely our blindness, our utter stupidity even more than our natural human weakness that hinders us from eternal life. We mistake the straw of words for the reality of things, as Leibnitz said.

And that of course is the challenge that all dogma presents. Unless we go behind the words and try to recapture something of the Christian experience that the definitions sought to keep alive, the whole of the *depositum fidei* can be nothing more for us than a grocer's window filled with dummies 'not for consumption'. Words themselves can obscure as well as reveal, and it is heartening that in Fr Baum's article in *The Ecumenist*, he refers to Pope John's distinction between the *depositum fidei* and the *modus enuntiandi*, and says: 'Because the formulation of doctrine is distinct from its content, the particular formulations of councils and popes, however authoritative, are not unchangeable. Infallible doctrine is definitive in the sense that . . . no doctrinal development, or further penetration of revelation, will ever negate it. But infallible doctrine is *not* definitive, in the sense that it *may* yield to new formulations that express more faithfully the *depositum fidei* and show more clearly how the doctrine is related to other aspects of divine revelation.' In such a demonstration lies one great hope that the Church may reach the unbelieving world.

Yet we recall with dismay that in *Mysterium Fidei*,

Pope Paul quoted with approval that definitions made of old 'are adapted to men of all times'. This is so manifestly not the case, that his approval forces us to the conclusion that he is out of touch with modern religious problems and ignorant of one of the main causes of unbelief in this century. That it plainly contradicts several remarks on the same subject made by Pope John is, I suppose, evidence that in the policy of the Church as communicator of truth, we have 'Stop: Go' as in any other government.[1] But whether Pope John realised or not the difficulties which reformulation of doctrine would present, or the problems which it might create, cannot alter the fact that he firmly believed in the necessity of such an undertaking if the Church were to cease to appear as 'a museum of ancient artefacts'. In John XXIII we had a Pope not 'bewildered by the Council', as Cardinal (then Archbishop) Heenan stated, but one who saw most clearly the failure of the Church to reach the unbelieving world.

A lively article entitled *What are we doing to Pope John?* asks very pertinently, 'Is he to be quietly shelved, to the gratification of those who sighed with relief at his death, blessing God for staying the frivolous hand that had already given such scandal, just as it was about to do more permanent damage? Are we still faithful to the spirit of Pope John?' It seems that many of us are not, and that in those influential quarters where he was con-

[1] Fr Gregory Baum, writes in *The Canadian Register*, September 25, 1965: 'Pope Paul's encyclical . . . is regarded by many as a sign that the Pope, by stressing the Council of Trent . . . over against the teaching of Vatican II, wishes to slow down the movement of renewal and reform . . . Since Pope Paul's terminology is so different from the *Constitution on the Liturgy*, it is not easy to fit his encyclical harmoniously into the conciliar teaching of Vatican II'. (Quoted in *Herder Correspondence*, December 1965.)

sidered to be a dangerous simpleton whom God obligingly removed in the nick of time, Pope John is being silently ignored '"out of fear perhaps"', as Cardinal Lercaro suggests, '"or out of anxiety to check, to canalise, to control, to divert, the flood of insight which that man let loose"'. The Cardinal would have us 'accept the whole John and set about realising the great man's vision'.[1] But we see already that many doors which he opened are being quietly and firmly closed by those whose idea of security is 'Back to the ghetto'. Yet the old ghetto can never be quite the same again.

What bearing will these matters have upon Catholic Christianity of the future? The recent news from the last session of the Council reports a speech of Pope Paul in which he declares, 'The Church lives! And here is the proof: here we have its breath (and) its song. The Church lives!' But we are given a photograph of the poor, weary bishops apparently in the last stages of *ennui* if not actually slumbering in the aula of St Peter's. We are told 'the fight has gone out of them'.[2] Whatever that may mean one thing is certain: the old orthodox Catholicism, as we know it, is dead. What form its resurrection will take is impossible to foretell; but every reflective Christian will have his ardent hopes during this period of transition.

There is more need than ever for the Church today. But although many Catholics are hoping for what Blondel called 'a purification of the religious sense and an integration of Catholic truth,'[3] it would be unrealistic not to understand that all organisations move organisationally, and that institutions have cares and problems

[1] From the text of an article in *Ruhrwort*, June 19, 1965, printed in *Herder Correspondence*, Sept./Oct., 1965.

[2] *The Catholic Herald*, November 5, 1965.

[3] *Op. cit.*, p. 32.

of which their members are largely free. Some of these cares form part of an argument against organised religion in general and Roman Catholicism in particular, that religious institutions inevitably introduce the factor of their own mystique with its attendant peril that what was founded as a means to an end may become an end in itself, activated primarily not always by a desire for truth but by what best preserves its mystique. Obviously, the greater the claims made by any Church, the greater this propensity will be. The Roman Church, burdened by too rigid a doctrine of infallibility, has the problem of changing her teaching on several matters without arousing the fears of the masses that the changes may be due to something more than 'doctrinal development'[1] —something, moreover, which challenges the inflexibility of the doctrine of infallibility. It must therefore be expected that for many a long year yet her prestige will demand that integrity must be obscured by various compromises until such time as the masses of the faithful are more prepared for the idea that the Church should, and in fact does, change her teaching on some matters of faith and morals; until the masses are able to understand that the loss of a legalistic view of inerrancy is not a matter that should affect their faith in the ark of salvation which will, by the aid of her mariner's compass, sextant and so forth, steer all on board towards safe harbourage in the end.

But is there not too little joy in organised religion and

[1] But the laity can no longer be hoodwinked by the 'edifying lie': by being told, e.g., that were the Church to compromise on her prohibition of contraception, this would be only a development of doctrine and would in no wise call into question the infallibility of the Church. How a development could ever result in a complete contradiction of the original doctrine must baffle all logic except that of the White Queen. Moreover, as Pope Leo told us, 'God does not need our lies'.

too much which blunts the eagerness of men's desire for God, substituting a disenchanted sense of duty; too much moral blackmail (however well-intentioned) in order that ecclesiastical laws shall be obeyed, presenting men with a legalistic God rather than one whose service is perfect freedom and who is above all infinitely desirable for himself and who cannot be worshipped truly through a sense of obligation? Is it not time that the Church should cease also to speak as if God were interested only in religion and had no other purpose but to oversee this ark of salvation? Is the moment not ripe too for her to admit that God should not be held responsible for 'sending' disease, deformed babies, destruction and disaster? Are Christians masochists that so many cling wholeheartedly to this belief, or are they influenced by the Church's fear of jeopardising belief in God's omnipotence? The problem of evil over against a divine Creator whom we call 'good' and know to be love, is always with us. But do we not make it even more insoluble by seeing his omnipotence from a purely anthropomorphic standpoint? Christ assured us that in this disordered and imperfect world we would have tribulation; but in a world in which God has ordained that every man shall be his brother's keeper, God works through secondary causes, through men, and it seems that he allows his omnipotence to be directly dependent upon men's free-will and co-operation. As Simone Weil has said, the good which God effects in humanity and the world as a whole over any period must be in direct proportion to the co-operation of men. (This resembles Spinoza's view that God works only through finite causes.) She believed that there was no possibility of there being more good than is afforded through this co-operation. Life on earth is the point of conjunction of good and evil, and the world is not to be thought of as a realm where God interferes between cause and effect. And for the rest of the problem we have to be content with a Socratic ignorance. Indeed, one of the just reproaches of agnostics is that Christians pretend to a far too great knowledge of God. *Si comprehendis non est Deus.*

This brings me back to the two points with which I began: the true basis of religion as an individual relationship with God, and the fundamental consequence of a man's conception of his Creator. These are two matters which, although of greater moment than anything else in the world, are apt to be smothered by the burdens which organised religion imposes upon its adherents. But without the constant awareness of this pre-eminence, all religions become no more than a tale told by an idiot, full of sound and fury, signifying nothing. One of the reasons for the widespread disbelief in God today is that organised religions are reluctant to urge the necessity for the breaking of idols. Of this necessity Fr Victor White, O.P., wrote in *God the Unknown*:

> 'Hide himself he [God] must, for so soon as we become satisfied with any picture or image of God we are in danger of idolatry: of mistaking the comprehensible image for the reality. That is why image-breaking is as much part and parcel of man's religion as image-making. All our images and concepts of God are stepping-stones which must be discarded if they are not to become idols.'

It would be more than superstition, it would be blasphemy to have any conception of the Deity which makes his nature inferior in any respect to what, with common consent, is assumed to be the highest in human nature.

And as to man himself, his salvation requires a passionate belief *ex animo* that his highest attribute, his power of loving—that which can best present him as made in the image of God—has its source in the divine love which immeasurably transcends the human. Does not the whole conception of the fate of men who finally reject God of their own free-will stand in need of fundamental re-thinking? That hell must be possible for men who have free-will cannot be questioned, but the nature and extent of the suffering which would follow such a choice needs far greater vision than that evinced by the old doctrine. We can learn much from the Orthodox Church upon this matter and upon the doctrine of Purgatory. Sir Leslie Stephen who constantly attacked Christianity for teaching a system of rewards and punishments, quotes this little parable:

> 'St Lewis the king, having sent Ivo, Bishop of Chartres, on an embassy, the bishop met a woman on the way, grave, sad, fantastic, and melancholic; with fire in one hand and water in the other. He asked what those symbols meant. She answered, "My purpose is with fire to burn Paradise, and with my water to quench the flames of hell, that men may serve God without the incentives of hope and fear and purely for the love of God." '[1]

Rewards and punishments do inevitably figure largely in Christian teaching, but they are never to be understood as anything which can be bestowed upon a man from the outside regardless of the state of his own being. The recording angel is nothing but the human soul which bears the mark of every thought and word and deed which is either Godward or directed away from him. All doctrines have to be shown as having their

[1] *Essays on Plainspeaking.*

foundation in God's essential nature. For this reason, the doctrine of limbo seems to be fading away. But we long for its burial—in unconsecrated ground.

Many Catholics look forward to the time when the Church which produced some of the greatest mystics will again teach her members the value of individual private prayer; giving them Fathers in God who will encourage them to learn of its progressive stages. Such prayer is the crying need of the world today, a world where increasingly the rush of mere existence drives out the source of life and ends are swallowed up by means.

May we hope too for some simplification in theology instead of an endless proliferation such as, for example, in the teaching about grace? Do we poor Catholic camels have to be burdened with distinctions in grace between habitual or sanctifying, actual, prevenient, efficacious, sufficient and congruous when all we need to know is that, as Barth remarked, grace is nothing but God's Spirit working in the human soul?

The Church as the consciousness of the Incarnation is owed a debt by humanity of which the majority know nothing. For what she has conserved for nearly two millennia all Christians render her undying gratitude. And if many deplore some of the methods by which she effected this conservation, her good faith is not rashly to be impugned. 'The Church', as Charles Williams remarked, 'committed herself, on the highest principles, to a breach of the highest possible principles'; for 'heresy was believed seriously to harm man's capacity to live and to love'. And 'there never has been found any method of driving out one devil—except by pure love—which does not allow the entrance of seven, as Messias had long ago pointed out'.[1]

[1] *The Descent of the Dove*, p. 107, Faber, 1939.

The future of the Church if it is to consolidate its remaining power by regaining some unity, must be founded on a mutual trust between the hierarchy and the laity. That many of the governed are suspicious of those who govern is not due to a revolt against authority in itself. The suspicion arises rather from the realisation that the Church still works secretly and is reluctant to take her children into her confidence. Admittedly, children must give some evidence of having arrived at years of discretion. Yet nothing more increases wisdom and understanding and, above all, love for a parent in a child's heart than the knowledge that he is trusted with the parent's confidence. Conversely, nothing repels love and trust more than being fobbed off with prevarications and equivocations in the cause of expediency.

Pope Paul is continually urging us to love the Church, but she will never be loved in the way she demands to be until there is a mutual trust between those who govern and those who are governed. 'Mother knows best' is a sentiment which is seldom pressed today in a civilisation where the young mature ever earlier. The maxim may inspire a certain trust and feeling of security in those still inhabiting the nursery, but to those who have left it a wise Mother will never pretend that she has invariably been right.

What has the Church to fear if she really trusts the guidance of the Holy Spirit? For he is the Spirit of Truth and the Spirit of Charity, and against these in the end the gates of hell cannot prevail. For ourselves as her members, might not our contribution be a working towards a purification of our own religious sense and an integration in ourselves of Christian truth?

'Begin to search and dig in thine own field for this pearl of eternity that lies hidden in it; it cannot cost thee too much, nor canst thou buy it too dear, for it is *all*; and when thou hast found it thou wilt know that all which thou hast sold or given away for it is as mere a nothing as a bubble upon the water.'[1]

[1] William Law.

The Future of the Female

BERNARDINE BISHOP

IN connection with this essay I recently put the question: 'What about the future of women in the Church?' to a friend, a loyal but liberal priest. 'That's easy,' he said, 'men have made such a mess of the Church the only hope is for women to take over at once and start afresh. The sooner we have our first woman Pope the better.' I propose to examine what was at the root of the exasperation he expressed and what he really meant by the solution he offered.

This is a critical time for women. The implications of their emancipation are still only half realised. It was inevitable that after the repression and enslavement to the purely biological aspect of her sexuality that Western civilisation has inflicted, woman's one idea should have been to deny all that she had previously stood for.

When women erupted between fifty and a hundred years ago into a man's world it was with no intention of redressing the balance. What they wanted was to become as men. Equality for women was the cry; it was left to a later generation to understand that equality is not equivalence. Initially the idea of feminine independence was largely an illusion, for it expressed no independence of the masculine values on which our social structure is based, but rather the desire to embrace and embody them. Women in the world today need to make a synthesis of their recently developed mental powers with their unchanging femininity. On this depends their fulfilment as women and the impact on civilisation of that distinctive and complementary approach we call feminine.

I shall leave that term in all its vague suggestiveness for the moment. Two girls, let us say, are now at a university. The first is reading geography. She throws herself into her work, cultivating her memory and powers of reasoning and planning her career. Her personal relationships are few and shallow. She is shy of men and develops a mixed attitude of fascination and intolerance towards her more social fellows. When she leaves college she goes into a job which requires nothing more of her than the correct functioning of her rational mind and the industriousness in which she has trained herself. As she becomes set in her ways it becomes less and less likely that anything will be able to impinge upon her that will awaken her to awareness of the feminine life within her. The second girl goes up to read languages, but changes after half a term to fine arts, which she has heard is the 'softest option'. She does a minimum of work and has a full social life, contemptuous of incipient spinsterhood where she sees it and of the 'suffragette complex' of her tutor. The teachers regret that university has turned her head, but actually the problem is far deeper than that. She is trying to express her femininity but can find no way of doing so except by being perpetually a sexual object. When she comes down from university she will rush into marriage, afraid of being mistaken for a moment for the sort of woman she has taught herself to despise. These young marriages have a bad outlook, probably partly because on the woman's side they are a response to psychological pressures rather than to a personal relationship.

Neither of these girls has solved the difficult problem of being a woman in the twentieth century. Their education has not helped them to do so. They have both been trained along channels worn into existence by generations of men. Both of them would have been assisted to personal fulfilment by some understanding of the feminine nature of which physical womanhood is at once a symbol and a manifestation. This is something each ignores, the first by tacitly denying its existence, the second by too crude an affirmation. It is typical of the stage of evolution women have now reached in Western civilisation that feminine fulfilment is still viewed exclusively as a biological affair. Spinsters are assumed without a second look to be frustrated, mothers the reverse. The truth of the matter is that a woman is fulfilled or frustrated according to whether the feminine nature from which her sexuality takes its character is being realised in her life. This is not a new idea. Indeed it is an old one, implicit in the vocation of a nun, who far from putting aside the attributes of her sex, is called the bride of Christ and by us Mother or Sister. It sounds paradoxical, but one of the oldest callings for women in the history of Christendom is culturally ahead even of our times, although of course the vow of celibacy makes it a special case.

Equally, there have been certain outstanding women who, without any help from the spirit of the age into which they were born, have made distinctively feminine contributions to civilisation and society, and have achieved things that no man could have achieved, and of which perhaps no man could have felt the importance. It is hard to imagine a legend springing up of the Gentleman with the Lamp. But these women are few and far between. What moves them has never been accepted in our culture. Emancipation for women was the first stage: feminine emancipation must be the next.

One can imagine that as women continue to have a hand in their own lives they will more and more find vocations appropriate not only to themselves as rational beings but to themselves as women. The antithetical elements represented in the two university girls, casualties of an era of transition, may reach a synthesis. Women may forge an educational system proper to themselves. Again, it is typical of the present moment that the idea of differential education for women should conjure up images of more cookery and needlework. When women are thought of as women, their place is, generally speaking, still in the home. There is room for radical reform in this field. Of course women must be educated for professions, although it is not inconceivable that in the course of time they may create new ones in response to needs that only they can come to see or see as mattering.

But the man is the head and the woman is the heart: so goes an old saying. We—men and women alike—have the education of the head; what is called for is the education of the heart. Men have educated Logos. It is for women to educate Eros. In our culture, Eros is confined to the erotic. What looks at us from every hoarding and advertisement page is raw material. The only approved manifestation of Eros is, at the highest, falling in love. The tremendous potential for good that lies and culturally lies dormant in the capacity to love cannot be taught; it is something too individual, and personal circumstances and psychology provide the material throughout a lifetime. Love (Eros), like intellect (Logos), is an educative power. It has in itself a dynamic force to evolve and to grow, to supersede personal gratification, to break down boundaries of personal preference, and to lead us to the centre of things where we are all one. It is the way to the sort of knowledge we call wisdom. This only life can teach, but what could be taught is the ability to learn. By it it has always been natural for a woman to orientate herself and evaluate experience and make decisions; in the old order its powers no doubt fructified in Nature-like unconsciousness. But woman is now highly conscious and rational, and needs re-education, or feminine neo-education, if she is now to regard as valid a non-intellectual mode of finding things out. We are all in danger of being inwardly cut adrift from what is closest to our hearts, but for a woman this is more damaging, and it is for women to redress the balance. It is inborn in women to know that love is a commitment of the heart more properly than an emotion, that in it there is fortitude, detachment, and that total acceptance that makes approval irrelevant: it is one of the things that fits them for maternity. It is a quality loosely called 'biological', especially by incredulous husbands visiting the nursery, but springing from the feminine nature that underlies a woman's biology. It could not be directly educated in school, but it could be prepared for the education of life, so that later experience could be fruitfully used, and even disappointments bring not bitterness, desiccation, and the determination never to give again, but unshaken orientation, a new flexibility and openness, and ever-deepening insight into the secret of *l'amor che muove il sole e l'altre stelle* (the love that moves the sun and the other stars). And in society, women might more and more carry into the bureaucratic conception and organisation of 'welfare' the love of neighbour.

'The only hope is for women to take over the Church completely and start afresh.' True to his epoch, my friend wants women to count more, but can't conceive of their doing so except in emulation of men. Women at their most characteristic are not given to forming hierarchical organisations. They act as individuals and on individuals. Unless personal complexes were involved in the utterance, my friend can't have wanted a switch-over from patriarchate to matriarchate for the mere sake of it. Underlying the vehemence of his reply, I suggest, was a desire that the feminine should be supplied to the life of the Church.

In repressing women, the Church, like society, has implicitly been repressing Eros values. In extolling men, the Church, like society, has implicitly been extolling Logos values. In both cases the repression of the female has been a symptom of a much further-reaching attitude of mind than mere misogyny.

We are moving very close to what we really mean by feminine. Here care is needed, or I shall soon be talking nonsense in a field already surfeited with it. I am not making a sweeping generalisation about women, who are individuals and various. The feminine is a part of human nature and of the world. It is an archetype. Women partake of it to different degrees, and in a balanced man a developed feminine component is necessary. Traditionally and poetically, it is in the earth, fertile to the seeds and subject to the sun. It is in the rhythms of Nature, and the continuous cycle of death and rebirth of the seasons of the years. On the biological level, it is in sexual surrender, loss of virginity, pregnancy and childbirth. On the specifically human level, it is in self-giving, self-using, passive creation, harbouring and protecting less secure lives, patience, trust and understanding. It is not in articulation, conceptualisation, invention, organisation, categorisation and exact measurement. It is in prayer rather than action and in contemplative rather than active prayer. It is in the Unconscious rather than the conscious mind. Sacramentally it is in the unleavened bread as it awaits the words of Consecration. Transcendentally it is in the whole of Creation labouring until the delivery in Christ.

We are regaining our trust in the feminine side. The trust will deepen, but the fact that we have begun to trust at all is one of the important things about the twentieth century. This new-found trust shows itself in many ways. Theologically, we find it in the treatment of Nature never as erased by Grace but as worked on and through by it. We find it implied in the recently defined dogma of the Assumption. We find it in Teilhard's emphasis on the inner purposiveness of Creation. It may not be fanciful to see it in the reinstatement of the laity, who have taken on a feminine and receptive rôle to a masculine clergy. We find it in Jungian psychology, where the workings of the personality are shown to have in themselves a spontaneous drive towards integration and wholeness, where symbols are accorded cardinal importance, and where the movements of the heart (the feeling function) are accepted as valid in the evaluation of experience and as necessary a part of human maturation as masculine Logos.

It is in this much wider context that the stirrings in the Church towards a revaluation of women must be seen. The trend is working both concretely and symbolically. Women are being granted status, and simultaneously the archetypal feminine is beginning to come into its own. On the concrete level we can see as straws in the wind the Church's sudden crush on marriage, and the contraception controversy. An altering attitude to woman is revealed. She is a human being and an end in herself, not merely a means to children, and has something beyond physical satisfaction to give her husband in sex. But one cannot really draw distinctions between concrete and symbolic manifestations of the single trend, for it is due to a revaluation of Eros that marriage is considered in a new light, and similarly the old idea of the primary and secondary ends of the marriage act. This is all splendid in itself and encouraging as a sign. But it is only the beginning. Woman and what she can give still tend to be taken seriously only in her ancient domesticity. And Eros, though allowed a new dignity and spiritual potency, is still only proper to the 'Bright/ And tiny world of lovers' arms'.

On the other side of the coin we see a movement in the Church which seems to revert to the Emancipation ethos, and the confusion of feminine equality with feminine equivalence. There has been a lot of talk recently about the ordination of women. My friend's remark: 'The sooner we get our first woman Pope the better', presupposes this innovation. Sacramentally and pastorally, the priesthood is a masculine vocation. When he administers the Sacraments, the priest stands for Christ. Christ is the embodiment of the archetypal masculine, to whom the individual soul, the Church and the whole of Creation stand in a feminine relationship. The vocation of a priest affirms his masculinity and calls him to be both a father and a lover. The ideal behind his celibacy must be that the functions of his manhood are generalised and raised to a higher level. If we lose sight of this we will end up with a mixed clergy of the neuter. Also—and this is another danger—the opening of the priesthood to women would make it less easy for them to develop that specifically feminine complementarity of which the Church now feels the need.

One can imagine a sort of underground of women deepening and amplifying the life of the Church in many ways. Nuns and other women could be called on to talk to seminarians about their experience of the spiritual life and of Christian life in the world, thereby assisting each of the young men to encounter his own feminine side, the anima without whose integration he will be unlikely to be able to canalise his sexuality into a non-physical affirmation of manhood. The long-term benefits of this would be far-reaching; individual priests would be converted from the idea of chastity as only a denial and a sacrifice, and hence would confront sexual and marriage problems with greater wisdom and equanimity. Women would have educated Eros in them. Men remain the confessors but women are suited to the rôle of confidante, and the time may come when each priest and bishop selects from among the nuns a sort of mother confidante to whom to take his difficult decisions and even his personal problems. Far freer and (this is very important) quite reciprocal discussions between priests and nuns could become normal. A nun has told me of the 'almost impercepible edge of contempt' nuns have to endure from a lot of priests; and she put this down, probably quite rightly, to the fact that so many of them haven't lived among women since adolescence. One might conjecture that the priests who despise women have consciously or unconsciously opted to despise their own sexuality, as the safest way of dealing with the problems it raises. Even if they escape palpable damage from this approach their parishioners will not, and in the long run the Church will not. Women have a tremendous part to play in the development of the priesthood, and they cannot do it best by joining it.

It is most encouraging to note that at the time of writing sixteen Council Fathers have made interventions demanding that greater importance be given to women in the Church. Recently Archbishop Hallinan of Atlanta, Georgia, welcomed the suggestion of a feminine Diaconate, and went on to say that 'Every opportunity should be given to women, both religious and lay, to offer their special talents to the service of the Church'. The idea of deaconesses is a creative one, but the phrase 'their special talents' is one that should be borne in mind. Unless this reform is tackled in the right spirit there will be a danger of parish priests regarding deaconesses as second-rate curates, a makeshift answer to the shortage of priests. Instead of being positive about their work they themselves would then be susceptible to resentments and a chip on the shoulder. Certain parochial activities, bingo for example, might be shoved on to them with a relieved sigh, more serious aspects of pastoral responsibility being regarded as above their heads. If the idea of deaconesses is to work, they must not be considered, even at the very back of our minds, as a sub-species of priest, but as fulfilling a function of their own, and a feminine one. Counsel for parishioners might become with the coming of deaconesses something very much more real than what is offered at the average presbytery today. Perhaps with this in view a course in psychotherapy and social work could be part of the training of deaconesses.

'Men have made such a mess of the Church.' I suggest that my friend was protesting, in metaphorical terms, against the one-sidedly masculine line of development the Church has taken. Unthinking trust in the feminine, in the processes of Mother Nature and the all-providence of Mother Earth, is a primitive, an infant and even an animal trait. The masculine is the agent of civilisation, and brings Nature and human nature within the grasp and under the domination of the rational and ordering human mind. Trust of the feminine that is conscious, however, complements and revivifies rather than obliterates masculine achievement, and represents a coming of age.

So in the Church. The first twenty centuries of Christianity, once the cycle got going, have been characterised by confidence in the masculine and suspicion of the feminine. The treatment of the sexes did no more than follow this trend. The mysteries of Sacrament and dogma have been pinned down so far as possible in intellectual formulations. Rules of conduct have been detailed and inflexible. The goal appears to have been a system to which individual experience is irrelevant. This served to protect the faith against pollution by personal emotional aberrations. It guarded against heresy. And it was evolutionally necessary. The Church had, as it were, to secure the ego before integrating the Unconscious.

In the sphere of faith this tradition devalued experienced response and in that of morals it discounted individual pressures. Increasingly during the past few years voices have been raised in protest against a too juridical and legalistic Church. We might interpret this as a sign that the Church is now ready to confront and assimilate the feminine side with no fear of being swamped by it. The last centuries have so established the collective will that it can stand a morality of liberty without libertinism resulting. Rational theology has so entrenched itself that the stability of the collective mind will not be endangered by any upsurge of irrational powers.

In the final etiolated stages of this tradition before the

pontificate of John XXIII, Catholics were being trained to use their minds and their wills, each functioning autonomously. The heart was not required of them. Mystery can be explained and explored, to some degree, by the intellect; it can only be experienced in the heart. Greater trust in the powers of the heart will create an atmosphere in which the faith can be apprehended directly, in the centre of the personality, sacrament as numinous experience, dogma as symbolic as well as intellectual truth, morality the external aspect of a fully lived out response to a commitment of love.

The hyperdevelopment of Logos brought about a distrust of humanity. This is understandable enough. God is masculine to humanity, humanity feminine to God. Distrust of the feminine bred distrust of Creation's power and purpose to respond to God's love. This basic insecurity is part of fallen human nature and can be seen in the propitiatory ceremonies of many religions. It reached unequalled intensity and refinement of expression in Judaism, the tradition that gestated Christ. Christ came to restore the trustworthiness of man.

In the gospels the word faith is used in the Eros rather than the Logos sense. The coming development will be another manifestation of our 'return to the sources'. In the gospels to believe always means to trust rather than to give intellectual assent. Moreover, trust in Christ signifies trust in the human as well as in the divine. When St Peter walked on the water he did not waver in confidence in Christ whom he believed to be the Son of the living God. His belief in God was not in question. 'Lord, save me', was his cry. What he doubted was himself, the fullness of his own God-given participation in that sonship, and for that he was rebuked: 'O man of little faith'.

Christ guarantees the reliability of Creation, the feminine partner. We know this, of course—in Christ we are all saved. But a feeling remains that our salvation rests on a propitiatory amassing of moral actions although it has been given to us to trust that our free actions undertaken in the devoted and developing commitment of our hearts will be in the truest sense moral. In this sense the integration of the feminine will complete the Incarnation.

The Broken Pitcher

An Essay on the Present Christian Crisis

MAGDALEN GOFFIN

THERE is a sentence in a letter written about sixty years ago by Lord Hugh Cecil to Wilfred Ward which sums up with uncomfortable accuracy the plight of Roman Catholics today. Those Catholics who had attempted to reconcile scientific knowledge with their religion had just been silenced and Cecil was remarking on the eventual uselessness of blunt contradiction, rigid suppression and the general campaign against independence of thought. 'I dispute with you,' he went on, 'because I think it very important that Roman Catholics should realise the fate which is fast overtaking them. They live emphatically in a fool's paradise....'

Because what is received is expressed in the idiom of those who first heard it, all religions which claim an historical revelation are extremely vulnerable to the onslaughts of new knowledge. The erosion of the traditional Christian statement was far more rapidly effected in those areas where the results of the scientific revolution were most widely disseminated. It is only a matter of time before a certain kind of education becomes universal and the process is completed. Yesterday Western Europe and North America, today Islam and Jewry, tomorrow the Christian communions of the Orient. Cecil was well aware how far the necessary attempts to disentangle the Christian faith from its traditional formulation had eaten into the vitals of Protestantism, and he foresaw that the longer Roman Catholics shirked the task the harder in the end would it be to accomplish. But his warnings, and the warnings of many like him went unheeded, and if the Roman Catholic Church finds herself today in a state of confusion, disarray, and doctrinal chaos unparalleled in her history she is but paying the price of her paradise.

Those under her care have found the reckoning expensive. No sensible person would lose his appetite if it were proved that Great Britain had never at any time been attached to the continent of Europe. But a religious mistake is very different from a scientific one. Statements of religious belief are vehicles for religious faith, the containers of man's most valuable possession. The forces unleashed by the General Council have shocked and unsettled Catholics all over the world but the peculiar religious pattern of this country has rendered it particularly sensitive to violent change. Everything has happened so quickly. People feel that somehow or other they are the victims of a sleight of hand, an elaborate conjuring trick, that when the patter runs dry, the arms cease to wave, the fingers to flutter, they will be smilingly asked to identify the object on the table as the one they had in their pocket the whole time. Not only has an acute crisis of confidence come into being but an animosity which sours the relationship between one group and another. At the root of it all are bewilderment, uncertainty, and fear.

When Catholics are taking up so many Protestant positions the apologist's task has become a nightmare. Knox's gay satire *Reunion All Round* no longer seems quite so sparkling; conversion stories with their grateful references to safe havens and Rocks of Gibraltar make painful reading. Educated cradle Catholics feel that both at home and abroad the reforming wing has sold the pass, opened the postern gate and betrayed the old religion into the hands of the very people who did the martyrs to death. What did the Archbishop of Paderborn mean when in answer to the key question whether Rome believed herself to be Christ's Church, he replied that it was only on the way to becoming so? How could Bishop Blomjous of Mwanza actually say that Catholics used to think that missionary efforts were directed to convert all men to live as brothers in a single Church, but now it seems that religious pluralism is part of God's plan? What did the the Constitution on the Church itself mean by suggesting that heretics and schismatics are in some sense incorporated into her? And why had the title for the Mass for ending schism been changed into one 'For the unity of the Church'? We cannot pray for what we already possess, for something which we must possess, if we are to call ourselves Christ's Church at all. For if the Church is not one, she is many, and if she is many for what cause then did the martyrs shed their blood?

There are others, perhaps more bitter than any, who have gone through all this before, and they are perplexed and disquieted to hear Protestant slogans on Catholic lips. They have escaped what they considered to be the ambiguities of the Anglican Communion Service, and do not like to read in a bishop's pastoral letter that the Eucharist is now regarded as a meal instead of only a sacrifice. It is with sinking heart they learn about new views of the priesthood which are now emerging from Rome. They can greet with no enthusiasm the opinion of a Consultor to the Council's Secretariat of Christian Unity that Catholics have now passed from a cultic to a ministerial understanding of the rôle of their pastors. They have rid themselves of the evasive answers and shufflings of Protestant clergymen who were uncertain if it were needful or not for Christians to believe in the miraculous draught of fishes, only to perceive an uneasy quivering in the branches of the Roman oak. They begin to entertain the horrible suspicion that the bright colours of the famous Second Spring were in reality but the last dying brilliance of autumnal foliage.

The less informed majority have been plunged into a conflict for which they were totally unprepared. Their world has been turned upside down. Encouraged to think of the Church as spotless they have been shocked to hear her criticised by her own children. Spoon-fed for generations they have been disconcerted to discover that some of what before they had been led to believe part of the deposit of faith has been relegated to mere theological opinion, that perhaps limbo does not exist and after all Adam and Eve never lived in an earthly paradise. Accustomed to laughing at Protestants for taking upon themselves an unlicensed commission to teach all nations without knowing what to say, they are confounded to hear their own trumpet give forth an uncertain sound. They are puzzled to hear Thomas More's 'lousy Luther' smoothly referred to as a religious genius. They are horrified to hear mention of inventions in the Scriptures, to understand that what they once took literally may belong to another order of truth whose existence they had not been led to consider. They are perplexed to hear theologians say there must be a return to the Gospels when it had never entered their heads to think Catholics had left them. They always thought the Church infallible (although sometimes a little more infallible than at others) and are thoroughly disturbed to find a priest, whose works their popular Catholic newspaper described as a 'must' for anyone who seeks to have an intelligent idea of the Church, point out that doctrinal statements are not only open to correction but stand in need of it. Having been told on high authority that the Church could no more permit birth-control than she could permit blasphemy they are bewildered to find the practice, under its new designation of responsible parenthood, widely debated even among the clergy. Any suggestion of mistake strikes at the root of their religious certainty.

The great divide, the real battle-ground, is between those who believe in God and those who do not. The people who swallowed uncritically a certain kind of religion will be the very ones as unthinkingly to swallow atheistic humanism. And these are the little ones for whose spiritual peace theologians tip-toed through the minefields of biology, history, psychology, and biblical exegesis, for whose undisturbed slumbers devoted censors sweated over their *imprimaturs*, for whose eternal welfare the mills of the Roman executive ground so exceedingly small. Whether after the Council some sort of control over free expression will be attempted it is impossible to tell. But what has been said, has been said. Issues once raised must be dealt with. And when the vernacular liturgy loses its novelty and papal travels seem as commonplace as the peregrinations of the Archbishop of Canterbury, not only will the urgency of these questions become more plain, but it will be perceived that upon their answer depends the whole future of Christianity.

Whatever its immediate results, in retrospect the Second Vatican Council will be seen to be a watershed in the history of religion as decisive as the summoning of the Estates General was to the Europe of 1789. Forced with brutal haste to grapple with problems other Christians have been wrestling with for centuries the Roman Catholic Church has discovered that the answer requires her to repudiate some of her basic thinking and so cease to be her historic self. By ceasing to be her historic self she has given the *coup de grâce* to the tottering superstructure of Christianity. From now on it will become more and more plain that however much accustomed allegiances may influence our thinking, the old confessional differences are anachronistic and fundamentally irrelevant. The lines of demarcation lie not between this or that Church, but between groups of people from any denomination who offer different solutions to those problems common to all.[1]

[1] Father Schillebeeckx in an article on the Council reprinted in *The Life of the Spirit* revealingly remarked that the conservatives' 'thinking and working stems from the self-same faith, the Catholic and Apostolic faith. And yet one sometimes gets the impression that (they) are speaking from a faith apart. One is astonished to find oneself more in sympathy with the thinking of Christian, non-Catholic, observers than with the views of one's own brethren the other side of the dividing-line.' There is no need for astonishment. In a very real sense the conservatives *are* thinking from a faith apart, or more accurately, a belief apart. To put the point another way, many Roman Catholics must find themselves more in agreement with the views of the Anglican (and therefore heretical) Dr Mascall than with the kind of evangelical Catholicism represented by Dr Küng. In his turn, Dr Mascall is religiously nearer the present Cardinal Archbishop of Westminster than he is to his fellow Anglican the Bishop of Woolwich.

As long as any single Christian communion claimed to possess the only certainly true solution this could not happen. But the most far-reaching result of the Council has been Rome's implicit abandonment of the one principle which had come to separate her essentially from the Reformed communions, seemed to provide a bulwark for the faithful, irritated her enemies, and in some curious and illogical way comforted those outside her boundaries. This principle was contained in her answer to the question which mankind has been asking through the ages: 'How can we know that what other people tell us about God is true?' 'You can know because God has committed to the Roman Catholic Church and to her alone the task of preserving and interpreting His final self-revelation without the possibility of definite error. The seat of revelation is the seat of authority. The source of revelation is God. Therefore, when the Church speaks with the voice of authority she is speaking with the voice of God. Go back and read the Shorter Act of Faith.'

But in an instant the Shorter Act of Faith rips off the sticking-plaster and exposes the nerve of our religious predicament. 'Oh my God, I believe in you and all your Church does teach because you have said it and your word is true.' It was just because much that the Christian Church said turned out not to be true, to be intellectually, morally, and imaginatively unacceptable to a consensus of informed minds that so many found they could walk no more with her. It is the gradual, reluctant, agonising realisation that neither Church nor Scripture is simply the voice of God which has lain behind all the religious struggles of the past three hundred years. The real conflict within the Roman Catholic Church today is between those who recognise this and have emerged from their fool's paradise and those who have not. It is between those who, in common with the majority of Christians,[1] are seeking to find another answer to this fundamental question and those who still think the old answer adequate.

Some Reformers in an attempt to establish their doctrinal *bona fides* used to appeal for support to the first four General Councils. In the same way, there is a tendency among some Catholic liberals to appeal to a purer, non-scholastic kind of Catholicism, to put the blame for all our discontents at the door of something which has been called 'non-historical orthodoxy'. In so far as non-historical orthodoxy means extreme papalism, an over-juridical approach to doctrinal formulations, a terror of criticism, intellectual dishonesty, triumphalism, Vaticanism, creeping infallibility, all that yesterday was confined to the classic Protestant rebuke, it is a legitimate label. But if we are to appreciate the magnitude of the present Christian crisis, we must have sufficient mental clarity and courage unshrinkingly to accept that what is happening within the Roman Catholic Church at the moment is not *primarily* an attack on non-historical orthodoxy at all. What is really in dispute today is Catholic orthodoxy, in other words that conviction about the nature of the Church which was once universally regarded as indispensable to the very existence of Christianity.

The traditional view has been stated with force and learning by Dom B. C. Butler, the present Abbot of

[1] Not all, however. For a number of Protestant sects the Bible is still without difficulty accepted as literal divinely revealed truth. And these sects, for example Primitive Baptists, Pentecostals, and Jehovah's Witnesses never compromised with Hitler or the Soviet Government. In many ways they display a missionary zeal and refusal of the illicit demands of the state which puts us to shame. Narrow streams run deep.

Downside.[1] The Church, explains the Abbot, is essentially a single visible communion of baptised persons, an historical, concrete society with a divinely established system of government. This society is, under certain conditions, infallible within the whole province of faith and morals, and is the ark of salvation appointed by God existing to the exclusion of all other such societies. Since she is essentially a single visible communion, there can be no such thing as schism *within* the Church; schismatics are in a state of separation *from* the Church. Unprejudiced scholarship has shown that the Christian Church thought of herself from the very beginning in this way, and there is in existence only one society which has, throughout her history, not only preached but acted on this understanding. That society is the Roman Catholic Church, and a schismatic is one who refuses to be subject to the Roman See which is unwavering in its call to all men to join her visible communion. While it should be remembered how much even Christians divided from her in good faith share in the grace-gifts which flow from our redemption, and borne in mind that elements of aids to salvation are found outside the Church, these elements are still 'things of the Church', ecclesiastical property, so to speak, which has got into unauthorised hands. Membership of the Roman Catholic Church is, objectively speaking, of universal obligation, an obligation which is as grave as salvation is important.

[1] *The Church and Infallibility*, Sheed & Ward, 1954: *The Idea of the Church*, Darton, Longman & Todd, 1962.

It should be pointed out that in these two books Abbot Butler is dealing with the intellectual justification, the rational basis, so to say, of the Christian Church, the institutional framework within which she lives her interior life, the container, not the contents. The deeper centre of unity, of course, lies in the Church seen as a community of prayer, this the author makes quite plain.

All this is, or rather was, the commonplace of Catholic apologetic.[1] Indeed, nothing else makes Roman Catholicism internally consistent. It is on these grounds she calls herself the one, true Church, thinks it sinful for Catholics to be educated in non-Catholic schools, frowns on mixed marriages, and keeps her orphans in institutions rather than permit them to live in the homes of those who do not share the faith. This is why the liturgy prayed that heretics and schismatics led away by the devil's deceits would reject their mischievous errors and come back repentant to the unity of truth. It is for this reason Catholics pray that England may be converted. And if a person received into the Church recites the longer Profession of Faith he says that, having before his eyes the Holy Gospels, 'and knowing that no one can be saved without the faith which the Holy, Catholic, Apostolic, Roman Church holds, believes and teaches; against which I grieve that I have greatly erred, inasmuch as, having been born outside the Church, I have held and believed doctrines opposed to her teaching; I now, enlightened by the grace of God, profess that I believe the Holy, Catholic, Apostolic, Roman Church to be the one true Church established on earth by Jesus Christ to which I submit myself with my whole heart. I firmly believe all the articles she proposes for my belief; I reject and condemn all that she rejects and condemns, and I am ready to observe all that she commands me.'

It is on account of this conviction that in the past ecumenism could imply nothing further than increased charity towards heretics, efforts to understand their point

[1] Abbot Butler's books are employed here for convenience of argument but readers might like to be referred to Fr A. Hasting's *One and Apostolic*, Fr S. Bullough's *Roman Catholicism* (Pelican Original), and Fr T. Corbishley's *Roman Catholicism*, in Hutchinson's University Library.

of view, confession of faults, attempts to curb a few extravagant devotions, a more flexible attitude and open-mindedness all round. But open-mindedness had a very definite limit. There could be only one-way traffic between a society which believed the teaching authority of Jesus Christ to be conferred exclusively on her and those whose Christianity was not only diluted but illegitimate. The fact of the matter is that little either was, or could be, heard about 'bridge-churches' until the chasm ceased to exist.

What is of importance is the clear-sightedness with which Abbot Butler stresses the significance of the traditional view. The idea that the Church is essentially a single visible communion indissociable by its essence is not only basic to the Roman claim, but if surrendered must lead to doctrinal liberalism of an extreme kind. For if we think the Church was wrong in this estimate of her nature and teaching authority, then she has been on the wrong track since the first Pentecost, when she went forth with the historico-dogmatic affirmation that Jesus had risen from the dead. Indeed, if she has been wrong and Donatists and Arians and subsequent schismatics are really part of Christ's Church, then the Great Councils were not ecumenical, and the Church, or 'whatever we mean by the Church' will have to go back and ask by what authority she excluded them, and consider if, after all, theirs was not a valid interpretation of the Gospel. Since any abandonment of the traditional view of the Church would succeed only in bringing 'into the field of question and uncertainty' some of the basic doctrines of Christianity there can be no possibility of a new ecclesiology. Although development might be possible within the existing ecclesiology, any proposed 'reconsideration' of a radical nature would commit us not to a genuine development of faith and theology, but to rejection of the past and therefore to a revolution in thought.

This is the orthodox position described by someone who is both an able theologian and very far from reactionary. There is nothing non-historical about it. Nor is there anything non-historically orthodox about the Catholic belief that we have certain knowledge of the laws of God and that, if history or experience conflicts with these laws, history and experience are wrong despite all evidence to the contrary. Abbot Butler explains that 'since in the objective order of things it cannot be God's will that we should attain salvation by accepting error, it follows further that the Church's dogmatic decisions are not liable to error'. This is precisely the difficulty and it was not the weakness but the strength of the traditional position which, when it was so painfully abandoned, left Christians struggling on the quicksands of doubt and uncertainty.

We may smile at Wiseman's naïve denial that Catholics resisted the progress of scientific investigation though they 'could not allow any doctrine of physiology to be taught which led to a pre-Adamite theory, or one of plurality of races, inconsistent with the doctrine of the Fall, Original Sin, and Redemption'. But this was only what Pius XII was to repeat in *Humani Generis*, and, granted the premise, was entirely logical. 'Than truth's own word there is no truer token.' When the Church speaks with the voice of authority she is speaking with the assistance of the Holy Ghost. It follows that, since the Holy Ghost can neither err nor contradict himself, if the facts of history, science, or human experience conflict with the formulation of that revelation, so much the worse for the facts of history, science, or human experience. If possible the facts are denied, if they cannot be denied, they are made to fit the formula; if they cannot be made to fit the formula it is suggested that after all the formula itself is not revealed truth but theological opinion. Newman put it succinctly enough: 'If anything seems to be proved . . . in contradiction to the dogmas of Faith, that point will eventually turn out, first, *not* to be proved, or, secondly, *not contradictory*, or thirdly, not contradictory to anything *really revealed*, but to something which has been confused with revelation'.

Acton thought Newman an artful apologist. He was not exactly artful, but he was devious and ambivalent. This was partly due to his general temperament and the possession of an intellect as sensitive to fine distinctions as the noses of others to delicate smells. It was due also to the fact that, although he stoutly denied it in the *Apologia*,[1] he was, as his private letters admit, 'fighting under the lash'. However, the most profound source of his ambiguity was that he never reconciled his intense conviction of the spiritual truth of Catholicism and the plain evidence that it was the historic Christian Church, with his awareness of the seemingly insoluble problems confronting the orthodox.

We all know to what lengths the determination not to make any attempt to reconcile modern knowledge with Catholicism was to drive the extreme ultramontane party, how Veuillot addressed the *Veni Sancte* to the Pope, and went so far as to substitute the name Pius for

[1] What would have happened if Kingsley had been a better informed and less crude adversary? Newman was well aware that truth for its own sake was not a virtue with the Roman clergy. 'Nothing,' he was writing about the same time as Kingsley's attack, 'would be better than an historical review. But who could bear it? Unless one doctored one's facts one would be thought a bad Catholic.' This last point is made together with some judicious comments on the whole controversy by E. I. Watkin in his book *Roman Catholicism in England from the Reformation to 1950*, Oxford University Press, 1957.

God in a really blasphemous version of an ancient hymn. But perhaps we do not sufficiently appreciate how generally unhealthy the atmosphere of the time was, recollect the flatulent and inflated language employed even by those who were attempting some sort of *modus vivendi*. Montalembert and Lacordaire were capable of addressing the Pope: 'Oh Father, vouchsafe to cast your eye on some of the lowest of your children who are accused of being rebellious against your infallible and mild authority. Behold them before you; read in their souls; there is nothing there they wish to hide. If one of their thoughts, only one, differs from yours, they disown, they abjure it. You are the ruler of their doctrines. Never, no, never, have they known others. Oh Father, pronounce over them the word which gives life because it gives light.'

It is obvious that people like Acton and Döllinger inherited a task which was as urgent as it was impossible to execute. As for Newman, his hands were tied behind his back. His right was fettered by the Roman autocracy, his left by his own conservatism. At the Munich Congress, Döllinger and his colleagues defended a liberal Catholicism, employing the same arguments and speaking sometimes in almost identical language as do our progressives today. These activities were smartly knocked on the head by the Pope, who by means of a Brief, put an end to freedom of inquiry by insisting that the researches of scholars should be conducted with reference to ecclesiastical authority, and that Catholics were bound, not only by dogmatic definitions, but by accepted theological opinion and the decisions of the Roman Congregations. Newman had no difficulty about acquiescing in the letter and principle of the Brief, although, characteristically, he dreaded their application and the prospect of being subjected to 'the dull tyranny of Manning and Ward'. The fact is that Newman's superficial disagreements with

W. G. Ward, and the manner in which his doctrine of development was used by some Modernists to cover their own notions about the mutability of dogma have obscured that half of his mind which was fundamentally conservative.

This great Cassandra of the nineteenth century, not only much more intelligent but far better informed than most of his Roman Catholic contemporaries, warned Christians over and over again that the forces of scientific knowledge allied with the all-corroding, wild, living intellect of man would lead straight to infidelity unless religion was placed on a far more secure basis than either Scriptural fundamentalism or personal experience in the evangelical sense.[1] Newman used natural religion, not as most Roman Catholics at the time, as a kind of buttress to revealed religion, but as its foundation, and no one was more sensitive than he to the difficulty of getting to the depths of an idea or more conscious of the inadequacy of doctrinal formulations. If he had been born a hundred, or even fifty years later when the issues were clearer, we should have had a defence of Christianity worthy of his genius. In the event, enormously helpful as he was in establishing a basis for assent to religious belief in general, when it came to the concrete, to the particular, to what agitated people, to the question how can we know revelation to be correctly stated, he could

[1] It is amusing to remember that in the charged and inquisitorial atmosphere which followed the suppression of Modernism, Newman's own conversion, that 'luminous certainty' experienced at the age of fifteen, the truth of which he was more sure about than that he had hands and feet, came to be regarded in some quarters with suspicion and alarm. A few attempts were (vainly) made to get Wilfred Ward to play down the whole episode in his biography. See Maisie Ward, *Insurrection versus Resurrection*, Sheed and Ward, 1937. To this book the quotation from Cecil's letter is indebted.

only repeat the traditional and implausible answer. '...I believe in whatever the Church teaches as the voice of God—and this or that particular inclusively, *if* she teaches this—it is this *fides implicita* which is our comfort in these irritating times.' Of what use was this to those Christians who admitted to themselves that they no more believed in an historical Adam and Eve, eternal torment, or the necessity of baptism for salvation, than they did in Jack and the Beanstalk?

The very clarity of Newman's arguments threw the central difficulty into relief. All the dogmatic developments over the centuries might be legitimate growth from the seed, but we can only know this for certain by appealing to the authority of those who are selling the flowers. Newman could but assume that there must be earthly teachers not subject to error. In doctrinal matters, the Church, acting through Pope and Councils, was the utterance of the Holy Ghost; the 'oracle of heaven'. Mankind is in fact offered the stark alternative of the chequer-board. There is only one authority in existence who can tell us all that human beings are capable of knowing about God and his plans for this world. That authority is the Roman Catholic Church. If a man does not accept the authority of Rome, he can have no rational basis, not for his general faith in Christianity, but for his personal belief. This is not to say he will not be saved, not to say he will believe in nothing; it is just that what he believes, whether he knows it or not, is in reality underwritten by Rome, by the very authority he consciously rejects.

In effect, Newman put a pistol, not to the heart, but to the head of Protestant England. If, as his gifted prose made only too plain, all the real arguments against Roman Catholicism were arguments against Christianity, then Christianity was as incredible as Roman Catholicism. He must have agreed with Abbot Butler[1] that a preliminary inventory of what is contained in the immutable essence of Catholicism is provided by the corpus of doctrinal definitions of ecumenical Councils and of the Pope teaching *ex cathedra*. So the mass of doctrinal definitions, the infallible utterances of the Pope, irreformable in their own nature not because of the assent of the Church, are part of the immutable essence of Christianity. Since verbal definitions are capable of almost infinite manipulation, in practice this implies consent to all that curial theologians at any given time more or less unanimously consider to be absolutely true statements of either doctrine or morals. Submission to the whole must follow, if, in the first place, it be once granted that there is such a thing as a definite revelation of doctrinal truth. And this is but a *preliminary* inventory. If one brought oneself to accept such a view, then one was sucked into Rome's secondary system, caught up in her devotions and indulgences, ordered about, subjected to irksome restrictions on freedom of scholarship, expected to participate in extravagant Mediterranean practices, to exchange Archdeacon Grantly for Father O'Flynn, and pay respectful attention when informed by the Pope that the Hebrew patriarchs knew all about the doctrine of the Immaculate Conception.[2] It was this complex of difficulties which made Roman Catholicism 'frankly impossible' for so many of the most sensitive religious minds of the past.

[1] *The Tablet*, September 1963.

[2] '. . . the Hebrew patriarchs were familiar with the doctrine of the Immaculate Conception, and found consolation in the thought of Mary in the solemn moments of their life.' Encyclical of Pope Pius X, October 1904. Quoted by Dean Inge, *Outspoken Essays*, 1919.

Nevertheless, Pope Gregory the Great had far more in common with Father O'Flynn than he had with Dr Grantly, and St Augustine of Canterbury would have made short work of Archbishop Sumner. Those who without reservation believed in the Christian creeds, who were convinced that there was such a thing as a definite revelation of doctrinal truth, should logically have become Roman Catholics. Such people rejected Roman Catholicism for reasons which were either superficial or basically inconsistent with their own position. To some the Gorham Judgment[1] made plain that 'the Church of England had forfeited its authority as a divine teacher'. What were the thoughts of the High Church Gladstone when, with his back to the fireplace and his face towards the disappointed Manning, he refused to put his name to the agreed protest? Gladstone was so horrified when he learnt that J. S. Mill had advocated birth-control that he withdrew his support from a proposed memorial. If he had lived to see Lambeth capitulate would he have become a Roman Catholic and contraception have achieved what a denial of baptismal regeneration had failed to do?

[1] A *cause célèbre* which began in 1847. The Rev G. C. Gorham was suspected of holding unsound views about baptismal regeneration. His bishop, therefore, refused to institute him to a living in his diocese. After lengthy litigation the case was referred to the Judicial Committee of the Privy Council which declared in Gorham's favour. As his bishop remained obstinate, in the end Gorham was instituted by the Archbishop of Canterbury, J. B. Sumner, who did not consider baptismal regeneration to be a fundamental doctrine of the Church of England. The case drew attention both to the theological uncertainties within the Anglican Church, and the weakness of having a secular tribunal act as a court of appeal in doctrinal matters. As a result many went over to Rome including H. E. Manning, the future Archbishop of Westminster.

As for Acton, it was all very well for him to call Newman artful, but was he himself free from muddle? Did the nineteenth-century *Rambler* Catholics know where they were going any more than our present day progressives? It was poor old Capes, exhausted from running backwards and forwards between Rome and Canterbury, who really put his finger on the point at issue when he said he was unable to accept 'a literal orthodoxy as an explanation of the great mystery of life'. The sad truth is that whatever temporary comfort Newman may have provided in those irritating times, since he depended on an assumption already exploded, to follow him, as the events of the last years have made plain, was to be lured into a state of illusory security.

For a variety of reasons, not the least because, as Jowett remarked, he had a kind of faith in knowing nothing, to go back to A. H. Clough[1] is to hear the twentieth century thinking aloud. Clough had listened to the growlings of Carlyle, read Goethe, made friends with Emerson, caught echoes of German philosophy, and above all had, as it were, perceived from afar the strained face of George Eliot as she sat patiently translating Strauss's *Leben Jesu*. Not for him the delicate cynicism of Jowett, the nervous acrobatics of Stanley, the circular scurryings of people like Acton, Gladstone, Newman, and Capes. Of course a literal orthodoxy could not explain the great mystery of life. It was patently inadequate, it had been proved wrong. If Rome did not know the truth, there was no reason to suppose Canterbury, or her dependents, derivatives and modifications, to be any the wiser. What else was there to do but become a disenchanted and dissatisfied agnostic:

[1] Katharine Chorley's *Arthur Hugh Clough: The Uncommitted Mind*, Clarendon Press, 1962, is a most interesting study of his life and poetry.

Eat, drink and die, for we are souls bereaved:
Of all the creatures under heaven's wide cope
We are the most hopeless, who had once most hope,
And most beliefless, that had most believed.

But a stark choice between orthodoxy and apostasy is as unreal as it is intolerable. Truth cannot hover between alternatives such as these. The world of thought and religious experience is not a Mogul moon-garden, a hedged enclosure of black and white. How did such a situation ever come about? If an answer can be given to this, we might be on the way to a solution of the whole difficulty.

Cautiously then, and remembering that such a vast historical structure as the Church cannot be wholly consistent in detail or practice, it might be suggested that from its earliest beginnings Christianity was faced with a problem which it never succeeded in answering. Seen from one aspect its whole history has been the attempt to resolve the tension which has resulted from two different but complementary answers being given to the question which inquires about the basis of religious certainty. On the one hand the interior assent of the spirit, the response of like to like; on the other the assent to the witness of an institutional Church which was presumed to embody the objective principle of doctrinal authority. The Christian Church was, at one and the same time, a community and a society. It was a community in so far as its unity did not depend solely on assent to a shared creed but on a shared life. It was a society in so far as its unity did depend on a shared creed and those who refused to subscribe to this creed were ejected, anathematised, and cast into outer darkness. But this is very far from saying that it considered the root of religious certainty to lie solely in its institutional authority. As long as it remained a comparatively small organisation more or less at peace with itself, it could run on both cylinders at once. Its certainty that its understanding of the work of God in Christ was true was founded upon acceptance of doctrinal authority interpenetrated by personal experience.

'The hint half guessed, the gift half understood, is Incarnation.' It would be a gross over-simplification to say that in its early centuries the Christian Church held exactly the same constricted notions about the nature of dogmatic statements as dominant western theologians came to hold later on in her history. 'If we are minded to reach a fuller theoretical understanding it is safer to go back to the original foundations resting it once more upon faith's primary insight rather than dogmas which were long ago formulated for the preservation of that insight.' These are not the words of a progressive Dutch friar or a professor from the university of Tübingen. They were written by St Athanasius.[1] Yet it was Athanasius' insistence on the truth which lay behind a certain description of the Son that helped to save Christianity from unitarianism. That is the puzzle. God is known in the order of experience before He is known in the order of theological proposition, but theological propositions about Him are the necessary concomitant of preaching the Gospel. And to proclaim is to dogmatise; an idea stated is an idea conceptualised, an idea conceptualised is an idea captured by its own statement, pinned to the board like a dead butterfly. It was this that made St Paul cry out about the glass darkly, a harassed Athanasius inquire where was the ear capable of understanding what lies beyond the power of man to express. But

[1] Quoted by John Baillie. *The Sense of the Presence of God,* Gifford Lectures, 1961–62. O.U.P.

as was to be remarked some one thousand five hundred years later, a Christianity without dogmas, precise and well defined, was more like a nervous disease than a religion. Some sort of expression there had to be, and indeed, as Abbot Butler has reminded us, apostolic preaching began with the historico-dogmatic affirmation that Jesus had risen from the dead. Christians did not butcher each other for the sake of an opinion, and however mistrustful they may have been about the suitability of the tools at their disposal, they never thought it possible for the Church consistently and solemnly to teach error.

In any field progress is best achieved by the integration of what has been perceived in fits and starts by a few, not by the crude confrontation of two opposed systems of thought. It is the slow, silent, consolidated advance of the human mind, bit by bit taking over one position after another, which is the mark of sound, organic growth. Humanity requires the gentle substitution of stronger lenses in the spectacles with which it observes the world. Violent replacement leads not to clear definition but to blindness. As the consequence of events not altogether within her control, the natural development of the Christian Church was stunted, and change, when it came, meant revolution.

It was not the discovery of Jupiter's satellites which really flustered the authorities of the Renaissance Church. It was a new attitude towards knowledge, life, and the world around us, the vigorous thrustings of an empiricism which was experimentally to disprove what was previously held to be fixed and certain. Intellectually and socially the old order was doomed. No longer would an external authority be able to impose a thought pattern on the community at large, no longer would it be able to gain assent to the truth of one particular map of the supernatural. For good and ill in the course of time an industrial society would possess both sufficient conscience and capital to educate the majority of its citizens in the same attitude and enable them to employ the same techniques. The pity of it was that the scientific method would continue to be used where its writ simply did not run, and that in the event its third-rate practitioners succeeded in substituting one *a priori* system for another.[1]

That the Church found herself immediately unable to reconcile what was happening with what she believed about herself is understandable. She could and would have come to terms, had she been given time to develop normally, to rediscover in peace the laws of her own being. But she was not given time. While she was still blinking in the light of the New Learning she was attacked on an entirely different flank by the Protestant reformers and naturally enough seized the most obvious weapons with which to preserve her identity. Already impoverished by diminished contact with the oriental approach,[2] the riches of her original thought were neglected and she suffered a loss of flexibility at the very time when the whole future of Christianity depended upon courage and vision. The energies which

[1] Brilliantly illustrated by a snatch of conversation between two little boys in William Golding's *The Lord of the Flies*:

'The trouble is: Are there ghosts Piggy? Or beasts?'

' 'Course there aren't.'

'Why not?'

' 'Cos things wouldn't make sense. Houses, an' streets, an' TV —they wouldn't work.'

[2] It is not without significance that some of the wisest speeches in the Council were made by Maximos IV Saigh, the Melchite Patriarch of Antioch.

should have been concentrated against a far more dangerous but remoter threat were necessarily used up opposing the more obvious foe. She was not to know that some hundreds of years later she would concede so much to this same enemy that the Lutheran Bishop of Berlin would be able to remark that if the Roman Catholic Church had been then what she is now, his leader would not have left her. But she was not then what she is now, nor were the Protestants what they are. Faced with a barbarous reaction against Catholicism all she could do was to put forward an elaborate statement of a position already undermined. 'Our stability is but balance,' sang Bridges, 'and wisdom lies in masterful administration of the unforeseen.' For the moment this had gone. A very nearly fatal shift of emphasis was made and tenaciously clung to. Since the Protestants were denying this, that, and the other, faith came to be regarded not so much as an act of loving confidence in the mind of Christ, but one of blind assent to whatever the Church said about him. Faith and its formulation were still more closely linked, and the infant called Science shuddered in its cradle.

In one sense the Reformation was an old-fashioned movement, out of date even at its inception. The Protestants pitched their tents on the débris of Catholicism, on what Matthew Arnold was to call 'poor fragments of a broken world', fragments which continually shifted under their feet. Exasperated and disgusted by what they considered to be an obese caricature of Christianity they fell piecemeal on Catholicism, concerning themselves in the first place with the righting of obvious wrongs, ridding religion of particular abuses, with getting Christianity to shed its fat. Ham-strung by their own disobedience they started with no consistent theory about the nature of the Church or the ultimate source of our knowledge of God. But they were one with Rome in believing that he had vouchsafed to man a definite revelation of unalterable doctrinal truth. Their only difficulty was location.

As long as the belief of Christians coincided with what seemed to be fact, although this was inconvenient and the cause of much interdenominational squabbling, it was not perceived to be the root problem it is. But as time went on and it became clear that Christians had attached their faith to much that scientific knowledge and a different kind of moral consciousness had shown to be false, the Reformers' lack of anything but an improvised ecclesiology exposed their nakedness.

If classical Protestantism had appealed to some purer religion which did not in the last resort depend on the authority of an institutional Church or the inerrancy of a Bible, it would have provided a more deeply thought-out alternative to Roman Catholicism and spared itself the débâcle of the nineteenth century. This was indeed attempted in isolation by the extreme Protestant radicals who wove their garment from a single but persistent thread drawn from the Catholic cloak. 'When my hopes in them [the Protestant ministers] and all men were gone,' said the Quaker George Fox, 'so that I had nothing outwardly to help me, I heard a voice which said "There is one, even Jesus Christ, who can speak to thy condition".' But the time was not ripe. The movement failed for a number of reasons, political and social as well as strictly religious, but most importantly because it remained a single thread, idiosyncratic and generally speaking, non-intellectual, unable either logically or practically to be worked into a fabric of sufficient strength to withstand the attacks of informed secularism.

These people, however, hit the nail on the head. They have left it to us to drive it home.[1]

The established Church of this country was fettered by those Catholic elements to which it so illogically, but in many ways so splendidly, clung. Anglicans were unable to defend their initial revolt by the Catholic principles to which they appealed against their own schismatics. Failing to find a satisfactory centre of authority not only had they no effective weapon with which to fight the doctrinal innovators within their own ranks, but until they looked beyond orthodoxy were powerless against the scientific assault. This challenge cut across the divisions within the ranks of the Reformers and obliterated the traditional distinction between the Catholic and Evangelical parties within Anglicanism itself. With some exceptions, the early response of all parties to the scientific threat was substantially the same as Rome's, merely far less effectual. Bishop Wilberforce was only Cardinal Wiseman without the hat.[2] As long

[1] Of course only from this aspect. Nothing could be worse for the future of Christianity than for Rome to shed the ostrich feathers but retain the habits of the creature. That is to say, go violently Protestant in worship but maintain a doctrinal rigidity in defiance of the known truth. George H. Williams has written an account of the extent and variety of the left-wing movement: *The Radical Reformation*, Weidenfeld and Nicolson, 1962.

[2] Wilberforce declared that men were in danger of being 'robbed unawares of the very foundations of the Faith' if they should be persuaded to 'accept allegorically, or as parable, or poetry, or legend, the story of the serpent tempter, of an ass speaking with a man's voice . . .'. His hearers could not have required much persuasion to believe in the truth of his last assertion. It is astonishing to recall that as late as 1931 Fr Messenger could seriously suggest that Eve began life as a dermoid cyst on Adam's body. And in the same year Ronald Knox was writing that he thought it rash to reject the literal truth of the story of Jonah.

as faith was identified with belief, revelation with whatever Church or Bible said about it, all attempts to put the Ark of the Covenant out of reach of impious hands were futile. Modern science could not but be regarded as a thief, a bogey, a long-legged Scissorman whose dreaded arrival signified the disappearance of yet another article of the Creed.

But what the Reformers lost in one way they gained in another. Since they were able to look beyond orthodoxy so much earlier than Roman Catholics, bolder spirits could the sooner evolve a more pliant and probing theology. Those Protestants who were able to throw off their Scriptural fundamentalism were able to join with Anglicans, and High Churchmen at that, in a common search with their Continental and American brethren. These people had reached about fifty years ago the point where Roman Catholics are now. The doubts and difficulties which so agitate Roman Catholics today have not been resolved, but they are rather *vieux jeu* to those who have been considering them for decades.

However, habits of mind are strong, and for many the more difficult the road the more urgent the need for authoritative declarations and definitive pronouncements. Of all the attacks on Christian belief probably the most deeply disturbing was not the Darwinian revolution, the study of comparative religions, nor, after the first shock, the over-confident assertions of Higher Criticism, but the sober application to the New Testament of historical and textual methods. As this knowledge gradually reached a wider public there were those who suspected that the Protestant approach was so open-ended that all would tumble out. They wondered in good earnest what exactly was historical about salvation history, and feared that if the Holy Innocents were not massacred and the flight into Egypt never took place, perhaps the events surrounding Christ's Nativity were not true either. If the angels by the tomb were the product of excited Hebrew imagination, there was nothing left but an inerrant Church to guarantee that the same could not be said of the Risen Christ:

> To such a process I discern no end
> Cutting off one excrescence to see two;
> There is ever a next in size, now grown as big,
> That meets the knife. I cut and cut again;
> First cut the Liquefaction, what comes last
> But Fichte's clever cut at God Himself?

Newman's pistol went on firing long after the hand which triggered it had crumbled to dust. As the shades lengthened it seemed that only one Christian community of any intellectual standing remained to provide a secure foothold, and many eyes were turned towards that flock whose peaceful grazing was undisturbed either by the prowlings of the wolf or by the reasons for his absence. But the wind blows where it lists and another poet has warned us what to expect when hot for certainties in this our life. An unlikely person summoned the Second Council of the Vatican and before so very long it was plain that orthodox, historical Christianity had become frankly impossible for Roman Catholics themselves.

As the Council drew to its close Dr Küng was able to remark with quiet satisfaction that for the first time in her history an official distinction had been made between the Church of Christ and the visible Roman Catholic Church. If there is a distinction between the Church of Christ and the visible Roman Catholic Church, where then may the Church of Christ be found? The opportunity missed four hundred years ago had come at last. The old religion was committed to just such a revolution in thought as must bring the basic doctrines of Christianity 'into the field of question and uncertainty', to a radical examination of 'whatever we mean by the Church', to seeking, with the rest of humanity, a deeper foundation for faith.

II

In the Book of Judges we read that after those who were fearful and afraid departed, only ten thousand of the Israelite army remained to fight the host of Midian. When these ten thousand were reduced to a mere three hundred, and the Midianites and the Amalekites and all the children of the east lay along the valley like grasshoppers and their camels were without number, Gideon spoke to his people. Each man was ordered to hold a trumpet in his right hand and in his left a pitcher with a lamp inside. In the middle of the night the remnant of Israel surrounded the enemy camp. On the sound of Gideon's trumpet each blew his own and at the same time broke his pitcher, so releasing the lamp by whose light he was able to engage the enemy.

Let us take that pitcher to be the traditional Christian statement, represented at its fullest and most consistent by Roman Catholicism. Long ago cracked, it has been our fate to witness its shattering. We can attempt either to fit the pieces together again or we can recognise that the pitcher has served its purpose, that time has done its work, and the lamp within was no longer protected but imprisoned. About us too the host of Midian lies as thick as grasshoppers and declares that the pitcher was always empty, that among the sherds we shall search in vain for a lamp. If this be so, then Christianity is yet another of man's illusions, and we would do well to stop rummaging among the pieces, but with dignity resign ourselves to darkness and our preposterous end.

If we are to reject Christianity, however, let us do so for weighty reasons. In the present state of our knowledge we are like people groping along the road in the greyness before dawn. We can see little of the path ahead so we are bound to stumble, take wrong turnings, explore tracks which lead nowhere. What follows makes no pretence to be anything more than a finger pointing in the direction from which the sun must eventually rise.

There is no other way but to start with the rock of which the institutional Church is the expression. That rock is the communion of the soul with God. This communion is an absolutely certain fact of human experience, attested by clouds of witness from all the religious systems of the world. It is as established as the fact of human existence, more certain than many hypotheses we accept in order to make sense of the world of physical phenomena. It can be denied, anything can be denied, and it is precisely what the hosts of Midian do deny. But here is the real chequer-jump, the move from black to white, the central assent from what is, to what is. Like our assent to the revelation of God in Christ, it does not depend on narrowly intellectual arguments but on experience, most emphatically not solely our own, but the collective experience of a multitude no man can number.

The essential self of Catholicism, the idea of Christianity, is but the extension and application of the essence of religion. Religion is man's union with God in prayer. The essential idea of Christianity is a profounder application of this truth. A vague hope and diffused perception have become concrete in the life, death, and Resurrection of Jesus Christ. Man can not only unite himself to God in this world but attain the eternal happiness of deification in a transformed existence. We have, perhaps, been too slow to adjust our perspective. If religion is universal, it is universal. In this vast cosmos God must have shown himself under a multitude of forms to millions of beings whose existence we can reasonably postulate:

> But in the eternities,
> Doubtless we shall compare together, hear
> A million alien Gospels, in what guise
> He trod the Pleiades, the Lyre, the Bear.
> O, be prepared, my soul!
> To read the inconceivable, to scan
> The infinite forms of God these stars unroll
> When, in our turn, we show to them a Man.[1]

A million alien Gospels. Our Gospels, essentially identical, would be superficially unrecognisable to those who live in worlds where five hundred years pass between succeeding springs, and Jesus goes by another name.

We know that all theology is contingent, but the central experience of God is not. The fact that we describe Christianity in Hebrew imagery or analyse it in terms of Greek philosophy is fortuitous. Had matters fallen otherwise God might have shown himself to man as a Chinese coolie, an African Negro, a Texan garage hand or a greengrocer from Southend. Incarnate love could blaze out just as well from an electric chair as it did from a wooden cross. And if it should be that there is

[1] Alice Meynell. It is difficult to understand how Jesus can be the centre of the *universe*.

Incidentally, although in the *Phenomenon of Man* Teilhard de Chardin is not altogether clear, he seems to suggest that man is not only the peak of terrestrial biogenesis but somehow the summit of the universe which would commit 'abortion upon itself' should the human race come to a premature end. If this means what it appears to mean then it is a strange example of cosmic *folie de grandeur*.

nothing intrinsically inferior in the female, the Word could have been made flesh in a woman, poured its light from a hospital ward or a village by the side of the Ganges. Such thoughts seem shocking to us only because we have attached our faith and love to what did happen, not to what might have been. But we should try to be consistent to the end, not take up one pair of spectacles one minute and discard them the next because they make us feel uncomfortable. If we are to ask what is essential about Christianity we must ask what is essential about Christ. It is sad that Christianity has been judged by the moral shortcomings of Christians, but far sadder that God's whole revelation to man has been rendered incredible by a timid and stagnant theology which pinned the Word to the letter and not the spirit of its utterance. This was in truth a failure of nerve, a refusal to take the Incarnation to its logical conclusion.

The light of the sun is filtered where it falls, the incarnation of divine reality is limited by the very conditions which make it actual. The mystery of God, Blondel reminds us, could not be violated even by revelation itself. '. . . truth, even though divinely inspired, cannot commune with human thought except by becoming incarnate in the contingent forms which make it little by little assimilable.' It is not a last ditch defence, or a dilution of the faith, or a betrayal of Catholicism, but a deeper penetration to remember how far our common humanity conditioned both Christ's formulation of his mission and our understanding of it. If the Word had been an African Negro he would have been as much, and as little, a product of his milieu as Jesus was of his. It would have been his mind and will to which the world gave its response, his spirit that captured us, not his human knowledge, his imagery, or details about the kind of organisation he or his followers thought would best achieve his divine purpose.

''Tis at the roaring loom of time I ply, and weave for God the garment thou seest Him by.' Primitive Christians imagined that the world was to come to an end any minute and that the elect would be gathered up into the heavenly Jerusalem.[1] That was how, as others have pointed out, they merged their Hebrew national identity with their supernatural destiny, the means by which the Jewish religion could be assimilated into the Christian, how what was beyond their understanding was brought into their imaginative grasp. Catholic Christendom thought that there was only one visible Church on earth and that was doctrinally inerrant. This for explicable historical reasons broadened into the notion that the Church of Rome with all her dogmas, devotions, and ecclesiastical structure was the more or less perfected incarnation of God's revelation. This gave it driving force. Without this illusion it would have lacked propulsion. For we start as nursery people and a child's whole development depends on stability, on what is true at the time for him. Historic Catholic Christian-

[1] No one who reads Père Daniélou's book, *The Theology of Jewish Christianity*, Darton, Longman, and Todd, 1964, can do so without an increased realisation of the extent to which a religion is expressed through the idiom of the time, how both dependent and independent it is of the milieu in which it arises. The evidence from the Dead Sea Scrolls has enabled us to obtain a much clearer picture than formerly of the thought background to the New Testament. The first Jewish Christians expressed their faith through what is to us a queer mixture of the bizarre and the familiar: speaking crosses, pre-existent churches, seven heavens, strange dwelling places of angels and demons, the descent of Christ to the world of the dead, his miraculous birth, his ascents and descents through the air. The Semitic form in which the Church first expressed herself has, of course, influenced far more than our creeds and angelology.

ity was, from this aspect, the spiritual equivalent of geocentric ideas in the scientific field. Christianity escaped from the national-spiritual exclusiveness of Israel to the international-spiritual exclusiveness of Mediaeval Catholicism, as little squeamish about the *massa damnata* as about the economic servitude of the bulk of mankind. We forget how dependent we have been on the imperfect, the unpleasant, and even the loathsome, what an enormous debt civilisation owes to slavery, appalling poverty, religious intolerance, credulity,[1] and even fraud. At a certain stage in its history Catholicity depended on the existence of spiritual serfs, on the silent multitudes who believed what they were told, lived as they were told, and died as they were told. It was that or nothing. Religion is as much the art of the possible as anything else. In the history of Christianity we can see the Franciscan failure writ large.

But attempts to force a partially exploded system of thought beyond the limits of the possible is a sign of arrested development and can only provoke that kind of revolution the Roman Catholic Church is witnessing today. The more the letter of the Christian statement came to be incredible, the more it had to be imposed from without, and the more the Church moved away from its original grasp of the Christian fact. It is now impossible to think that God's self-revelation can be

[1] Would we now be enjoying the basilica at Vézelay in all its beauty if it had not been for some fairy-story about St Mary Magdalen? The possession of a fragment of Our Lady's chemise given by Charles the Bald undoubtedly enriched the cathedral at Chartres. We owe the glories of Compostela to delightful nonsense about St James the Great and a miraculous Spanish trip undertaken by the Blessed Virgin accompanied by angels bearing a marble pillar. See T. D. Kendrick's carefully documented, amusing, and appreciative *St James in Spain,* Methuen, 1960. The fruits of human folly are by no means always sour.

translated into guaranteed, uncontradictable truth statements, perpetually to be understood in the same sense. We cannot admit that Roman Catholic bishops are, in the words of a Doctor of Theology, 'as a body not allowed by God to teach what is wrong on matters of faith and morals revealed by Him', or that 'a definition by the Pope himself is sufficient to inform us of the truth'. This is an oppressive challenge to Roman Catholics. And it is the reason why, when a minority of people are fighting to establish the validity of any religious truth whatsoever, when we should be employing all our energy in considering such fundamental questions as the nature of the spiritual and natural world, what we can believe and what are our grounds for believing it, Catholics waste their time fretting about so paltry a matter as methods of contraception.

There is no reason to be fearful and afraid. We know well that Christianity is full of paradoxes, is indeed based on the greatest paradox possible, a God transcendent and a God incarnate. These things can be reconciled not on the surface, but in the depth, not in the letter, but in the spirit. Those of us who are in doubt about the kind of infallibility the Church possesses might find the answer has already been given in the paradox of the Incarnation.

It does not shake our faith in the Word made Flesh one jot to say that Jesus was completely ignorant of modern physics, nor should it disturb us in the least if it came to be shown that he believed in a discredited and to us fantastic cosmology or in the imminence of the Second Coming. He could do nothing else but express himself in terms of current ideas. He was not infallible, that is to say incapable of making an erroneous statement, either about the phenomenal world or the world we cannot see. If he had been he would not have been human and the Incarnation a sham. It is not within the competence of human language to make absolutely inerrant statements about spiritual reality beyond exact thought. God does not come to us in that way and, if we think he does, we are looking in the wrong direction. It was Christ's insight and spirit which were infallible, his whole presence, his total impact. So it is with his Church. The same principle applies to both, because humanity is their medium. But whereas Christ was utterly transparent to the Holy Spirit, the Church in the world is not. What came to her already under the veil was obscured still further, not only by the imaginative and intellectual presuppositions of successive centuries, but by sin and spiritual obtuseness. The servant is not greater than his Lord. If one whose spirit was perfectly united to God, could not, because he was human, express that spirit perfectly, how much less should we expect to be able to do so. The Risen Christ was freed from the inevitable restrictions of mortal humanity, and in good time, so too shall we. Let us not take upon ourselves now what belongs to the Church Triumphant. The Incarnation, the Church, the Eucharist, are all part of the same mystery, in their 'far depths does shine the Godhead's Majesty'. But the depth is not the surface.

Divine revelation cannot be identified with any verbal expression of it, whether it comes from the Church or is found in Scripture, but only with what lies behind it all, the truth to which both are pointing. This is often said but we have discovered it to our cost. And indeed a literal infallibility is as impossible to sustain with any degree of integrity as is biblical fundamentalism.

Doctrines of faith which refer directly to the nature of God suffer from an inherent imperfection. Dogmatic statements about morals, although they may involve ideas about God, are not in themselves stating something that lies beyond conceptual formulation. When they are wrong, they are wrong simply because man's ethical discrimination has been slow to develop. Morals are not divinely revealed but are discoverable through the exercise of right reason. Christianity never claimed to have given the world a unique moral code. Neither pagans nor Jews were strangers to the two great commandments, but by linking them together, showing us that where love is, so is God, Christianity deepened and made them more meaningful.

In general the Roman Catholic Church has been a constant, and in that sense, infallible witness to these commandments, but their application in given circumstances has not been so happy. History makes plain that, in common with other Christian communions, the Church rarely rose above the accepted standard of the best thinkers of her age, and, alas, frequently fell below it. In fact, owing to the natural conservatism of any institution, the humanist claim that the correction of some of the ugliest social evils has been achieved by non-Christians and atheists in the face of clerical opposition, is only too well founded. When enunciating particular rules the Roman Catholic Church has not spoken with the voice of the Holy Ghost but as the child of her age, at times officially commanding what we now see to be moral error.

When we remember the economic structure of the society into which Christianity was born, it is not surprising to find that the Church taught us it was right to own slaves, but we must admit that in permitting this she was condoning what we now recognise to be a particularly nasty violation of the natural law. Nor has her moral guidance been consistent in detail. Although in the ninth century Pope Nicholas I condemned judicial torture as contrary to divine and human law, later on in her history she not only officially commended the practice but employed it herself, both in her proceedings against heretics and as part of ordinary criminal investigation in the Papal States. This is common knowledge, and so is the fact that the Church once taught that those who did not belong to her visible communion had no hope of seeing God, that people who differed from her in theology had no right to spread their opinions or even to live, that it was possible for man to endure unspeakable sufferings in hell for ever and ever. We are all aware that exegesis has forced her to accept views of Scriptural inspiration she formerly condemned over and over again, and that there was a time when usury was solemnly forbidden in Council after Council.

It was only because in the past she changed gradually, because events moved so much more slowly, and but a few either bothered or were educated enough to read her history that these changes were not as obvious as the conclusion to be drawn from them. But a General Council is today acted on a world stage. One of the reasons for the extreme difficulty in getting the decrees on toleration and freedom of conscience passed was the reluctance of many bishops to make manifest that what had been condemned by a succession of Popes was now approved. If the dreary debate over contraception achieves nothing else, it will at least expose the frailty of a position which can only be defended by verbal manipulation or suppression of the facts, and if the lesson is learnt, it will be one which, once assented to, serves to deepen not destroy our Christian life. To wish for the impossible, to regret that things are not so simple as we once believed, is to forget what happened to the Son of God in the desert, to ignore the bitter vigil in the garden, to misunderstand what it means to be a pilgrim.

It is a lesson, moreover, which once learnt not only

reminds us of the price we pay for our humanity, but helps us in our efforts to achieve a deeper foundation for our assent to the truths of the Christian faith. We have seen some of the disastrous consequences which resulted from the traditional view expressed by Abbot Butler: 'Since in the objective order of things it cannot be God's will that we should attain salvation by accepting error, it further follows that the Church's decisions are not liable to error'. It is in the nature of man to accept error. It is the nature of faith, so to speak, to live itself into the knowledge of God. No theologian would of course deny this. But by so firmly attaching faith to belief irreparable harm is done. Should it be proved that any one of the Church's decisions was erroneous then the whole system collapses. Apologists have to spend a great deal of time trying to make out that it was not the Church's decision but the decision of only a handful of people in the Church, alternatively that she did not teach it but only seemed to teach it, or that it was not error but only seemed to be error. Because the whole thing has become a package-deal those who remain unconvinced by such arguments think all is doubtful and go out in despair.

The validity of Christian truth surely does not depend upon supposedly inerrant statements made about it or any other more or less external evidence. It depends, like our assent to the existence of God and the fact of our communion with him, on experience, as indeed did the faith of the Apostles. And by experience is not meant just feeling, surface emotion which may fluctuate from one day to the next, but those profound intuitions of the head and heart which Coleridge called our higher reason. It was on Peter's faith the Church was built, not on his detailed expression of it.

It is useless to appeal from the authority of the

Church to the authority of Scripture and back again. It is as useless to expect to be convinced of the reality of the Resurrection solely from the Gospel accounts as it is foolish not to assent to it on the ground that these accounts are contradictory, *ex parte* statements written only by believers many years later and that they contain untruths and distortions. It is vain to lament that the primitive Church casts its shadow between us and the historical Christ. Not only can we expect nothing else, but the Christ we already know is the Christ who matters. Taken as a whole and related to that primary experience of God, to that spark which lightens every man who comes into the world, Christianity bears all the marks of truth. As Dean Inge has written: 'We have then two guides, which are not two but one. We have the spiritual faculty, which, as Plotinus says, all possess but few use, the privilege of communion with God in prayer; and we have "the mind of Christ" as revealed in the records of his earthly life . . . the witness of the spirit is behind both.'

The Roman Catholic Church in the historical order is the source of our knowledge about Christ, but it is not for this reason we believe what she says about him to be essentially and fundamentally true, any more than we believe *King Lear* to be a great play on the bare word of a teacher or publishing house. The play speaks to us itself, and it speaks as a whole despite inconsistencies, imperfections and doubtful renderings. Nor does it fundamentally matter to the reader if Bacon were the author and not Shakespeare, or that later hands have added or excised portions of the text. A good teacher can draw our attention to depths of meaning, to what better scholars than we have understood from it, can above all, mingle our minds not only with the author's, but with the minds of those who over the centuries have meditated on what the author is saying. A bad teacher will mangle and maul the text in such a way that we never want to read it again. But rightly taught our assent to its poetic reality will come from within, from a certainty which answers to its corresponding witness from without. Both are necessary, not as the halves of an apple which once cut remain separate, but as two eyes directed to the same object.

A child's response to external stimuli is not automatic and invariable. It is conditioned by the reactions of those about him, by their whole approach to the world in which he finds himself. This is what is meant by the mind of the Church. Out of the depth of her own experience she shows us the things of Christ so that we may grow up, and by becoming part of that mind, show them to others. But let us remember that it is not the textual critics, important as they are, who help us most deeply to appreciate the play but those who understand it in terms of human experience. For that is what the play is about. In the same way, if we want a deeper understanding of Christianity, we must go, not to the theologians, important as they are, but to the saints. For that is what Catholicism is about.

Christianity is a picture, not a diagram. It is a picture made up of numerous strokes, the over-all effect of which is compelling. Its truth or falsehood does not stand or fall as a result of the obliteration of this or that brushmark, the historical truth of one particular miracle or another. The persistent difficulty however remains. What about the liquefaction? How can we know we are not going to end up with only a smudge on the canvas? Clearly, it does not matter in the least if demons did not really inhabit swine, or fishes swim about with coins in their mouths. But Christianity is not a revelation of purely mystical theology. There are doctrines in which what is affirmed, although mysterious, is a fact belonging to the order of sensible experience. Either Jesus was born as a result of sexual union or he was not, either a body laid in the tomb on Friday had disappeared from it the following Sunday or it had not. These affirmations may and do involve spiritual intuitions—the value of virginity when consecrated to God, the existence of an order of being unimaginable and inconceivable to us now, into which the Risen Lord enters with his body—but they are far from being images beyond exact thought. Those Modernists who made out that such doctrines had only a prayer-value, that they were valid because they fitted in with the requirements of religious consciousness, were using the poetic analogy not to throw light on the whole Christian event but to evade a particular problem.

Perhaps we have made a difficult matter even harder for ourselves by failing to make a sufficiently clear distinction between an event and the explanation of that event. We might do well to ponder a remark of Keats's. The Established Church in England as it was at the start of the nineteenth century was unlikely to capture someone of Keats's temperament. The man who so finely described this world as a vale of soul-making, on his death-bed groaned in agony against the 'malignant being' who denied him faith, that 'last cheap comfort any rogue or fool may have'. But it was he who praised 'a Negative Capability, that is when a man is capable of being in uncertainties, mysteries, doubts, without any irritable stretching out after fact and reason'. Some Christians suspend judgment about the fact of the Virgin Conception. No one, however, can suspend judgment about the fact of the Resurrection and remain a Christian. But while only the spiritually blind can remain indifferent to the overwhelming evidence we have of the power of the Risen Christ and the decisive effect it had on the Apostles, only an utter fool would dare to say exactly what this involved in the physical order. Revelation is one thing, the manner of it another. We are all very much more children of our age than we care to admit. We are not now in a position to answer these questions. Perhaps our descendants will be surprised at our solemn doubts and irritable attempts to find the connection between spiritual and material energy. Baffled we may be by the effect of the Incarnation upon the material world, but let us mark time, be content to wait until we can see the next bend in the road, not on any account abandon it altogether.

Uncertainties about the categorical truth of parts of the Christian creed are intensified for Roman Catholics who feel bound to give their assent to what the majority of people within the Reformed Churches consider to be merely pious opinion. At the time of asking Ullathorne his notorious question, 'When has a definition of doctrine *de fide* been a luxury of devotion and not a stern painful necessity?' the dogma of the Immaculate Conception had already been defined, and Newman must have known that its promulgation had been very far from a stern painful necessity. The fact is that the three *ex cathedra* papal pronouncements, the Immaculate Conception, personal papal infallibility, and the Assumption of the Blessed Virgin were not defined for this reason at all. But because a doctrine may have been defined for the wrong motive this is not to say it is false. No doubt the motive behind a number of excellent social reforms has been unconscious envy of the rich; the ecumenical movement would never have got so far if the Christian Churches had not been threatened from without; and perhaps our present insistence on good works is strengthened by unacknowledged scepticism about ever arriving at theological truth. Although the dogma of the Assumption, as commonly understood, places Roman Catholics on the horns of a dilemma, what lies behind it, like many supposedly Roman Catholic accretions, is part of the Christian faith, and as such is closely connected with the difficulties under discussion.

Roman Catholics have always asserted, and for obvious reasons are asserting more emphatically today, that the Church has never defined *de fide* any doctrine not found in Scripture or tradition. If the Assumption is thought of as an historical event in the sense of Pius XII's preamble to the definition, that is to say that Mary's physical body did not corrupt but was somehow immediately after her death changed into a glorified body, then all scholars are agreed that there is no Scriptural evidence, implicit or explicit, for such an occurrence. And if tradition is understood as the mind of the Church meditating on and interpreting Scripture, what is not there cannot be meditated on, what is non-existent cannot be interpreted. If by tradition is meant the now unfashionable view that it is a separate, non-written, Apostolic handing on of truths, then no tradition of this nature is discernible. Late legends are not Apostolic tradition. This is a particularly Roman Catholic dilemma. Some Catholics, for these reasons and on the ground that it widens the breach between Rome and other Churches, have gone so far as to regret that the doctrine was ever defined. But if a thing is true, it is true, and to play it down is not ecumenism but appeasement.

The central difficulty is for Christians to believe in the resurrection of the body at all. We know, if only from the Letter to the Corinthians, that this is an ancient problem, but what troubled a few in the past is now universally difficult. 'On the resurrection morning, soul and body meet again' is not now so much devotional as grotesque. We have no imaginative replacement for the old images of trumpets and tombs, and when we try to think how it can happen our minds are weighted by mediaeval speculations about beasts and fowls which carefully restore all the human flesh they have devoured. Much has been written on this subject, little with profit. If the notion of resuscitated bodies rising from their graves at some far-away future date is absolutely incredible, the accepted exegesis of heterosomatism, that is that we have true but new bodies, does not get us over the difficulty. The idea of the organic identity of the total human person which lies at the heart of what this doctrine is trying to tell us implies, as does the resurrection body of Christ, the existence of something bodily but not materially identical. The answer will come and we must leave it at that.

An opinion prevailed in some Jewish circles that the bodies of the righteous had anticipated the eschatological resurrection and that theirs was already accomplished at the time of Christ's. Some Roman Catholic theologians, notably Karl Rahner, have suggested that Mary is not the only human being already to possess a resurrection body. If we take the matter further and say that whatever a resurrection body may be, it is already possessed by all united with God in heaven, then there is no reason why Our Lady, who as the Scriptures certainly tell us was the mother of the Incarnate Word, should be excepted. The objection that it is unmeaningful to celebrate a state common to all in heaven is groundless if we take the Assumption, as it should be taken, in its entire Christian context. Most closely united to God of all the saints, Mary preeminently represents the Church. In celebrating her

Assumption we are in fact celebrating the triumphant assumption of the whole of glorified humanity.

This view, although it by no means obviates the difficulty about the nature of a risen body which must vex all Christians who recite the Creed, does dispose of some too superficial Protestant criticisms and save Roman Catholics from their initial dilemma. And, it might be added, from the degrading kind of apologetic which talks about the absence of body relics, or suggests that devotional tales are evidence. But if the juridically minded can take comfort from the fact that it is only the actual Definition not the preamble to which they are bound, such an interpretation involves an explicit repudiation of the idea that Mary's body did not corrupt in the tomb. We must take our choice. We can either make the attempt to swallow a literal orthodoxy, the patent incredibility of which in all likelihood will lead us sooner or later to reject all, or we can digest, not what we alone in any given mood feel to be palatable, but what, if prayed and lived, fits into the whole experienced pattern. Dogmatic statements unless realised in prayer are as boring as someone else's dreams, and as absurd as another's love letters.

Those who choose the last must, however, take the consequences and openly acknowledge that no living authority possesses the faculty of describing the Christian event without the possibility of error. And this is what those Roman Catholic theologians who are stressing the fact that dogmatic statements are partial, fragmentary and open to correction are really saying although they do not care to put it so bluntly. But we cannot have our cake and eat it, and the attempt to do so is a further cause of the confusion within the Church today. This is understandable, for those who are trying to deepen our hold on Christianity have not yet arrived, they are travelling. Like all Christians, indeed like millions who walk under no banner, they are in labour with they know not what. They have in front of them the spectre of Modernism, the insubstantial wraith of doctrinal symbolism, the nagging fear that what was born in wisdom could die in doubt, a vision of an exodus without a Moses, a crusade without a Christ. The last thing they want to do is to separate themselves from the visible Church, yet the logic of their arguments seems to be leading them away from her. So they have to persuade themselves that a solution to the problem can be found within the existing framework, that new ideas can be clothed in old terminology, harmony achieved by playing two entirely different tunes on the same fiddle. For those who always thought the Emperor naked, these tactics are a legitimate target for ironic amusement. For those, however, who are convinced not only that Christianity is the sole answer to the world's despair, but that the Roman Catholic Church is the one community of sufficient strength, vitality, and spiritual genius to take the lead in such a renewal, they are both distressing and mistaken. Distressing because a situation which is perplexing enough is still further obscured; mistaken because reconstruction can be achieved only through the facts and not by evading them.

It does not help anyone if we shroud our misgivings in cloudy language about reinterpretation of divinely revealed dogma or refer vaguely to some fresh thinking about the extraordinary and ordinary *magisterium* which is somehow and at some future date going to be ingeniously reconciled with the letter of traditional teaching. Rahner has remarked that a great deal of the Constitution on the Church will require 'a very subtle theology' if it is to be reconciled with her previous doctrinal pronouncements. Do we want our subtle theology to be employed where it is needed—to help us solve genuine problems about faith and its formulation, the necessity of some sort of doctrinal authority and discipline—or are we going to waste it on fruitless attempts to reconcile what cannot be reconciled on the surface but only in the depth? The Catholic renewal is often feared on the ground that it will lead to heresy. This is to put the case the wrong way about. It would be more open, more courageous, show more real faith in Jesus Christ and the future of Catholic Christianity, to recognise that we must go through surface heresy to reach that ultimate truth, which, because it is true, is the real meaning of non-historical orthodoxy.

When she had finished reading the *Apologia* the agnostic George Eliot described how it affected her 'as a revelation of a life—how different in form from one's own yet with how close a fellowship in its needs and burthens—I mean spiritual needs and burthens'. All those whose wills are tuned in love to something beyond and greater than themselves are part of the vast fellowship which we describe when we talk about the people of God. This is the root of all things, and if we trust the Holy Spirit, we can be certain that what is now hidden in the earth will one day put forth green shoots. In the far future Christianity will reach out to embrace not only Jews, Mahommedans, and Buddhists (who are already essentially so close to us), but farther still to include those multitudes who dimly recognise a God they cannot name.

The immediate future is another matter. For all Christians it is sombre, and for Roman Catholics dark indeed. Accustomed for so long to looking at the statement of their faith through a single lens they cannot be expected immediately to accustom their eyes to stereoscopic vision. Nothing can prevent the conflict between those who still think the Roman Catholic Church alone is the vehicle of doctrinal truth entirely free from error, that the word of the Church is simply the word of God, and those who with equal sincerity perceive that the time has long passed for such an answer to be sufficient. Unless fundamental readjustments are made all the battles fought in the Anglican Church during the past hundred years will be repeated in the Roman. We have yet to come to terms with biblical exegesis, the function of ecclesiastical authority, and questions raised by what is called situational morality.[1] If we fail to find some point of rest between a rigid and inhuman code-morality and complete antinomianism, the consequences will be grievous. One of them will most certainly be a distressing and basically non-religious controversy over divorce.

Browning's bishop called the Catholic faith the most pronounced, fixed, precise, and absolute form of faith in the whole world for working on the world. Take what you like and pay for it, as the proverb remarks. If we have paid heavily for one kind of Christianity the price of the other will be far steeper. A religion based on experience can never be so immediately effective as one based on authority and, in this tale of two cities, will be far more difficult to integrate into the fabric of an institution. If, however, for a significant minority of souls institutional religion will always be a licking of honey off thorns, we cannot therefore accept an over-simplified contrast between a religion of the spirit and a religion of authority. We cannot do without the institutional aspect of religion but we must appreciate that, like the creeds, it has a relative and protective

[1] Although its elaborate moral theology is one of the most hateful features of Roman Catholicism, its exponents never lost sight of the principles behind 'situational morality'. The two aspects were simply not integrated.

function. Abbot Butler reminds us that 'the instinct of the faithful is to look for or to depend upon an infallible *magisterium*—if it were not so the Catholic Church would not be the immensely vigorous and powerful thing it is today—'. But this, in the event, has not only proved a short term view but has tended to result in a kind of lessening of authority very far from the author's ideal. It has led to the notion that ecclesiastical authorities are only to be respected or what they say really believed when they speak infallibly, that it is quite safe to dismiss those utterances bearing the non-infallible ticket. Far greater respect is paid to an authority which understands the limits of its competence than one which by claiming more than the community is able to grant, succeeds in casting doubts on its right to speak at all.

We should bear in mind that much Christian history was the result of accident,[1] and this applies not only to its theological, liturgical, and devotional development. A divinely established structure of government can only be one which brings us closer to God. This generation is not more wicked and adulterous than any other, but too many stars have gone out for it to follow a single one with any confidence. It feels that all variations of Christianity have been tried and not one of them works. The theological virtues may not be much in evidence today, but, of them all, perhaps hope is the most neglected. To us now it may seem ludicrous to think of the

[1] The Catholic liturgist Edmund Bishop in a moment of irritation called Rome 'an embodied and *organised egotism*: one of the greatest (I am apt to think *the* greatest—as a *system*) the world has ever seen'. Allowing for exaggeration, how much of this is due to the Italian temperament? How much to the ambition of any theocracy? If the executive of the Catholic Church had by another accident settled in London, or Madrid, or New York the history of Christianity might have been very different.

Pope acting in the rôle of Moderator of the Free Churches. Not so long ago we would have laughed at the idea of a world police force. But just as the sovereign state is now seen to be an anachronism, so in the end will the notion of sovereign churches and gunboat theology. It is not the moral scandal of divided Christendom which strikes us now but its stupidity. In a sense which was both intended yet not intended by those who first thought of it, we are all indeed in Peter's barque. Each historical denomination has its part to play in keeping it afloat. Nor ought we to try and enforce uniformity. The reasons why a person is attracted to or remains within a certain religious tradition are frequently more profound than any he articulates. He has grown nearer to God through customs of worship and habits of mind which may appear trivial to outsiders but are essential to him, since they have become part of his inmost life. Whatever the form of the Church of the future it must make room for divergent groupings and different schools of thought.

To say that there is not one true Church in the old meaning of the expression does not imply in the least that all religions are equally good, that is to say, express the same amount of truth about God. Very far from it. A man may indeed find nourishment in some narrow sect while a Roman Catholic starves in front of a table spread out with rich food. But that judges the man, not the Church. Nothing could be more foolish than to imagine that because Catholic Christianity overbid its hand, it is now a declared bankrupt. Nothing could be more stupid than to think that because history does not guarantee religious truth, therefore what was done and thought and lived and prayed in the past is completely irrelevant to us. New knowledge means new ignorance. The unreflecting conservative may be a dangerous bore but the unreflecting liberal is an unmitigated disaster. Political tyranny is equally odious whether it comes from the right or left. In the sphere of thought and religion intolerance from the left is more deeply mischievous because it destroys, not merely obstructs. The works of the condemned Modernist George Tyrrell are not now neglected. But from his unquiet grave comes this warning: 'Ask the liberal to paint the glories of the New Jerusalem which is to arise on the ruins of the old and the pencil falls from his fingers on the blank sheet . . .'. And blank sheet it will surely be, if we rush from one extreme to the other, if in despair we surrender the supernatural and substitute a friendly society for religion. To forget that Mary has chosen the better part is a far more deadly compromise with the spirit of the age than any denial of a number of the articles of the Creed. It is to betray Catholicism at its very roots. For there the whole thing begins and there it ends.

Because we have been mistaken about living oracles, inerrant churches and infallible books it does not mean that we have been misled all the way along the line. On the Thames Embankment the horses driving Boadicea's chariot point towards the Houses of Parliament. Despite fire, pillage, false starts and many backward turnings we can discern, not an imposed pattern, but a real continuity in the history of this country. We cannot, however, be certain that we will not end up as slaves of a so-called democracy or as victims of foreign aggression. But looking back over the history of the Roman Catholic Church we can perceive over and over again, not a literal infallibility to be sure, but an infallible life principle, a constant correcting of the compass, a persistent orientation which is an infallibility of vital direction, although not of conceptual statement. Now the dust has settled no thinking person would say that the cause of Christianity would have been better served if Gnosticism, Montanism, Pelagianism, Arianism, or Protestantism had captured the Church. Viewed from a distance we can see that each of these was a one-sided development of a truth. In the long centuries which lie ahead historic Roman Catholicism will be seen in just such a light. There is a sense in which if the Church has to live, she has to die, if she is to recover her vital direction, she has to lose herself in the open sea.

We must not deceive ourselves into thinking that the voyage will be an easy one. The traditional objections to a radical reappraisal of the nature of the Church voiced by Abbot Butler have by no means been satisfactorily answered. If they had been, there would be no problem. If his solution were the right one, there would be no problem either.

In many ways we seem to have reached an impasse, existing as we do 'on this isthmus of a middle state', in the twilight between knowledge and ignorance. But we have the full witness of the heart and conscience to Christianity, and, if the witness of the intellect is fitful, that is the meaning of faith. There comes a time in all human endeavour when the shell resists the beak of the bird, when old images and concepts seem unable to bear the weight of their deeper significance and an entire impulse hangs suspended between that which was and that which is to be. The great Church which dyed our minds with the love of God and his Son is torn by doctrinal dissension, a light which shone before men for nearly two thousand years is growing dim. With singleness of purpose, utter humility, we must go back to the original foundation and rest our understanding once more upon faith's primary insight. Then that light which in reality exists beyond time and change will most surely illuminate the untrodden world towards which we move.

> We shall not cease from exploration
> And the end of all our exploring
> Will be to arrive where we started
> And know the place for the first time.

Love and Morals

JOHN M. TODD

I. THE DIMENSIONS OF THE PROBLEM

THE fount from which all morality springs is love. Utter self-giving. Nothing held back. Always giving of our best, not only to those we love, not only more dramatically to those we find it difficult to like—but also less dramatically but perhaps more demandingly to those to whom one is largely indifferent. Eight to ten hours a day it is not easy to give unreservedly of 'one's best' to those with whom one works, whether to one's equals, or to those over one or under one. But indifference is not really a possible option for love.

What can this unqualified sort of love really mean in practice? We have to work out some kind of rationale. Otherwise the whole thing just becomes a 'counsel of perfection', a synonym either for an unattainable ideal or for the specialised life of religious vows. Is the unqualified love to which Jesus calls men really a practical possibility? The occasional shining example, the saint, the man or woman completely committed, cannot give us a detailed key to daily conduct or the solution of difficult decisions.

Morality is the rational application of love to the situations in which a man finds himself. But it is difficult to make up 'loving' rules. There may be more than one 'loving' option in any given situation. And the danger arises of mistaking a set of rules, a morality, for love itself. The purposes of morality being to enable men to love each other, the observance of rules by themselves becomes phariseeism. The observance of rules of behaviour merely for their own sake involves the risk of betraying and degrading the very love they were intended to promote. Rules and conventions, whilst essential, are very dangerous things. This was the burden of Jesus's denunciation of those religious people who loved by rote. In many ways it is more comfortable to live by rote. But it is not the way of life recommended in the New Testament. The first of the Downside symposia studied this subject. In his introduction Reginald F. Trevett wrote, about the conclusions reached at the end of the symposium:

'. . . All forms of "categorical" morality, whether religious or philosophical, are either tyrannical or powerless, according to circumstances, corrupting those who impose them and stultifying the souls of those who accept them. All codes of morality are valid only in so far as they allow and encourage men to love with utter self-giving. A moral code is not therefore truly a way of life until it is accepted, and accepted freely, as making it possible for love to liberate us from imprisonment in the closed world of the individual or social self. There are immediate consequences both in the field of the exercise of any authority whatsoever, and in the whole sphere of personal relations. There is no abstract morality. This man or that woman are the subjects who make moral judgments and act upon them.'[1]

What are the situations in which men and women find themselves? What are the problems? Sexual relationship, racial discrimination, war, advertising policy, industrial organisation, delinquency, prison policy, housing, old people, school and neighbourhood problems, medical problems of life and death. These commonly pose the crucial moral dilemmas today. The problems facing each individual are increasingly 'socialised', closely related to the changing social context in which he lives. It may be asked whether Christians have anything special to offer. Surely we need to work, like all other people, for whatever arrangements may seem most likely, in the circumstances concerned, to promote the full social and individual self-realisation of every person. At many points, commonly perhaps at most points, these arrangements, this optimum structure of society towards which a Christian will work is likely to be identical with or similar to that towards which a humanist student of human requirements will work. A sufficiency of food, clothing and shelter still remains to be achieved for vast numbers of people. And the more thoroughly a scientific study of human needs is undertaken the closer in practice its conclusions can often come to a statement of needs posited by a Christian. A

[1] R. F. Trevett in 'The Symposium', the introductory chapter to *The Springs of Morality*, edited by John M. Todd (Burns & Oates, London, and Macmillan, New York, 1955). Much of this volume would serve as further reading for the present article.

perfectly efficient business manager, and a completely Christian business manager, would often follow practically identical courses of action in the strictly objective sphere. Long-term efficiency takes account of the nature of a man as thoroughly as possible.[1]

Someone might make out a case for saying that the 'socialised' moral problem is only a distraction to hide the real personal moral problems—broken marriages, young people and sexual behaviour, mental breakdown. Obviously every moral problem is indeed a personal problem for each person involved in it. It is also true that a very large number of people have unsatisfactory personal relationships, both in and out of marriage. And more people suffer a breakdown in mental health than ever before. Clearly every one of these cases needs a healing hand; for most of them professional attention divorced from love is less than adequate. But this only highlights the socialised nature of the problem. The great majority of all these cases do in fact require the attention of what we call 'the social services'; they are too numerous to be left to purely haphazard spontaneous attention.

All these cases, all posing moral problems of some kind, are due in great part to the rapidity of social and economic change. One or another conventional guard rail has disappeared. There is no organic community helping the individual towards a choice of one course of action from a fairly small selection of options. He gets less and less sense of positive direction from the community.

The growing disappearance of a conventional acceptance of monogamy, in the form of Christian marriage, is presumably a major factor. The Christian belief that

[1] The note on chapters 13 and 14 in *The Springs of Morality* discusses this problem.

the sexual relationship should be exclusively sacramental is held by a steadily decreasing proportion of the population. But the resultant problems are essentially similar to all the other problems caused by rapid social and economic change, such as delinquency, neighbourhood problems, etc. They all need study; and the Christian will only bring a valuable contribution to the sexual problem so long as he does not come in an attitude of horror, and encumbered with taboos.

Is the definition of our aim as 'social and individual self-realisation' adequate? It depends. The Christian if he uses any such term must always carry over into it the full Christian definition which involves the reference to love and complete self-giving; for him self-realisation in its fullest sense must tend towards this. While the Christian works for particular social goods, the ultimate reference still dominates; there are no minimum conditions for love. And the strictures against categorical morality quoted above apply equally, perhaps even more so, to social as to individual categories. There is no social, political or economic mechanism or community formula which will automatically ensure a good life.

II. THE CHRISTIAN MYSTERY

It is the purpose of Christian love to elicit a response from all men and to co-operate with every other human and religious insight and affirmation. But it has a unique significance and its own precise historical origins. Christian morality cannot be transformed into a mere universal abstract plan of human morality. At its extreme points it makes demands against which a humanist morality could raise arguments of moderation—one thinks of the Austrian conscientious objector, Jagerstätter, or of St Francis. This personal response is in answer to a specific historical revelation. Christian principles, intended for all men at all times, have their own reference documents and their reference events.

The only way to identify this love seems to be to attend to the words which were originally spoken of it, and to the historic events which were their accompaniment. They cannot, strictly speaking be 'described', but only repeated and re-told. This love is something that asks man to recognise it, and to believe in it.

> 'How blessed are those that know they are poor;
> the kingdom of heaven is theirs'[1]

> 'Do not suppose that I have come to abolish the Law and the prophets; I did not come to abolish, but to complete. . . . Unless you show yourselves far better men than the Pharisees and the doctors of the law, you can never enter the kingdom of Heaven.'
>
> 'You have learned that your ancestors were told: "Do not commit murder . . .". But what I tell you is this: Anyone who nurses anger against his brother must be brought to judgment. . . .'
>
> 'You have learned that they were told, "Do not commit adultery". But what I tell you is this: If a man looks on a woman with lustful eye, he has already committed adultery with her in his heart. . . .'
>
> 'You have learned that they were told, "An eye for an eye, and a tooth for a tooth". But what I tell you is this: "Do not set yourself against the man who wrongs you. . . . If someone slaps you on the right cheek, turn and offer him your left. . . ." '
>
> 'You have learned that they were told, "Love your neighbour, hate your enemy". But what I tell you is

[1] This translation, as all others in this essay, is taken from the *New English Bible* by kind permission of the Oxford and Cambridge University Presses.

this: Love your enemies and pray for your persecutors; only so can you be children of your heavenly Father, who makes his sun rise on good and bad alike, and sends the rain on the honest and dishonest. If you love only those who love you, what reward can you expect? . . . And if you greet only your brothers, what is there extraordinary about that? Even the heathen do as much. You must therefore be all goodness, just as your heavenly Father is all good.'

. . . .

'In your prayers do not go babbling on like the heathen, who imagine that the more they say the more likely they are to be heard. Do not imitate them.

Your Father knows what your needs are before you ask him.

'This is how you should pray:
"Our Father in heaven,
Your name be hallowed;
Your kingdom come,
Your will be done,
On earth as in heaven.
Give us today our daily bread.
Forgive us the wrong we have done,
As we have forgiven those who have wronged us.
And do not bring us to the test,
But save us from the evil one." '

. . . .

'No servant can be slave to two masters. . . . You cannot serve God and Money. . . .'

'Pass no judgment, and you will not be judged. . . . Why do you look at the speck of sawdust in your brother's eye, with never a thought for the great plank in your own? Or how can you say to your brother,

"Let me take the speck out of your eye", when all the time there is that plank in your own? You hypocrite! First take the plank out of your own eye, and then you will see clearly to take the speck out of your brother's. . . .'

This was not entirely revolutionary talk. Jewish teachers had already been going beyond the law of a tooth for a tooth for some centuries, and had set up a principle by which a man was not to insist on his own rights, but to follow a way beyond that of normal 'justice', to follow instead a way of 'righteousness' which was related fundamentally to the idea of God's 'holiness'. There was something else however in these words of Jesus that was quite new, though at first difficult to define: 'When Jesus had finished this discourse the people were astounded at his teaching; unlike their own teachers he taught with a note of authority'. Instead of merely spelling out a commentary on the Torah, Jesus was evidently propounding what amounted to a radically new way of life. It was not, in other words, a matter of whether this act or that act was right or wrong, nor even a matter of the high ideals of the best of the traditional Jewish teaching; it was a matter of a searching examination of oneself and a radical re-orientation of the self in an attitude of self-giving. And from words of authority those who listened were led on to witness 'authoritative' events which commanded the same astounded response. The note of unique authority continues on from this first confrontation with the love to which in their hearts people immediately responded, to the final revelations at the gathering in the upper room of the chosen followers:

'If you love me you will obey my commands; and I will ask the Father, and he will give you another to be your Advocate, who will be with you for ever—the Spirit of truth....'

'There is still much that I could say to you, but the burden would be too great for you now. However when he comes who is the Spirit of truth, he will guide you into all truth....'

'But it is not for these alone that I pray, but for those also who through their words put faith in me; may they all be one: as you, Father, are in me, and I in you, so also may they be in us, that the world may believe that you sent me....'

'Father I desire that these men, who are your gift to me, may be with me where I am, so that they may look upon my glory which you have given me because you love me before the world began. O righteous Father, although the world does not know you, I know you, and these men know that you sent me. I made your name known to them and I will make it known, so that the love you had for me may be in them, and I may be in them.'

We are on the road which, begun in the Judaic understanding of God's creative act, continued in God's historical call to Abraham and the setting apart of the Jews, leads from the first celebration by Jesus of the sacrament of his body and blood through his death, his resurrection and the outpouring of his Spirit on his followers and their total renewal; to the growth of the Christian community and its spread through the Roman Empire. It is a road which leads to the ability of one of the followers to re-express the love which was the message of Jesus:

'And now I will show you the best way of all.

'I may speak in tongues of men or of angels, but if I am without love, I am a sounding gong or a clanging cymbal. I may have the gift of prophecy, and know every hidden truth; I may have faith strong enough to move mountains; but if I have no love, I am nothing. I may dole out all I possess, or even give my body to be burnt, but if I have no love, I am none the better.

'Love is patient; love is kind and envies no one. Love is never boastful, nor conceited nor rude; never selfish, not quick to take offence. Love keeps no score of wrongs; does not gloat over other men's sins, but delights in the truth. There is nothing love cannot face; there is no limit to its faith, its hope, and its endurance.

'Love will never come to an end. Are there prophets? their work will be over. Are their tongues of ecstasy? they will cease. Is there knowledge? It will vanish away; for our knowledge and our prophecy alike are partial, and the partial vanishes when wholeness comes. When I was a child, my speech, my outlook, and my thoughts were all childish. When I grew up I had finished with childish things. Now we see only puzzling reflections in a mirror, but then we shall see face to face. My knowledge now is partial; then it will be whole, like God's knowledge of me. In a word there are three things that last for ever: faith, hope, and love; but the greatest of them all is love.'

III. CHRISTIAN MORALITY

Of itself St Paul's description of love was not a sufficient guide for everyone. When he had spoken to them of love he had still to move on into specific behaviour problems. Should Christians continue to be Jews? Ought they to continue the rite of circumcision? What of the ten commandments? The answer was clear in principle.

Jesus had not come to deliver a message of esoteric individualism; he was no anarchist. He came to deliver a message to a particular society and he came as a fulfilment of a promise to that society which had understood itself for a thousand years as a people specially chosen by God. Jesus's message assumed this understanding as the truth, confirming and fulfilling it. Because of this, many things, taken for granted in a Jewish milieu, are never referred to by Jesus. He takes the whole traditional Jewish set-up for granted, the goodness of marriage, for instance.

The ten commandments were not abrogated, nor the historic call to the Jews. But it was also clear that Jesus's message was an explicit condemnation of any society which thought of a set of rules as being the complete fulfilment of man's religious needs. St Paul wrote to Timothy: 'We all know the Law is an excellent thing, provided we treat it as law, recognising that it is not aimed at good citizens, but the lawless and unruly, the impious and sinful, the irreligious and worldly . . .'. But the underlying principles of Jewish life were implicitly recommended in the Christian revelation.

So St Paul answered the problems put to him and provided his questioners with the casuistry they demanded. Christians were not to worry about eating meat which had been offered to idols. They hadn't done the offering and it was still good meat. But if other people got upset then it would be better not to eat it, or not publicly; the consciences of others should be respected.

Then they wanted to know about politics. Jesus's many references to his Father, St Paul's explicit hope, in the early days, of a quick finish to history, could have led easily to an exclusively apocalyptic attitude, a belief that all human arrangements, politics included, are irrelevant. This could have meant a practical attitude of either apathetic indifference or complete intransigence. But Jesus had set a policy of realism, of living with facts, and keeping them in their place when he called for a coin of the Roman occupiers of his country and pointed out that since the coin belonged to Caesar it did not seem in principle morally outrageous that Caesar should collect taxes in such coins. St Paul tells his Christians to be good citizens.[1] God has willed or permitted all things and human society is no exception. Injustices should be put right, but there is no call to overthrow society completely, only to reform it. So too with slaves; they should be good slaves. One might object: 'What of the freedom of the sons of God?' The answers would be that as a slave a man or woman might enjoy more personal freedom, have a more appropriately human life than by making a living in some other way. Moral absolutes are not patient of expression in terms of generalisation about any given situation. The notion of slavery is a blasphemous outrage against the freedom of choice inherent in human relationships based on love. But this is not to define slavery finally in terms of any particular thing or person that enslaves. One must not transpose the generalisation in such a way as to say that a particular social and economic institution of slavery is so much more evil than the only alternatives that all slaves must immediately be released. The results could be more evil than the slavery.

These judgments about conditions as being 'more' or 'less' evil need to be partly reached through, and always related to, the experience of men and women living in the conditions concerned. Self-realisation cannot be weighed accurately in a balance which is intended only to estimate degrees of 'freedom' by means of some abstract formula. We need statistics; we need sociological

[1] But see the reference to political authority in the Note at the end of this essay.

analysis. Moral assessments have to be based on the fullest possible survey of the facts, and the most penetrating analysis of them.

Decisions about moral problems need to be reached by a rational process. They are not to be reached by some *ex cathedra* 'revelation',[1] that is not by any merely prophetic utterance from established ecclesiastical authority. A decision about some problem, related say to immigration or nuclear war or housing, is taken after a rational process of deliberation on all the facts and principles involved. Then the decision has to be accepted by all those whom the decision has in view. If the decision is to be put into practice in the fullest possible way, that is in a human way, in a loving way, it has to be fully accepted by all the individuals concerned. Their consciences have to accept the decision. This can only happen if the reasons are fully understood. The arguments accepted by authority have to be as fully accessible as possible to those to whom the rules are recommended. There must be 'communication'. Good communication is a rule which all human societies nowadays understand to be a necessity; it is a rule which should be followed most of all by the society of Christian love. Rules should be seen to be an application of that Christian love for which the Church exists.

For these reasons the Church should take the greatest caution in basing moral rules on 'the natural law'. In every case exposition of the 'natural law' must be really convincing. If the exposition does not convince, the argument should be examined again. This is what has been happening for the last thirty years in the spheres both of the regulation of births and of warfare. Preceding the public discussions of these issues in recent years have

[1] See reference in the Note at the end of this chapter, to the conclusion reached by Elizabeth Anscombe on this matter.

gone two or three decades of intense thought and private discussion among individuals who have found the arguments normally appearing in Catholic books to be unconvincing. Gradually the number of such people has grown; thought and discussion on the points concerned have been more and more widespread. Finally attempts have been undertaken at authoritative levels to understand anew what the Christian revelation must mean in the situations in which men find themselves today, situations truly unique not only in the way that all human situations are unique, since they are situations of unique individual people, but unique in that such situations have simply not faced human societies in past ages.

Implicit in what we have said must be the certainty that in morals there are always borderline cases. It is clearly quite impossible, on the basis of our previous arguments, to make a list of all conceivable human actions and divide them into sections, one good, and the other bad. This is not to say that reason can *not* see clearly in the majority of human actions whether these either promote the interests of love, or impede them. Night is recognised as night; day is recognised as day—but as Dr Johnson pointed out, there is a twilight time; attempts to bring casuistry to bear at this time bring the whole business of casuistry (the unravelling of individual cases) into ill-repute. It is obvious to the common sense that twilight is neither daylight nor night time. In such cases the individual conscience must take its own difficult decision, assisted by all the advice and help of every kind that fellow Christians can give, priests and laity alike. But it would seem wise for this assistance to be given in another way than by means of command. In these situations the Church is searching its own communal conscience; to attempt to impose a particular course of action when large numbers of Christians are honestly in doubt about it seems to be a contradiction of the Church as described by St Paul and by Vatican II in *Lumen Gentium*. Christians think of God as their Father, as Jesus taught them to do; they believe in humility before facts, and submission when the authority in their own Church speaks. The question at issue here is whether in these difficult cases the Church believes that it should speak gently, even tentatively, wherever possible as it were 'taking the sense of the meeting', or whether it is committed at all times to providing a cut and dried decision in terms of command. Personally I cannot see any basis in Christian revelation, or in reason, for the latter option. It would seem to imply a kind of 'oracular' privilege for ecclesiastical authority, a right to add to the teaching of Jesus which the Church has always disclaimed.[1]

Morality is not essentially the putting into effect of rules recommended or prescribed by authority. It is a loving response to the needs of others. Often enough what is needed today is intense study of the facts; without this no theoretical exposition is likely to be of much value. What lies on our conscience today? Among other things that half the world is rich and the other half poor. The standards of love given us by Jesus are mocked by this situation. In spite of its complexity, this situation stings the consciences of many in that they believe that we ought to be sharing among all people the wealth of the world. All should have the necessities of physical life and the opportunity to live as befits a human being. Within some western countries the gap between rich and poor has got smaller. But in the world at large the gap is larger.[2] Within western countries themselves much still

[1] See again the Note at the end, concerning the relation of Revelation to morals.

[2] For an immediate appreciation of the currently deteriorating

remains to be done. There is a vast severely underprivileged class in America; in England there are small sections of people undergoing less remarkable but no less intense suffering, often related to housing difficulties. The rich countries are pouring an important part of their wealth into producing weapons of destruction and into preparations for possible war. Interwoven with this problem is the rapid increase of population in the countries already suffering from lack of essentials. The late Pope John described what needs to be done in general in his two encyclicals *Mater et Magistra* and *Pacem in Terris*. But the detail depends on the collection of facts and their analysis. Without the certainty that a complete and accurate picture is available and that a thorough study has been made of all the possible solutions it is impossible for the individual citizen to take up significant positions on these subjects, beyond purely negative decisions based on respect for life. For instance the population problem is not to be solved by compulsory euthanasia of any classes of people. On the other hand the sheer difficulty of getting the facts into an accurate and comprehensive analysis should not be taken as a reason for preventing or not attempting direct attempts to help. Individual initiatives can sometimes be the means of breaking through vast and apparently insoluble problems. An individual driven by compassion, determined to relieve suffering, can lead to a new social or economic structure which no amount of formal planning can achieve. Such things as Oxfam, or Cheshire Homes, or international voluntary service overseas usually owe their inception to the dedication of an individual determined to overcome all obstacles. His success may depend on the support he gets from ordinary

situation, see *Planning Prosperity* by Ronald Brech (Darton, Longman & Todd, 1964), and the diagrams illustrating Ronald Brech's article in this book.

citizens, in other words his loving response to the needs of others.

The 'right of innocent life' is a moral reference put forward recently in relation to abortion but largely ignored in relation to war. But the arguments have often proceeded in an unreal world of abstract theory, where no account is taken of the fact that every human situation has its own special and unique tensions, history and prospects. Such tensions do not represent something exceptional. They are on the contrary normal. Every human situation is unique and personal, and every one has its own history and prospect. In all arguments about abortion and about war such phrases as the 'right to live', or the 'rights of innocent life' always have a twofold resonance. We are not in a world where it is easy to say that any particular death has been caused by an action which is clearly murder. This is an example of an area of moral problem in which the Church is searching its conscience at the moment. In such cases, as big a place as possible has surely to be left to the individual conscience. The advice given by Christian authority should not be prescriptive or binding on all. Great latitude needs to be left to the individual conscience. When moral laws are set up in highly problematical areas the result is that we have precisely that loveless categorical morality referred to on page 116. Conscience must remain essentially supreme and not virtually subordinate as has been liable to be the case when Catholic authorities while stressing the rights and duties of conscience, have so emphasised the duty of a person to 'instruct' his conscience correctly that the original freedom of conscience has in effect been overlaid; this has occurred for instance in the case of conscientious objection where one or another ecclesiastical authority has often taken up a position in complete opposition to this right; in countries such as Italy, where the Church is dominant, it has been effective in preventing the legal recognition of this right up to the present day.

A particular rule is only convincingly put forward as moral if it can be seen to be a reasonable proposition, and one which in some way furthers the great purpose of love. But a moral rule put forward by a Christian authority needs also to have that peculiar authority which the teaching of Jesus had. We have seen that the compelling element was a new kind of self-critical, self-giving love, a new kind of 'righteousness' connected with the holiness of God. It received its authentic note in the person of Jesus; it had the impression of being self-authenticating at the same time as being completely self-giving and completely holy.

Those who stand in authority in the Church—and this includes parents as I have argued elsewhere[1]—have this burden. It is not only their authority as ecclesiastical superiors or as Christians exercising a particular function within the body of Christ, but as visibly holy Christians which should give their teaching its full authenticity. The Vatican is not some kind of Christian Delphic oracle—nor are Catholic teachers or Catholic parents. Christians have to expound, apply, and 'develop' the teaching of Christ—and they may not 'improve' it. They, and especially those in authority, must follow in the steps of holy truth, not rejoicing in authority for its own sake.

The moral initiatives of Christian authority need also to have about them both an historical and an existential contemporary character. We may not say that because a certain formula was convincing two or six hundred years ago it cannot be controverted or improved on. All the formulae of moral theology are no more than means

[1] 'The Authority of the Layman' in *Problems of Authority* (Darton, Longman & Todd, 1962).

towards the rational application of love to the daily circumstances of individual men and women. On the other hand past practice should never be jettisoned without the most careful thought. All history is in some sense sacred history.

St Paul was a good example of a self-authenticating Christian authority. He was something of a worker priest of course—'we did not accept board and lodging from anyone without paying for it; we toiled and drudged, we worked for a living night and day, rather than be a burden to any of you—not because we have not the right to maintenance, but to set an example for you to imitate. For even during our stay with you we laid down the rule; the man who will not work shall not eat.' Paul's preaching was never a merely reasonable morality. It was indeed always reasonable and argued; but it was always done in the full Judaic and Christian context. This new Christian behaviour was for the purpose of bringing 'the universe, all in heaven and on earth, into a unity in Christ' . . . 'so may you attain to fullness of being, the fullness of God himself'. And it had always about it the authentic Christian dimension which we refer to in the word asceticism. The Christian should keep in training. There is a personal and social value in moral discipline and there is a special Christian value in all suffering in that it can be united with the Christian sacrifice, with the cross, with the Mass; it can be made fruitful through prayer.

Asceticism is a moral dimension for which the modern world is perhaps waiting more than any other. Pope John charmed a whole world with his deep humanity, the fullness of a human personality come to marvellous ripeness. Then after his death we had revealed to us in his *Journal* the tedious, deadly seeming routine which he had used as his training—throughout his life. The daily routine of rosary (repeated Hail Marys, Our Fathers and Glory Be's, along with meditation on gospel incidents), daily self-examination—the latter hammered home with robust simplicity, the recitation of the psalms and prayer of the breviary, etc.—all without any mystical high-lights or special activities other than the occasional intensification of the same exercises in silence during an annual retreat. I offer no suggestion here as to how men and women of the twentieth century should approach this matter. But the principles of asceticism do not change. In the past centuries a tradition grew up by which the occasional individual Catholic would seek a special spiritual way and would ask a priest to be his or her 'spiritual director'. This tradition needs modifying now so that communities, rather than individuals only, have some such access to the holy tradition, to a deliberate spiritual training. In some sense it is already happening in the form of Christian study and action groups which have been in the last few decades springing up, having their roots in prayer, public and private.

It is important for such groups to be quite simply Christian or human groups, not in any way official ecclesiastical organisations, and to undertake action in the public sphere simply as groups of people who want to put right what may be wrong. There must be no question of some kind of ecclesiastically inspired pressure group. The problems—housing, racial discrimination, advertising abuse, the international problems etc.—all cry out for Christian commitment. Such commitment has to be rooted in preparation really adequate to the purpose. The problems of violence for instance, both on the international level and amongst individuals and small groups, might perhaps be countered by groups inspired by the recently revived tradition of 'non-violence'. This could mean a lifetime of dedicated training. But it is not the purpose of this article to make out a list of priorities. These things hang together. A sick society is related to sick morals in every person who makes up that society. If no one trusts another, if no one can be trusted the society falls apart and can only survive by tyrannical imposition, by the imposition on a categorical basis of rules which no longer spring from men spontaneously.

But if I do not wish to make out a list of priorities, I do think that the muscles of society need exercise and renovation. Many of the 'old English' structures have come near to ossification. The drugging effect of the mass media has to be thrown off and men and women made to realise again that a single person or a single group, if determined to think for themselves, can change society. If sufficient people realise this and have the courage to follow their own beliefs, political and economic positions known by everyone to be inadequate but thought equally to be impregnable can be threatened and reformed overnight. If the Roman Catholic Church can do what it has done, in the way of reforming itself, society at large can do the same. But one may ask whether the Roman Catholic Church has really changed itself. One would be right to ask. The changes so far are mostly still on paper; the beginnings of a revival of the tradition of communal worship, and of social responsibility are to be seen. But it is true that the structures, the very organisation of the Church, will have to be changed in the coming five years if proper effect is to be given to Vatican II, and the kind of moral approach outlined here to be accepted. Catholics have still to put their own house in order. And their efforts as individuals or groups in the world will be suspect until their own affairs are conducted on a level of justice comparable with the best civilised standards and on a level of charity compatible with the gospel. And they will need to find their leaders, that is their bishops, by means of some more regular and more appropriate process than that which is followed today.

I have attempted the impossible, an outline of Christian morality for today. Although it was published ten years ago much of the book I referred to at the beginning, *Springs of Morality*, is still closely relevant. I end with a quotation from a piece of exceptional value from it by Dom Sebastian Moore. It contains a couple of generalisations at which specialists may shudder but it makes the essential point. 'It is a sobering thought that Communism is the first real attempt since the feudal system to construct a complete human polity—and it should be a danger signal to us that we find such an attempt so easy to condemn on theological principles. We should remember that the moment Christian charity becomes for us essentially an idea, albeit a sublime idea and one which we intend to put into practice, God too becomes an idea. Ezra Pound says of St Ambrose: "St Ambrose didn't rise suddenly and without forebears. A transition from self-centred lust after eternal salvation into a sense of public order occurred somewhere and sometime" (*Guide to Kulcherm*, p. 43). "A travesty of the Christian notion of salvation" we readily reply, and miss the fact that Pound, just there, is probably seeing more in St Ambrose than we do: namely that wonderfully precise care for human polity that flows from real charity.'

Note

I have omitted consideration of many aspects of Christian morals; some theologians will think I have left aside essential considerations. It may be said that I have begun to outline a Christian 'situation ethic'; I should be happy indeed if so. I have avoided discussion of any of the great issues in detail. One thinks of the political issue and the notorious *presumptio juris* (the State must always be presumed to be right if there is any doubt at all) which had to be controverted anew at Vatican II (session IV). Professor Cameron once wrote on this:

> 'In one crucial instance, then, we may be sure that there cannot be a presumption that obedience to political authority is a duty. If we are to hold that in this instance there is a reasonable presumption that obedience to political authority is a duty, we may as well print in all editions of theological works in which the moral problem of warfare is discussed the following rubric: Notwithstanding anything to be found in this book that may appear to contradict it, the maxim *My country, right or wrong* is to be taken as the supreme guiding principle' (*Problems of Authority*).

Then I have left the sexual issue largely aside. For this one must start with a theology of the Christian sacrament.

I have not faced fully the traditional dividing line between Christian morality and natural ethics, the idea that the former, being in some way absolute, involves the statement of a morality which is not arrived at as a result of consideration of consequences as an overriding factor. On this the reader may usefully consult 'The Philosophical Concept of Morality' by Dom Illtyd Trethowan in *Springs of Morality*. He refers to the rôle to be played by Christian Revelation. The reader will find further discussion of this in 'Authority in Morals' (*Problems of Authority*), a chapter by Elizabeth Anscombe. She has a powerful paragraph about the impossibility of the revelation of moral truths *per se*:

'What there does not seem to be room for is moral

truths which are *per se* revealed. Given the facts about original sin and the promise of the possibility of a man's joining his sufferings to those of Christ, the goodness of severely ascetical practices, so long as they do not damage the body or its faculties, is obvious; there is no such thing as a revelation that such and such is good or bad not for any reason, not because of any facts, not because of any hopes or prospects, but simply: such and such is good to do, this is to be believed, and could not be known or inferred from anything else. How can one instruct an archer to aim at an unseen target? There would be no room for that knowledge by connaturality which is characteristic of the understanding of a virtuous person, in such a case; no room, therefore, for understanding application of what one believed to be right or wrong.'

The Heart of Unity

T. L. WESTOW

WHAT kind of unity are we pursuing? There is no doubt that unity is fundamental to Christianity. The words, 'That they be one', appear at the very climax of St John's Gospel. Since the pioneering efforts of the Abbé Couturier these words have been so much used to foster the ecumenical movement that they have assumed a colour or a slant which seems to make them the exclusive preserve of those who are concerned with the reunion of all Christians. It may, therefore, not be altogether superfluous to remind people that there were no divisions in the Christian body when Christ spoke these words, if, indeed, one can already at that stage of his human existence talk of 'Christians'. The words do not, therefore, apply primarily to Catholics and Protestants, nor even to Jews and Christians. They can only refer, according to the context, to the people of God at large for whom Christ was praying. One can go further. This people of God was not yet organised in structures or what we would term today a 'society' or 'association'. In other words, Christ did not directly address them to an institution called the Church, as this institution was as yet non-existent. He simply addressed them to his followers, actual and potential.

On the other hand, there is only one community which is composed of 'Christ's followers, actual or potential', and that community is the community of all mankind. Even the Conciliar Constitution on the Church (ch. 1, n. 3) recalls John xii. 32 : 'When I am lifted up from the earth, I will attract *all men* to myself'. The union which Christ had in view, was the union of all men, of the whole human community. Now, behind these words, 'That they all be one', there lies the implied but unspoken realisation that mankind is torn apart by every kind of division.

Now, it appears to me that in too many sectors of the ecumenical movement as we know it today there is a tendency to think of this wished-for union too exclusively in terms of theological encounters, common worship, ecclesiastical structures, in short, in terms of somewhat external factors such as theology, ritual and ministry. This is rather a pity. The divisions, not only between Catholics and Protestants, but also between Catholics and Orthodox, and Buddhists, and Hindus, and primitive religionists, are not, and cannot be, limited to such simple divisions as are shown in theology, ritual or ministry. These divisions are historical, they have created attitudes, they were caused by preliminary attitudes that were already widespread when the divisions broke through, by cultural differences, by social conditions. They were not isolated features, standing apart from the broad current of a developing nationalism, economic mercantilism, and the disintegration of a common language or any *lingua franca*. The divisions cannot even be limited to that. They go right down to the roots of each person, his situation, his biological and psychological and educational and environmental antecedents. And I cannot see for the life of me how we can walk around with the illusion that we can achieve unity in one little and rather dark corner of our concrete existence without at the same time tackling the whole broad field of that communal existence which is the very air we breathe. To put it briefly and sharply: the 'reunion' of all Christians cannot be isolated from the unity of mankind, and I am not afraid of adding that it will simply not come about without progress in this unity of mankind. If, therefore, we want to look into the future of Christianity, we are bound to train our sight on this universal union.

Inevitably we turn towards Rome and wonder whether the Council has made any impact in this direction, because if not, then the prophetic effort of Pope John has largely failed, as so many prophetic efforts have failed throughout religious history.

One might say, although it is an exaggeration, that the main impact of the Council has been made indirectly by our great theologians. If Pope John intended this Council to concentrate on self-examination and self-criticism within the Church, let us frankly give credit where credit is due, to our great theologians. They have to be praised, not only because their honesty and integrity made the bishops listen to them, but even more because so many had prepared themselves by years of painful and laborious work long before there was any mention of a Council. They are only criticised by those who do not bother to read them. And as the extraordinary success of their international review *Concilium* shows, they have opened a thousand windows and a thousand doors, and have no intention of abandoning this vigorous effort simply because the Council is over. I would almost say that they have not only forced the Church as a whole to have a good look at herself, but they have managed to remain identified with this Church and, in so far as I have met them, have remained genuine persons with open minds, humble, and endowed with that indispensable 'charisma' of the Christian, a sense of humour. However untranslatable their style may sometimes be and with whatever elephantine elegance Theology sometimes takes a stroll in the garden of the soul, they are exemplary in their integrity, their love of Christ and the Church, their deep humility.

The theologians, then, certainly have opened the door. And who would deny that in the astounding progress made in the field of ecumenism, of the membership of the Church, of the relations of the Church and the World, of the rôle of the laity and the training of priests and missionaries, they have certainly steered towards that unity of mankind which I mentioned before? On the other hand, the major task has still to be tackled. In spite of their exhilarating freshness of outlook and their generosity of temperament, they are still theologians in the old sense of the word. They are still very conscious of being clerical theologians. The subjects are still very much the old subjects, however newly looked at and dealt with, and those subjects are still very much within the structure of the institutional Church. Nobody doubts that these subjects are of vital importance. One has but to think of the consciousness of Christ, of the relation between episcopacy and papacy, of the historical evaluation of such important Councils as those of Constance, Trent and Vatican I, of how to celebrate the liturgy in a way which encourages active participation, of evangelical counsels and spirituality. Yet, all these subjects are still very domestic, very clerical, very pastoral. And it is this the ordinary educated man or woman feels only too sharply. The result is that when we get studies that go beyond these rather severely 'theological' subjects and try to enter into the science of life as such, in the concrete environment where the Christian witness must be borne by the layman, there is a stumbling and fumbling which leads to disappointment. The root of it all, but this is only my own opinion, lies in the fact that as clerical theologians, leading their sheltered existence in organisations and institutions that are still wholly imbued with the old spirit, they have not completely escaped the reproach of living in an ivory tower. And I don't think they will until their lovable personal humility has been transferred to their profession, in other words, until they realise that theology is neither above nor apart from life in the concrete; when they realise that they are persons, adults, male, scholars like any other scholar, citizens with a vote, in short, that they are, before everything else, ordinary layfolk in the theological sense of ordinary members of the People of God in this world.

This is an important point because I am strongly convinced that Karl Rahner, for instance, is still an individualist. His close dependence on Heidegger, the background of the philosophical tradition which goes back in its individualism via Kierkegaard to Gabriel Biel and Ockham, means that he does not have the feel of the human community as a live unity composed of adult human and free persons who share in the same communal responsibility. He has large views, he talks about the universe and mankind. But mankind is still 'Man' for him, in the sense of eighteenth- and nineteenth-century rationalism, really 'everyman' as an individual writ large. But for practical conclusions, there is a vast abyss between a mankind understood as a generalised individual, and a mankind understood as a live community of free persons endowed with responsibility for each other and for all. It seems to me that this is the reason why so much theological labour still seems mainly irrelevant and sterile. It seems to have no effect whatever on the Catholic political world, the de Gaulles, the Salazars, the Adenauers, the Francos and the military dictators of Latin America; and because these theologians seem to refuse to admit the reality of the political world they have apparently no effect either on the baroque system of the Curia, as has been painfully evident during the Council. Whether we agree with it or not, the Curia represents the political aspect of the institutional Church in outlook, behaviour and contact with the world.

Nevertheless, while it seemed vitally necessary to make this point, the stirring within the Church is most certainly due to the work of such men as Rahner, Schillebeeckx, Congar, Küng, Metz, Schoonenberg and many others of that calibre.

All this is reflected in the concrete results of the Council. We have Constitutions on the Liturgy, on the Church, on Ecumenism, bolstered up by various decrees and continuity commissions, but, for instance, the decree on the Mass Media was nowhere near the level of the more strictly theological ones, and there are serious lacunae in the Schema on the Church and the World—which, to start with, should have been entitled 'The Church in the World'.

One can only be grateful for the great progress that has been made. How different the Constitution on the Church looks from what used to be written in manuals of dogmatic theology of the days of Pohle and others. But most ordinary Christians do not doubt that the major achievement of the Council lies deeper, and is the fruit of Pope John's vision. His *aggiornamento* was never meant to be a simple kind of up-dating: he, above all, realised that one could simply not 'up-date' the Church without a stringent process of self-criticism and re-valuation. No society, whether religious or secular, can be healthy without continuous self-examination. To have brought this about at such a high level is not only an astounding achievement of Pope John; the glory of it must go also to those theologians and those many bishops whose integrity corresponded to that of Pope John. The People of God must, by their nature, constantly shake off any clinging to man-made creations and man-made structures, so that the faith may remain alive and the Spirit of Christ make it fruitful.

Here one recognises another step forward towards unity. For this unity demands above all honesty and sincerity. It is fatal to confound sincerity with fanaticism, as is so easily done. Sincerity demands as a first condition that we be ready to expose our motives and our principles to fair criticism, and that we be willing to adapt ourselves to such criticism. And here one feels a certain pride in one's Catholicism. I, for one, do not know of any instance in the whole of history, ecclesiastical or secular, where an examination of the communal conscience was conducted on such a scale, in front of such a universal audience and so ruthlessly. This sincerity, this openness to God's saving activity, this basic humility surely are the features of a People of God, that even the fiercest of prophets would applaud? And what has happened? Instead of losing prestige, the Church has become a reality that all the world is willing to accept as a reality. And, I must confess I find it a pity that I see no such readiness to accept a public examination of conscience in any other religious body, although there are signs that it may come, as in the moving

Lutheran letters published in *The Unfinished Reformation*, edited by the great Hans Asmussen.

In spite of all that has been said so far the main advance towards the unity of mankind has not been made by the theologians and the Constitutions and decrees of the Council. It has been made on the level of ordinary secular life, inside and outside the Church. In so far as the Church is concerned, it started timidly with the peace efforts of Benedict XV and grew in clarity and determination during the pontificates of Pius XI and Pius XII, till it finally broke through with Pope John XXIII. The very context in which Pope John set the whole of this Council of his was that unity of mankind, to which he addressed his *Mater et Magistra* and his *Pacem in Terris*. This line was firmly continued by Pope Paul, in his repeated denunciation of nationalism and its evil consequences for the modern world, and above all in his great statement to the United Nations Assembly in October 1965.

In spite of the wrecking attempts of various members of the Security Council, almost since the beginning of the U.N.O., this great organisation has grown into a veritable international political body whose purely human activities have brought to the world, mainly through its many flourishing international agencies, an awareness of the unity of mankind which has never existed before in human history. It is through the work of these Agencies that all over the world ordinary men and women became involved in the hunger, disease, poverty, ignorance, exploitation and lack of communication through lack of education, which beset two-thirds of mankind. The Development Decade, the Freedom from Hunger campaigns, the Disarmament campaigns and many other enterprises have pierced the smugness and egotism of Western individualism. It is at this point that

Pope Paul's statement acquires the significance of a religious witness. Whatever may be criticised in the speech, Pope Paul did present himself as 'your brother', and not as a superior. He is 'the bearer of a message for all mankind', and speaks 'in the name of the great Catholic family'. He obeys the command to 'go and bring the glad tidings to all peoples. And it is you here who represent all peoples.' He says that his message is 'first of all, a solemn and moral ratification of this lofty institution'. He also makes his own 'the voice of the poor, the disinherited, the suffering', and, though Vicar of Christ on earth and the principal representative of the Catholic Church, he generously admits: 'The peoples of the earth turn to the United Nations as the last hope of concord and peace'. And then comes the historic declaration, revolutionary certainly from the Catholic point of view: 'We would almost be tempted to say that your chief characteristic is a reflection, as it were, in the temporal field of what our Catholic Church aspires to be in the spiritual field: unique and universal. In the ideological construction of mankind, on the natural level, one can conceive of nothing superior to this. Your vocation is to make brothers not only of some, but of all peoples. . . . Is there anyone who does not see the necessity of coming thus progressively to the establishment of a world authority, able to act effectively on the juridical and political levels?'

Here we have a man who does not talk about 'Man' conquering nature, or 'Man' conquering his own fate. For Pope Paul mankind is not an abstraction, a generalisation, it is a live community composed of persons, equal in the sight of God. The theological link between his words and the kerygma, the Christian witness, lies in the use of the word 'brother'. My comment on this is short: why have the theologians of

Concilium so far not seen that a thorough overhaul of our traditionally individualistic attitude towards our brother is utterly indispensable if they want their new look on Christian thought to be relevant to the practical and concrete witness in which the salvation of the Christian lies? But so far, there has been no article in *Concilium* on the 'brother'. Are they afraid of the consequences of the inherent logic of the commandment of love? Or is it that, while having a generous measure of heart and head, they in fact lack the lay experience which is the crucial point for any relevance? Or are they afraid of admitting that many have discovered this truth for themselves outside the Church and, having found there a solid anchor for their personal life and personal responsibility, have put us, who have the great 'Formula', to shame in the sight of our own conscience and in the eyes of God, the Father of all mankind?

This side-stream of the development towards unity which arose before the Council, led up to it, and then was allowed to run parallel with it (as the shocking hesitations among the Fathers showed when they debated conscientious objection, for instance), has nevertheless run close enough to it to make us hope that, once the Council is over, whatever it may have achieved will be developed and interpreted in the light of the great new awareness of the existence of a brotherhood of mankind.

The basic importance of this point is not difficult to see. If as Christians we are wholly committed, on both the ecclesial and 'secular' level, to a witness which embraces our brother without preference or favouritism, we are, by the same token, committed to see 'evil' in all those factors which lead to division instead of unity. These factors are complex and rarely isolated, which means that it would appear to be hopelessly unrealistic if we conceived of the ecumenical movement as something which can be achieved on a clerical or theological level while we keep on cherishing our colour-bars, our armaments, our militarism, our class distinctions and our unjustified wealth. And this shows a new facet in this new awareness. For, today, we no longer divide on purely external factors but on ideological ones: national sovereignty, racialism, capitalism, communism, Nazism or Fascism (in any country), and fundamentally inspiring all these, individualism. This means that we cannot ignore the fact that our theology should concern itself with all this, for, indeed, it concerns our basic interpretation of Christ and his kerygma, and baptism is no excuse for ignoring it.

This view of unity as the all-embracing unity of mankind was not born of theological speculation. It sprang up, spontaneously, from a direct lay experience, the experience of the last war. In order to make this point clear I wish to tell about something which happened to a friend of mine, because it is typical of many incidents which all together constitute that lay experience I mentioned. As a small boy my friend lived with his family in the Moselle province of France. His father had to decide whether to flee to the south or to stay put in his village when the German armies flooded the country. He stayed put. The SS occupied the village. After a few months his mother was taken to military headquarters for interrogation. Nervously she submitted. She was questioned again and again, and the fifteen-year-old boy saw his mother slowly disintegrate until she went completely mad. At that stage the boy himself was forcibly conscripted into the German army, and in despair he became one of 'them'. The hatred, however, which he saw around him was so relentless and merciless that in the end, young as he was, he told himself that this simply could not be 'life'. He switched back, and as soon as the war was over he betook himself to the seminary of a modern congregation of priests. Studying and experiencing the liturgy, he saw there the means of spreading love among the ordinary people by making them see, hear, eat and drink it. His individual way of saying Mass, which would be wholly approved of by the new Constitution on the Liturgy, was frowned upon by his Superior in Rome and for many weeks, shortly after his ordination, he was only allowed to say Mass in a house chapel with no one present except the server. He returned to France and continued to work out and live by his principles, this time with the blessing of his Superior. He naturally fell in with the Taizé community where, until recently, he used to take groups of students from Paris and other places, for two or three months a year, and so continues to spread his version of ecumenism.

And, curiously enough, the experience of the Taizé community runs along the same lines. Roger Schutz went from Lausanne to France in August 1940 to be in the middle of the misery of war and occupation. Alone, he looked after refugees who shuffled from one zone to another by sheltering them temporarily in an empty building at Taizé. He determined to start a community after the war, but his plans were vague. When the occupation of France settled down, more or less, he returned to Switzerland, to Geneva, where he lived with a small group of similar-minded young men, among whom was his right-hand man, Max Thurian. After the liberation, in the summer of 1944, he returned to Taizé and set up house for abandoned children: social work again. It was only after a while that he began to concentrate more on ecumenism as such. But the curious thing was that his brand of ecumenism had wholly grown out of the concrete social experience of the ordinary people. The words which stand written large near the church of Reconciliation proclaim the universal view of unity as I tried to sketch it above. They read: 'You who enter here, be reconciled: the father with his son, the husband with his wife, the believer with the unbeliever, the Christian with his separated brother'. You will notice, he does not say 'reunion'—the term that had been more or less appropriated by the theology-dominated ecumenism of before the war—but 'reconciliation'. He does not begin with reconciliation between Christians: that aspect comes last. It seems to suggest that Schutz, too, considers this ecclesiastical ecumenism to come about as the fruit of a deeper reconciliation, one that must take place first on the ordinary human level, in the lay experience. This is underlined by the attitude of the Taizé community towards their environment, which consists of small, relatively poor farmers who, for the last two hundred years, have lived in a traditional hatred of the Church since the bad end of Cluny. There are seven parish churches in the immediate neighbourhood, with only one priest to serve them because nobody comes. In order to 'reconcile' them, the community has set up a co-operative system of farming, in which the members of the community take part but have no more to say than the other farmers. When the usual donations began to pour into the community, given by the kind of Christians who try to elude their personal guilt and responsibility by giving away some of their superfluous money, Roger Schutz made his community proceed to a collective examination of conscience. As a result they decided unanimously not to use those donations but to pass them on straight away to the peasants of Chile and the peasants of Patmos. They were quite determined that the example of wealthy Cluny which had driven the ordinary people to exasperation and to hatred should not be repeated at Taizé, only eight kilometres away from Cluny.

Finally, to show that these are not isolated instances, one has but to look at what happened in Holland. There the occupation drove Catholics, Marxists, Calvinists and humanists together in one common purpose and one common experience. They began to know each other, to understand and to appreciate each other. They became conscious of their power as responsible laymen in a society which others may try to direct or control but which they themselves run in their own concrete existence. The result has been that a new Christian awareness has grown out of that lay experience and that theology began to open its eyes on the true facts of life and to follow the lines indicated by that experience. Theology did not precede the experience. And if it is said by mean people that the Dutch are restless Catholics, one should remember what Cardinal Alfrink quietly pointed out in Rome, namely that 80 per cent of the Dutch Catholics are practising Catholics, while only 5 per cent are practising in Italy. In England we have, it is said, some 53 per cent, which is still a long way off 80.

This lay effort towards the realisation of human unity is something which is still hopelessly underrated by our theologians. And here England certainly is worth studying. When Professor Halmos wrote his book on *The Faith of the Counsellors*[1], he pointed to a phenomenon which is no less Christian for being anonymously so. The stream of voluntary workers who devote their time and energy, unbeknown, to fellow human beings is still swelling. The peculiar implications of such movements as the Samaritans, a movement which has already spread

[1] Constable 1965.

to more than twenty countries, East and West, and even behind the Iron Curtain, have not been fully explored. The Samaritans work on the principle that the first aid in human distress is never the official, whether of State or Church, but the ordinary neighbour, the 'brother'. The reason is psychologically sound: the first communication in distress is that which is made on the uncomplicated level of ordinary and direct human experience. In this experience, which lies below whatever science and pastoral work may discover, they can share with the outcast, the depressed, the man-at-the-end-of-his-tether, the human being as such. And it is at this level of direct human experience that man realises, becomes conscious of, this basic human identity which links us all together into one community. It is also clear at this level that it is a *drawback* to be an official, to be 'qualified', to be a representative of authority, to be seen as an embodiment of a 'structure' rather than as a live human being without any pretensions and without any presumptions. It is vital to be aware of this drawback if we want to understand the paramount importance of what I call the 'lay experience'. And, lastly, it is on this level that the word 'brotherhood' acquires a significance which is not imposed from above or from without but is directly experienced from within, without any argument. It is, therefore, at this level that man opens up as a person and as a communal being. It is here that he reveals himself as a person precisely in so far as he shoulders, without further complications, immediate and effective responsibility for his brother. And where this is done simply and ungrudgingly man discovers Christ in his brother in the way Christ must have meant it when he pointed to the final and ultimate test of discipleship and witness in Matthew xxv. 31 ff.

It is here, therefore, that the unity of mankind lies buried; it is here that it must grow, and it is from here that we should approach the whole Christian message. Because this aspect of the lay experience is so strong, and so universally testified in these modern days, I find it difficult not to see here the Spirit of Christ pursuing what we call today his 'salvation history'. It is here that the development in the Church as shown in the papal directives of the last twenty years converges with the development on the secular (or should we say: 'political'?) level in the United Nations and in such wholly modern movements as the World Voluntary Service. It is therefore from this point of view that we ought to look at the future of Christianity. And the consequences may be surprising.

The first point when we consider the function of Christianity in the future is that the opposition between Church and World will vanish. This will come about because the world will be recognised, not as one society —the secular (political?) one—opposed to an ecclesiastical society, but rather as the field within which the witness of Christ grows. The Church will shed more and more the false secular imitation of a nation-state, it will no longer be described as 'the perfect society' on the basis of Aristotelian philosophy. It will rather aim at being the life-blood of Christ flowing through the veins of the human community. The princely and somewhat pagan titles and ranks and dress and pomp will gradually be abandoned as being foreign to Christ's witness. The Christian will be much less anxious to compare himself with others and mark off the boundaries which set him apart from his brother. He will rather be preoccupied with the only thing that matters, that is, the responsibility for his brother which he has assumed in

Christ's stead when he received baptism, confirmation, ordination, or marriage. Some of this can already be read between the lines on the People of God in the Constitution on the Church. Some of this is already put into practice by some far-sighted bishops who have set precedents that will impose themselves on the rest of the ecclesiastical body. It is true that the very architecture and decadent culture of Rome and Italy will remain for some time the stony embodiment of a period when the Church saw herself as the supreme Nation-State. But the Rome of the Renaissance will die the death of Constantine and the see of Peter will become more and more a centre and inspiration of love and forget the corruption of power. The hierarchical structure of the Church which for so long was the dominant feature of the Church, both in the East and in the West, will deflate itself on its own accord without violent religious conflicts and the essence of the Church as the People of God will come to life. This means that the Church will become more realistic, will identify herself more and more with the concrete existence of the human beings that make up the human community. As long as the Church looks for security in outward and man-made structures, she will merely be a society in competition with other societies. The more she competes on this man-made level with other societies, the more she will adopt the ways, views and attitudes of the other man-made societies. That is why it is so difficult for us today to distinguish in the Church what is merely a man-made and rather pagan accretion to the basic simple structure which she needs, from what is genuine Christian development. Words like 'power', 'authority', 'teaching' are commonly used in such a wild and indiscriminate fashion that they have almost lost all meaning except the crudest.

Now, when the overblown and overloaded structures gradually sink back into their true, very modest, significance, the result will be that all the life and energy that first went into propping up the structures, the power, the secular prestige, will now be released for the genuine live witness of Christ. Instead of being constantly in opposition Christian life will identify itself with the life of mankind as such, and Christ cannot work his universal salvation of mankind through us until we have in fact identified ourselves with mankind as He did. And this is really the most extraordinary point in Church history, since Constantine, and certainly since Charlemagne and the later Middle Ages, that the more the Church emulated the crude, pompous, frequently inhuman structures of a basically pagan feudal society, the more hierarchical she became, the more she lost contact with the real people, the real mankind, and the farther away she grew from Christ precisely because the basic significance of Christ is that he identified himself with mankind unto death—a radical identification without which Christianity is a pretence, a really repulsive pretence because of the implied hypocrisy and even blasphemy. It will be a long haul back to Christ, but we are on the way.

That this is, by the grace of God, the way in which the Church is beginning to shape seems to be borne out by many factors which anybody can observe for himself. Let us look at the notion of 'authority' and what happened to 'authority' during the Council. To start with, and almost by universal implicit consent, the Council has steered clear of the type of definitions which used to gladden the heart of William Ward in the last century. Instead, we have descriptions, illustrations, repetitions in different words. There were too many bishops who, frankly, had no more theological maturity than the average priest, and there were others who had so much of it that they were perforce a minority, and there were a good many who simply took the best—but wholly human—way out, which was to treat those matters as they would be treated in any human gathering, namely by bargaining, finding a formula, spicing the lot with enough rather too human intrigue to set the tongues wagging. Of course, there was the Mass of the Holy Spirit every morning, and who would dare deny that all assisted according to the grace given each and the response given by each: no differently from the way any other Christian assists at Mass (alas, it was just 'assistance' (not communion) for the bishops and the *periti*). One came out of St Peter's and one asked one of them why such and such a phrase was added to the text voted on, and the answer would come quite frankly that it was in order to make 'the others' agree to another section of the text. No doubt, the Holy Spirit was present, but is there any bishop or theologian left who will still maintain that conciliar texts are a sort of second-rate revelation, and represent 'the' teaching of Christ completely and finally? Yet, how many theologians said exactly that in the past when any tiresome opponent was finally and utterly disposed of by quoting a text from Trent or Vatican I? How many bishops would still hold that they can speak with final authority when fellow-bishops contradict them in their own right? The authority of the Christian Church is without any doubt derived from Christ, but what exactly does this mean when it comes to personal claims and personal statements? Modern theologians, historians, philosophers and scriptural scholars were not born yesterday, and the truth they so laboriously and unremittingly pursue will prevail, without any respect of persons, high or low.

And all this again is exhilarating, because this truth, which in any case cannot be caught in a temporary formula, is not endangered but begins to come alive, to enter realistically into the human experience, and so humbly mixes with mankind in the market square, overjoyed at the opportunity of a dialogue. And so the truth unifies instead of divides: men work out the truth *together*, in their concrete experience, and this is precisely what is meant by 'truth' in the Bible, an aspect of salvation history in operation.

Once authority has become more humble, more human and more Christian, the glamour of the clerical position will decline sharply. The first stage will be a sharp and long overdue separation of the cleric from the priest. The cleric is very much the relic of a feudal society, but today there is not a single field left where the priest can claim advantages and privileges over any other educated human being. The scholar, the philosopher, the scientist, the sociologist, the psychologist and the psychiatrist, the social worker, the welfare officer, the probation officer, the marriage guidance worker, the doctor and the nurse—all these people deal most adequately with the ordinary human field of ordinary human experience, and there is no reason why theology should not become a humble specialised discipline taught, along with others, at every university, and that will be the death-knell of all clericalism. As a result, the priest will become more modest, more identified with the People of God, probably sharing their human experience by earning his bread and marrying or not marrying according to the way God calls him to. The bishops will no longer be able to combine ruling large dioceses as if they were little kingdoms with doing their job in a way which is relevant to the experience of the People of God. Canon Law, that rather regrettable imitation of the purely secular law, still more regrettably called 'sacred', will become equally deflated, and be reduced to a relatively small number of principles, and far more will be left to the practical judgment of the man on the spot, priest or bishop, who is the president of the liturgical assembly. And this is as it should be, since nothing is more incomprehensible to the People of God than the sight of grown-up, intelligent men who have to ask for permission on every possible occasion. How this can be counted as a virtue is as much a mystery as the idea that a Christian should not be an adult human being with an adult sense of responsibility. And in this way, the disappearance of clericalism will lead to a truly Christian integration of the priest in the community of men and consequently strengthen the unity of mankind.

What about the sacraments? The sacraments have been given much attention in recent years and at the Council. There is no doubt that the essence of all the sacraments is a strengthening of the Mystical Body of Christ in every way. Unfortunately, a certain over-physical interpretation, too common in the past, led to a somewhat frightening amount of superstitious treatment, a popular view which came very close to sheer pagan magic. Today the theologians have again brought out the true Christian interpretation of the sacrament as a personal encounter between Christ in glory and the receiving Christian. This has given more strength to the objective reality of the sacraments whilst at the same time driving home that this reality cannot transform us unless and as far as we stand open to that total commitment into which Christ wishes to draw us. And as this total commitment of Christ lies in his total identification with mankind as a whole, in his death and resurrection, it becomes obvious that the sacraments flow into our concrete existence as members of the community of mankind. This truer and more demanding interpretation of the sacraments will lead to greater vitality in the reception of the sacraments, and by that very token probably to a less quantitative estimate of sacramental values and to a less exaggerated use of what are called the *sacramentalia.*

All this really means one thing: Christianity, and Catholic Christianity in particular, is becoming more conscious of its pristine nobility and vitality; it is becoming more conscious of the fact that the only thing which gives it meaning is to create and continue and develop the live witness to the Father of all mankind through Christ, his Son, in the Spirit. It is quite astonishing when one looks at the religious literature of the past, particularly in the field of apologetics, how much the emphasis on faith came to override the reality of concrete existence. This was only possible when we began to confuse the essence of faith, which is unquestioning surrender to God's faithfulness in his promise, embodied in Christ, with the man-made attempts to pin certain intellectual aspects of it down to dogmatic formulae. This was bound to happen when different 'faiths' —an expression which is really nonsensical—began to compete for adherents and moved away from real life to a separate intellectual battleground. Hence theology seems to have ousted the live witness. By the same token the reality of Christianity disappeared from the immediate field of concrete experience with the result that so many millions have come to look on it as noble and good but, unfortunately, irrelevant.

To illustrate this point, let me tell about a small incident. A first-rate theologian talked to a friend of mine. The theologian was wholly wrapped up in ecumenism and was indeed an authority in that field.

My friend, having developed a rather live social conscience from which he, quite rightly, cannot exclude the field of politics, happened to mention the business of the Oder-Neisse line. No sooner had he mentioned the words than all ecumenism was forgotten and, in the actual concrete test of ecumenism in the question of national hatreds, the German theologian rejected any possible compromise between Germany and Poland. Does this not show that our theologians are still, though unwittingly, disporting themselves in an ivory tower?

There is no possible doubt that if the live witness, which Christ demands of us, is really taken seriously, the Church will have to identify herself with the human experience within which lies her essential task. Nor, so it seems to me, can there be any possible doubt that this concrete witness, within this concrete experience, is borne principally by the ordinary layfolk. It is they who represent and are the People of God at the crucial point of existential decision. It is their conscience, their commitment, their maturity that decide the fate of the Church as Church. And as this experience lies wholly wrapped up in their immediate share of the experience of the whole of mankind, they carry the brunt of Christ's advance. It is they that are most immediately the 'brothers' of the sick, the poor, the dispossessed, the distressed, they are the carriers of that love which has primacy over faith according to St Paul. They are immediately and personally involved in the wider experience of those who do not explicitly recognise Christianity but in whom the Spirit of Christ so often works his hidden wonders of salvation to shame those who try to monopolise Christ as an individualistic possession. It is through this new realisation of the people of God as such, that the Church will become humble; that faith, in the true sense, will dominate structure, instead of structure strangling the faith. The Spirit of Christ will flourish in an abundance of charismatic and prophetic purpose, and there will again be room for vision.

Union will then grow, not from the periphery, but from that root, the *radix Jesse*, which is Christ, the revelation of God within mankind.

Towards a New Integrity

ANDREW BOYLE

TOWARDS the end of the recent Vatican Council's final session, when most of the participants were already chafing with ill-concealed impatience to resume their normal pastoral duties, an eminent English-speaking prelate disclosed his anxiety about the future to a non-Catholic writer friend of mine who chanced to be visiting Rome on business. They had been discussing, among other things, the unwieldy nature of the conciliar machinery which was put to its severest tests whenever a controversial issue came up for debate; and, after marvelling together at the results achieved on paper in spite of this elaborate, antiquated machinery, they turned to the future—and to less easily calculable matters of translating theory into practice.

My friend belongs to that small, highly unfashionable

group of outsiders who continue to admire, in the romantic spirit of Macaulay, the image of the Roman Catholic Church as a rock-like, impregnable structure defying all the winds of change blowing idly and aimlessly about it. At a turning point in history, when only the Communist States present a visible front of disciplined unity, dedicated to the subversion of all spiritual and human freedom, he found it astounding and deeply disturbing that the Church of Rome should have seen fit not to tighten but to loosen the bonds of its own members. Having himself passed the stage of utter disillusionment with the fruits of material affluence, and believing that such fruits, in the non-Communist world especially, are filled with the seeds of self-destruction, he could not resist expressing his own doubts about the effect on Catholics throughout the world of the Vatican Council's more progressive reforms. A Church so determined to enter the modern world, to come to terms with that world, and to make it practicable for its adherents to do so, was courting disaster.

Such a change of policy could hardly have been chosen at a worse time. With his thoroughly jaundiced view of human nature and his conviction that most human aspirations are foredoomed to disappointment, my friend could see nothing but harm in the Council's plans for modernising the Church. He could not understand how, and I can almost hear the well-modulated voice selecting the words with care, 'the entire edifice of the Church can be prevented from crumbling if the process is allowed to go on to its logical conclusion'.

To do him justice, the attentive prelate did not wholly accept my friend's extremely pessimistic opinion. But the gloomy trend of the conversation did induce him suddenly to express a strange misgiving of his own. He had been surprised, he admitted, by the weight of support in favour of drastic reforms in the outlook, the structure and the administrative machinery of the Church. He was not referring, of course, to the clash of views often heard in Council debates. Divisions between progressive and conservative Fathers were different. These he had grown used to; they were only to be expected. He had been less prepared, however, for the comparatively strong underswell of progressive sentiment among laymen and clerics in his own archdiocese. It evidently caused him some alarm. In the past, he said, Catholics spoke out on Church matters only when specifically invited to do so. Criticism had been confined to a few cranks and rebels whom nobody took too seriously. No doubt the Council had produced its own special atmosphere of self-questioning in the Church at large; it seemed that the uneasiness stirred by clashes in the Council on subjects which had once been regarded as undebatable articles of faith was spreading rapidly.

'I formerly supposed that the majority of Catholics would be opposed to changes,' he said. 'All their training and habits of mind suggested that they would go on clinging to what was old and tried and familiar. The main difficulty, as I saw it, was bound to be persuading them to accept gradual changes, and this could only be done with care. The actual situation today is different. Too many people for my liking apparently want to make a clean sweep in too much haste and regardless of the dangers.'

The revealing dilemma of this prelate is understandable. It is probably quite common, notably in the developed countries of the West where, for the first time since the Reformation, a large and growing number of laymen are now at least as well educated as their spiritual leaders and sometimes better. The tendency of laymen to think for themselves, whereas a mere generation ago it was still the undisputed right of the Bishops and clergy to do the thinking for them, has certainly been stimulated by the debates of the Council. The process cannot in the nature of things be easily reversed; and it has created new problems of an unprecedented kind. Enormous courage, vision, patience and tact will be required on the part of the ecclesiastical authorities to rise to the challenge without intensifying the accompanying stresses and strains on the faith and loyalty of their people. Is it too much to hope that the Bishops and Clergy will interpret the signs of the times correctly? Will they succeed in solving misunderstandings that could imperil everything achieved in Rome during the four sessions of the Second Vatican Council? The answers to such questions will vary from country to country, from diocese to diocese, and from Bishop to Bishop; success or failure will hinge on the character and outlook of individuals, and on the use they make of the moral and spiritual authority that is theirs by right.

An episcopal ruler of conservative views and instincts may be tempted to sit back and do nothing, on the time-worn pretext that prudence is a cardinal virtue and impetuosity a vice. A liberal-minded Bishop may conceivably cause anguish and disruption among the majority of his people by taking the diametrically opposite course and trying to reform too much too quickly. It must be added that there are many Bishops who share my non-Catholic writer-friend's conviction that here lies the broad road to anarchy, disintegration and the ultimate erosion of stability and truth. One may expect from them a traditional touch of asperity and rigidity in introducing major reforms as it were by divine right. Their actions may result in forcing the critical minority to conform or quit, and the silent majority to obey; but the long-term consequence will surely be to multiply and aggravate the problems of their successors.

Between these two extremes there will be numerous variants; but no matter how any individual Bishop seeks to implement the awaited changes, none will ever be sure again that he has placed his particular area of the Church beyond criticism. For the spirit of honest and open criticism is perhaps the healthiest and most important phenomenon that has erupted throughout the Church since the late Pope John invoked it by summoning his Council. That spirit can no longer be exorcised or suppressed at any one point without hurt to the whole Christian body.

If one decision of the Council more than another can be said to have given rise to considerable uneasiness among Bishops, priests and compliant laymen in the Catholic Church at large, it is undoubtedly the declaration on religious liberty. That decision, of course, was inevitable. It was certainly long overdue. Other Christian bodies and sensitive outsiders welcomed it with relief. Here was a sure sign that the Catholic Church was indeed determined to change her ways. Yet not a few progressive Catholics had instant reservations. They foresaw what a traumatic effect the decision would have on the minds of most of their fellow-Catholics, indissolubly wedded as these are to the old authoritarian ways.

Allowing for the fact that the theologians will be busy possibly for years working out the practical implications, it is not hard to understand why local ecclesiastical authorities have been reluctant even to mention the subject to their people. Religious liberty was all very well as a theoretical principle. The Church has always upheld the abstraction, and taken care not to honour it in practice, wherever her writ happened to run, on the ludicrous pretext that 'error has no rights'. Now, it appears, the

Council's decision to admit practice with principle is causing acute embarrassment and uncertainty to a formidable number of Catholics. The reader may well ask why.

There are at least two interlocked reasons for such a reaction. The first of them bears on the instinctive attitude, bred in the bone by tradition, of the average Catholic towards his non-Catholic neighbour. During the four and a half centuries since the Reformation, the Catholic Church has been on the defensive, most of all perhaps when in the act of striving to purify and renovate herself. 'Hence,' in the words of Hans Küng[1], 'we see much of the Catholic reforms displaying itself as *reaction*, in the sense of a restoration aimed at maintaining what was established and restored according to the pattern of a superior past, with the consequent danger of stunting and fossilising the fullness of Catholicism.' This work of 'conquest for the Kingdom of Christ' has been carried on intermittently until our own day. The reforms lacked the essential Christian prerequisite of charity because they were at any rate partly shaped to 'combat Protestantism'. They were not devised 'as a means of reconciliation and reunion but as an armament programme and a plan of campaign'.

The main achievement of the recent Council was to remove nearly every trace of militant and sectarian bias from its reforms, thus enabling the regenerative force within the Church to be released at full pressure for the first time since the high middle ages. The declaration on freedom of conscience was to that extent revolutionary. It was at once an admission of the Church's failings in the past and a statement of positive intent to preach and practice the fullness of Christianity in the future.

[1] *The Council and Reunion*, pp. 114–115, Sheed and Ward, 1961.

It is never an easy matter for any person to own up to his or her faults and shortcomings. For the Catholic Church to do so, before the watchful eyes of the whole world, seemed to require a miracle of grace. The Council Fathers certainly owned up in the name of the Church; but it may be doubted whether one Catholic layman in a thousand yet realises that this historic happening took place, committing him to the hopeful consequences. It is one thing to pass a resolution. It is quite another to make its sense and significance understood by your entire people and clergy, notably if you happen to be a cautious or conservative-minded Bishop prepared to procrastinate. The fact that the Church has embarked on a dynamic programme of renewal, rooted in the love of God and one's neighbour, has not penetrated to the mass of ordinary Catholics in Britain, for example, where the ecclesiastical authorities are still as reluctant to speak about the true dimensions of the Council's achievements as they were to promote its positive aims while it was in progress.

Fear of causing needless anxiety, unrest, doubt and misgiving among simple people noted for their loyalty and unquestioning respect for the said authorities may help to explain this extraordinary conspiracy of silence. It hardly excuses it. Indeed it may give rise eventually to far worse difficulties since it establishes two standards of truth, one on paper for the benefit of sceptical outsiders, the other in practice for members. The Bishops in question seem to have forgotten a further factor. There exists in Britain, the United States and Western Europe a strong minority of Catholics willing and able to think for themselves. Are the patience and divided loyalties of these men and women to be stretched to breaking point? Must they become the victims of heedless complacency on high?

This leads us to the second reason for the doubts of many churchmen regarding religious liberty in practice: their instinctive fear that it will undermine belief itself. If the Church is, in practice, still in two minds about the expediency of acknowledging openly that its inner life in the past left much to be desired, and failed on numerous occasions to measure up to its divine ideals, will it not be still more untimely to allow individual members freely and openly to ventilate their own personal misgivings as Christians? It is reasonably clear already that such misgivings abound. But the habit of parading them in public is quite new and still alien to the post-Reformation tradition, at any rate in Britain and North America. If bishops and priests resent public criticism of administrative decisions, however much these may be faulty and thus ripe for honest criticism, they can hardly be expected to welcome with open arms admissions of uncertainty about points of doctrine and moral teaching. The scandalising of 'weaker brethren' is regarded in official quarters as a heinous error. The weapon of scandal is a strong and handy one which the authorities may well be tempted to use indiscriminately in their own defence and on behalf of the alleged 'weaker brethren'. But repressive measures cannot be imposed indefinitely. The obligation to live up to the new and difficult promises made on behalf of the Church by the Council applies to Bishops as much as to their lay critics.

A change of heart on the part of the authorities will be believed when education of the 'weaker brethren' begins. Then we may see a final abandonment of the bad old English Catholic habit of damning public disagreements as a form of treason. The mentality of the catacombs or the religious ghetto dies harder here than anywhere else in the West, including the United States and even Ireland. There are sound historical explanations for this appalling immaturity which I have no space to enter into here: but the most noticeable outcome has been the barrier of respectful and almost servile reticence protecting the Church (in the outmoded, narrow sense of the Church authorities, whether parochial, diocesan or national) from the faintest breath of criticism or complaint. That this is still true in a land like England, which yields a fair annual crop of distinguished converts to Rome, should surprise nobody, since converts are not infrequently regarded with suspicion and usually lapse into impotent silence rather than give witting or unwitting offence. Let us not forget that Newman, that much-tried model of patience and visionary erudition, was spoken of in his day at the Vatican as 'the most dangerous man in England'. That foolish and insensate charge is still levelled against lesser men in our own day.

Part of the trouble is that Bishops and priests are seldom told more than is felt good that they should be told, so entrenched is the misplaced reverence in which they are commonly held. The apocryphal saying attributed to a layman who warned a Bishop on the eve of his consecration: 'Beware my friend, you may never hear the truth again' has a recognisably authentic ring, like the bitter jokes that circulate in Soviet Russia at the expense of the régime. When there is wide room for disagreement on official lines of policy, allegations of disloyalty—and worse—descend on the heads of critics honest enough to take issue with the authorities. Quarrels are all very well, runs the usual excuse, but only when kept inside the family.

'It has been suggested with a good deal of plausibility,'[1] says Fr Herbert McCabe, O.P., 'that disloyalty is shown, not indeed in disagreeing with, say, the known views of a particular Bishop or local hierarchy about

[1] *Honesty in the Church*, p. 11, Constable, 1965.

nuclear war or birth control or the necessity of denominational schools, but in publishing one's disagreement "outside the family" in, for example, the secular press.' The prompt steps taken by the authorities not long ago to silence two priests who were courageous or treacherous enough—it all depends on the point of view—thus to air their personal opinions on the birth control controversy amply bear out Fr McCabe's words. Laymen find it easier than priests to cross swords in public with the authorities because, unlike priests, they are not bound by any oath of obedience; and I take leave to doubt whether in future priests are likely to be better off in pleading the right to follow their consciences. Until Church leaders themselves learn to face the truth without fear, and strive to put love in its proper place as the supreme guide to Christian living, the rigours of the Church Litigant will go on harrowing all believers.

It might help if a simple attempt were first made to understand and overcome some of the less agreeable manifestations of what an English Benedictine priest, Dom Sebastian Moore, has cleverly characterised as 'A Catholic Neurosis'. For without such an attempt, it may prove impossible to carry out what to my mind is the second most important of all the reforms approved by the Vatican Council—that aimed at closing the gap between the Church authorities and the laity.

Dom Sebastian, in drawing up a list of some of the more peculiar aspects of English Catholic conduct, has referred to the 'tendency on the part of us priests to be allergic to frank discussion on matters which are at once important and personal, ranging from sex to real difficulties with the faith. The effect is that people encounter, at a certain point, a barrier which is not so much the limit of orthodoxy as the limit of the priest's willingness to talk as a man.... More often than not the preferred alternative is to keep right off important subjects and to cultivate a sort of impersonal *bonhomie*—a tendency that is especially marked in clerical gatherings.'

Is it astonishing that Dom Sebastian felt equally constrained to observe 'a tendency for young Catholics to remain strangely immature', and to conclude that 'the Church of today is still waiting to enjoy that "sanity in religion" which is to be found, mixed up with all sorts of heresy, in the reformed Churches'? Neuroses can be cured, especially if they are the product of environment and the obstinacy of habit; the cure will begin and become effective in the Church here and elsewhere only when the Church authorities admit to their share of responsibility for past failings—and let more daylight and fresh air ventilate a system that has been hermetically sealed for too long.

Pope Paul VI, in his encyclical letter *Ecclesiam Suam* was at pains to stress the risks attending what he called 'the great transformations, upheavals and developments' of mankind at the present day. 'All of this,' he said, 'like the waves of an ocean, envelops and agitates the Church', so that 'a danger bordering almost on vertiginous bewilderment can shake the Church's very foundations and lead men to the most bizarre ways of thinking'. The Pope's concern about 'bizarre ways of thinking' precisely reflects the concern of that non-Catholic writer-friend of mine who has seen in his lifetime the slow erosion of belief in Christianity as a direct product of religious license. Once upon a time it was the minister who often erred in his desperate eagerness to lend Christianity a bright new look, causing the late Ronald Knox to note with astringent fairness: 'Dogmas may fly out of the windows but congregations still don't come in at the doors'. Today, it is apparently the turn of the existential Christian, including the so-called maverick Catholic, to play fast and loose with the teachings of his Church. Where there is agitation and flux, there will be the danger of drift and evasion of responsibility.

But the crisis is a crisis of integrity as well. The authorities of the Catholic Church, at every level, may conceivably convince themselves that the only safe interim solution is a reversion to traditional rules, sanctions and coercive measures, putting reform into cold storage until sanity and docility are restored. Should they do so, they will have themselves to blame for rocking and even capsizing the barque of Peter, as has happened more than once before in various local waters throughout the history of the Church.

Boldness, not timidity, is needed. As Hans Küng emphasises in his latest work:[1] 'How is the Church with her message of freedom to be regarded as credible by men if she does not show herself a dwelling place of freedom? How is she to show herself as a place of freedom unless freedom shines out everywhere through her institutions and constitutions, her ministries and ordinances? It is of decisive importance that the Church's free nature should not be impenetrably covered and displaced in men's eyes by her unfree unnature.... More than ever today, in this century of totalitarianism, the Church must avoid even the merest appearance of totalitarianism, authoritarianism and absolutism with a religious colouring to it.'

By boldly trusting the laity; by treating them as people worthy of trust, in the true spirit of the Council's decisions, rather than as mindless children; and by giving them a voice and a place in the business of reform, the authorities stand to gain far more than they

[1] *The Church and Freedom*, pp. 19–20, Sheed and Ward, 1965.

will lose. Faith itself is a permanent, living risk. This is more true now than ever since it entails the right to take a long, cool look at the nature of one's own belief. Clashes and divisions inside the Church are therefore bound to continue with increasing frequency and sharpness. They should be open clashes, otherwise the taint of evasion and a devious integrity will attach to them. In the past, because of the unnatural gulf separating bishops and clergy from laity, many of the tensions in the Church sprang from faulty communications: frequently the authorities either did not know what was simmering below the surface or did not want to know.

The defect is one that can be found in all closed systems. Yet who can ignore the lamentable fact that the Church has repeatedly become an obstacle between the conscience of the individual and his God? And who can deny that such tragic dilemmas will multiply if there is any return to the religious ghetto with its robot discipline and penny-in-the-slot values? Here again the Council has pointed the way ahead. In the Constitution on the Church and its rôle in the modern world, it is emphasised that 'God founded human nature originally as a unity and has resolved to bring together into one all his children scattered far and wide. This was the errand on which God sent his Son.' How well this accords with the views of those critics, including many outside the Church, who point out that Christ died not for Christians in general and Catholics in particular but for all mankind!

The Church, looked at in this broader light, ceases to be a narrow, self-centred minority group shut off from the rest of the world. It becomes instead 'the seed of unity for the whole human race—for each and all the visible sacrament of saving unity'. In other words, the Church exists for mankind, not mankind for the Church, which means that the only Church that matters is an open Church in which men can worship God in perfect freedom, without restraint, without deviousness and without hypocrisy. This is the ideal put forward by the Council. Nothing less will do if the Church is not to be indicted by men inside and outside as little better than the whitened sepulchre of the Pharisees.

A Church that is still ridden with the regulations of canon lawyers, still bound by the trappings and ornate conventions of those long centuries when her rulers were often earthly despots as well, will be tempted to go on exacting the wrong sort of tribute from her subjects. There is little virtue in the mechanics of a dumb and unthinking conformity. Of course, to discard what is old simply because it *is* old would be a fruitless exercise. Indeed the argument is sometimes heard that Catholics have as much right to be proud of the regal splendours, the ancient ceremonial, the curial discipline and the innumerable rules and institutions that have come down the ages to them as the citizens of any nation are of their history and inheritance. This is a poor argument. It can be a double-edged one, especially to anyone conscious of the vaster spiritual patrimony which the majority of uninformed Catholics have not yet begun to recognise as their own.

There is more than a grain of truth in the gibe ascribed to an eminent English churchman about a hundred years ago that 'the conversion of England will come when the Catholics of England become Christians'. Nor should the curious lesson be forgotten that Cardinal Manning, when the Papal States were in peril, misguidedly wanted to have the Temporal Sovereignty of the Pope defined as an article of faith. Nobody with the slightest sense of history will dispute that the moral authority of the Pope has increased enormously since the Papacy ceased to have a vested interest in the politics of Italy and Western Europe. Now that the opportunity is at hand to simplify and streamline the internal administrative machinery of the Church by voluntary means, who can seriously dispute that there are anomalies to be removed, abuses to be checked, extravagances to be corrected and a vital change of heart to precede them all? I personally am extremely dubious, for example, whether the Council performed any useful service in unanimously supporting Pope Paul's proposal to promote the beatification of his two predecessors. The proving of sainthood rests finally with God; it seemed to me to be carrying the divine prerogative beyond the limits of common decency when it was implied that the beatification of Pius XII would please conservative Fathers, who were evidently displeased at the success of the progressives' moves in favour of the beatification of Pope John. Whether the solemn process of raising saints to the altars in any case has much to commend it these days as a spur to Christian Unity is only one question among hundreds that deserves open and responsible discussion.

At the local level, too, such tangled administrative issues as mixed marriages, the appointment of Bishops, the education of the clergy, denominational schools, and the ecclesiastical rota courts with their antiquated and sometimes extraordinarily inefficient methods of handling marital cases, cry out for thorough revaluation. Bishops and priests will be judged (and will deserve to be judged) by their readiness to seek expert lay advice before jumping to conclusions and imposing decisions. Consultation with the laity may result in decisions that are just as wrong as those now taken by bishops or priests ruling in splendid isolation. There can be no harm in this, provided that lay cliques and obsequious 'yesmen' are actively discouraged. It is high time that the Church's local leaders acquired sufficient courage and humility to be able to say 'We don't know', or 'We made a mistake'.

There is a paradoxical sense in which my non-Catholic friend's rosy picture of the Catholic Church as a once-powerful spiritual bastion, recklessly throwing its doors open to the untender mercies of a world that has lost its way, represents almost the exact opposite of the complex truth. Today, and for decades to come, the struggle for renewal will take place more and more in that vast, unmapped and inaccessible arena where the hearts and consciences of individual persons are busy working out their own salvation. The rapid pace of modern technological development has already outstripped the slow efforts of the hierarchy to adapt themselves to it, so that the parish is now seldom more than a handy service or filling station, except in thinly peopled country districts.

The diocese has become the realistic unit of the Church's organisation; yet the aloofness of the Bishop and his chapter in many instances makes the diocese as it stands a remote and ineffectual pillar of authority which hardly touches the lives of ordinary people at all. The isolation will continue until, on the initiative of the Bishops themselves, the best available lay brains and energies are harnessed to the common task of broadening the still exclusively clerical committees which administer many dioceses. Much can be learnt from other Christian bodies in this sphere: much will have to be unlearnt first. For the present obsolescent administrative machinery is the legacy of a smug philosophy of contempt for this world and its values, everything—including the diocesan machinery—being subjugated to the overriding and frequently narrow preoccupation with personal salvation.

Disenchantment with modern ways is strong among the clergy in countries like Britain where historical memories of the penal days once actively fostered the ghetto mentality. As a result, many uninformed laymen are indirectly encouraged to live on in confusion of mind, uncertain how best to combine their dual rôles of loyal Catholics and good citizens. The duality frequently drives the more spirited out of the Church altogether, especially when they stumble over religious doubts or moral difficulties. I myself know of many cases of the kind. Equally, the effect on the fanatic is that he may think of himself as 'a living extension of the Church' almost in the sense of an undercover agent working among and against the enemies of God. For the vast majority, however, living under the strain of this double allegiance to a Church which seems to despise the world, and to a world which no longer mocks or persecutes but merely ignores the Church, the easiest course must be to go on living a double life—that of the Christian on Sunday, that of a puzzled or even full-blooded worldling on the other six days of the week.

The tug-of-war between spiritual and secular, eternal and temporal, supernatural and natural, is as old as mankind. It is the emphasis laid by churchmen, now on one side, now on the other, which varies through the ages according to circumstances and tradition. In a long period of siege, such as that from which Rome has only recently emerged, the mind of the Church naturally bends to the eternal at the expense of the temporal; and the official bias of philosophers, theologians and canon lawyers has until recently been steadily towards that end. I, who am no theologian, philosopher or canonist, cannot be expected to predict how or where the official bias of teaching will change; but change it must if the Church honestly intends to live up to the promises of the Council.

There can be no room for that anthropomorphism which reduces God to unworthy and barely acceptable levels, which converts grace into a monolithic Church monopoly not unlike some nationalised industry, which continues to treat indulgences, the modesty or immodesty of dress, the attendance or non-attendance of clerics at theatres, as serious examples of spiritual legislation, and which strains the credulity of many Christians beyond the point of ridicule. Honesty and integrity demand revision of a whole multitude of such anachronisms.

The time has at least come to ensure that the rising generation will be spared them since, as the young American writer, Michael Novak, has so shrewdly observed: 'the greatest difficulty of the layman in the Church is the dishonesty in which he is constantly forced to live.... A dishonesty which begins at school or in catechism classes where he memorises definitions that he does not wholly accept, since often he does not understand them. But correct answers win good marks, and if he asks the teacher unsettling questions he is labelled rebellious or impertinent. The same system of falsehood characterises most of his experiences in the confessional.'[1]

Faith may be a fact yet it remains a marvellous, personal mystery. Abstractions of the traditional kind simply add an element of glib uniformity and deep individual confusion to a mystery which has become mummified. The workings of grace in the depths of the human personality are always mysterious, often paradoxical. It is humbug to go on pretending that grace is a Church monopoly when there are so many 'good

[1] *The Open Church*, p. 354, Barton, Longman and Todd, 1964.

pagans' and 'natural Christians' in the world, whose unorthodox integrity often puts the practice of professing Catholics to shame. Was it not partly from the past inspiration and example of the secular world that the Vatican Council drew courage enough to discuss such controversial themes as religious freedom? Was it not the zeal of non-Catholics in the teeth of past Catholic intransigence which made all the running in the ecumenical movement until Pope John at last gave the movement his spontaneous blessing?

As an institution once accustomed to the exercise of absolute and sometimes wrong-headed authority the Catholic Church is not finding it at all easy to acclimatise herself to conditions in a free, pluralist society. Breaking with the habits of a lofty isolation must create tensions and anxiety, if not strife. Alongside the gift of faith which the Bishops are naturally anxious to safeguard there stand the forgotten reservoirs of hope and love. If these are patiently tapped, for the greatest good of the whole free community of believers, then the Church cannot fail to fulfil the moral and spiritual rôle awaiting it. Individual insights will then amplify and enrich dry, often meaningless decrees and formulas; philosophers, conscious of the existential liberty of the individual person, will no longer have what Péguy called 'the politicians of the spiritual life' marshalled against them. Theology will become positive instead of negative. Men will then grow more secure in their beliefs, readier to serve a Church which acknowledges them at last as adults, happier and better integrated as members of that wider human family whose common Father is God.

Economic Planning for the Church

RONALD BRECH

THE world is experiencing prosperity on a scale unprecedented in history. The developed countries are battling with affluence. Even the many developing countries, which by Western standards are still desperately poor, are much richer per head of population than ever before.

The problem with prosperity is that it is relative. If one country has a much higher standard of living than another, the one looks rich and the other looks poor. Riches and poverty are defined in terms of aspirations, and aspirations are determined by what other people have got. Because of this, material wealth can lead to envy and even strife. But if it is dominated, it can be used for higher things.

The United States enjoys a much higher standard of

living than any other country in the world and for this reason it appears to set the trend in social values and conduct. But the other countries are not becoming 'Americanised'; it is merely a case of 'the United States has been there first'. As Britain and the other countries of Europe, as well as Canada, Australia and New Zealand, follow the United States at varying distances and varying speeds, their psycho-socio-economic environment transforms itself in the same way and to a similar pattern as the American environment did, say, ten years earlier.

The Church in its mission in the world has to live in this environment and use it to improve its own pastoral effort. Its administrative structure must be so designed as to enable it to do so. It must keep up with, even be ahead of, changing social conditions, if its pastoral mission is to be made really effective. For this reason any discussion on likely changes in the administrative structure of the Church requires first a description of the changing environment in which the Church has to operate.

Here, Britain has been taken as the template. But what is said about Britain applies equally forcibly to the Church in Europe, to the Church in the United States and to the Church in the developed countries overseas. The world is shrinking in size and one country's problems are in essence similar to those of another, once the external embellishments have been discarded.

I. BRITAIN'S RISING STANDARD OF LIVING

Britain is in the throes of yet another economic and social revolution with a rapidly rising standard of living and its consequent impact on social values. The standard of living between 1955 and 1965 has been rising at a compound yearly rate of nearly 2½ per cent and between 1962 and 1965 of nearly 3½ per cent. If the compound growth rate of 3 per cent a year is maintained, the standard of living will double in less than twenty-five years. The last time the British standard of living doubled, it took seventy years from 1890 to 1960, and the rate of increase during this period was accelerating in such a way that the rate between 1890 and 1930—forty years—was the same as that between 1930 and 1950—twenty years—and as that between 1950 and 1960—ten years. Such a degree of economic change is bound to bring with it certain social problems, since social values and customs tend to change at a much slower rate.

But this economic revolution has not affected *all* the people to the same degree. The country's income structure has become more equal, with the lower income groups benefiting relatively more than the upper income groups. This can perhaps be best seen from the accompanying diagrams.[1] The proportion of numbers of incomes is shown along the base, and annual incomes per head up the vertical. Diagram 1 shows the income structure for 1938—a triangular shape with the bulk of the people in the lower income groups. Diagram 2 shows the income structure for 1960. The shape has been transformed from a triangle to a hexagon—the structure is becoming more equal. The normative shape, given genuine equality of opportunity, is a diamond (◇) which represents the normal distribution of ability in society—a few geniuses at the top, a few cretins at the bottom and the mass of average intelligence in the middle. When the income structure achieves this shape

[1] Reprinted from *Planning Prosperity* (Ronald Brech), by permission of the publishers, Darton, Longman & Todd Ltd.

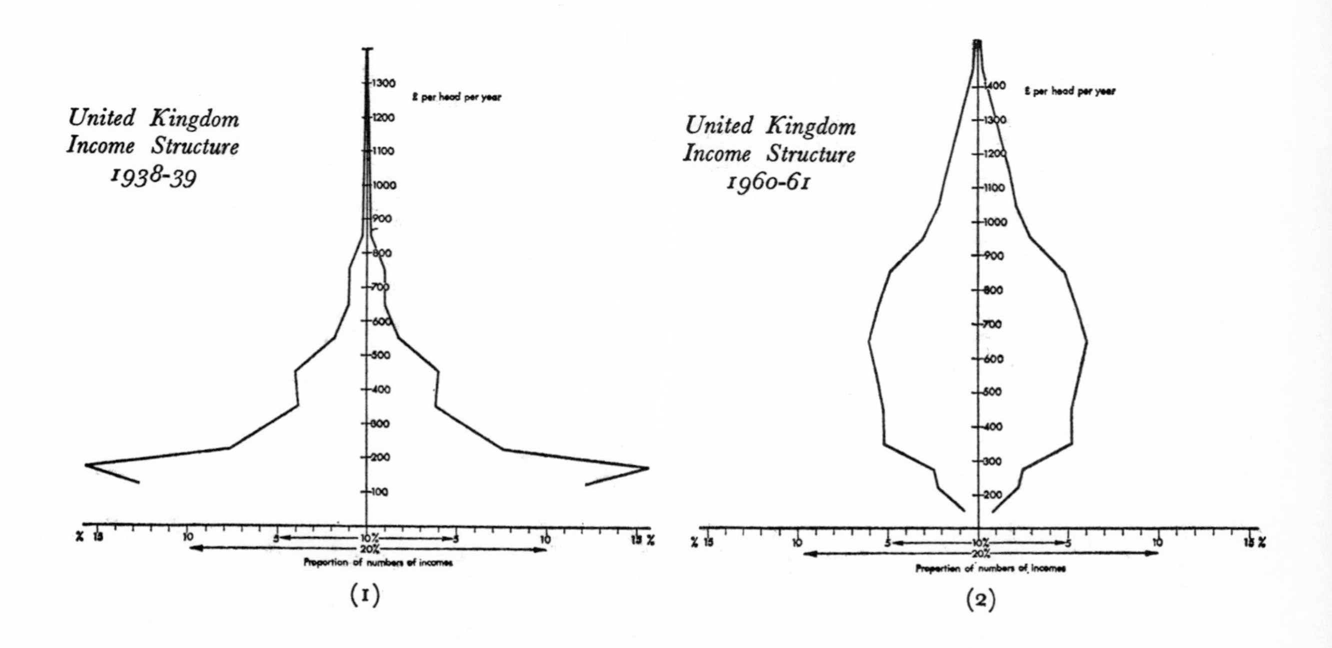
United Kingdom
Income Structure
1938-39
£ per head per year
1300
1200
1100
1000
900
800
700
600
500
400
300
200
100
% 15
10
5
10%
20%
5
10
15 %
Proportion of numbers of incomes
(1)
United Kingdom
Income Structure
1960-61
£ per head per year
1400
1300
1200
1100
1000
900
800
700
600
500
400
300
200
% 15
10
5
10%
20%
5
10
15 %
Proportion of numbers of incomes
(2)

(as in the United States), it heralds the emergence of the mass middle-class.

The present growth rate in the British standard of living implies that within the next twenty years, the income structure will have achieved its diamond shape and society will become politically more stable with most of the power and most of the wealth in the hands of the masses. But this transformation will bring with it—indeed, is bringing with it—a number of social changes.

The most important is the change in the structural relationships in society. In the past, people's positions in society were determined by property-ownership, whether land or means of production, which, through the incidence of inheritance, meant that position was determined largely by birth. Nowadays society is becoming consumption-orientated, where position is determined by income—income related to ability. But income has to be expressed outwardly so that people can recognise their relative positions. Hence the emergence of status symbols—usually durable consumer goods: the house, the motor car, the swimming pool. A consumption-orientated society is much more flexible since aspirations rather than actual income (especially given hire purchase) can determine one's social position. With increasing equality of opportunity and the decline of inheritance, the accident of birth is giving way to ability and endeavour as the determinants of one's position in the social structure.

Secondly, the social changes are determined by demographic trends. The rising standard of living is being accompanied by a rising birth-rate. In the vital marrying-age group (15–25) already the young men outnumber the young ladies and society is tending to become female 'dominated' as the superfluity of young men compete for the scarce hands of the young ladies.

The male members of society are becoming more fashion conscious and using cosmetics in the guise of men's toiletries. The competition for young ladies (coupled with the ease of marriage through relative high earnings of younger people and hire purchase) is reducing the model age of marriage; it is already below twenty and will soon reach eighteen. As the unmarried young people are economically able to live alone, and as the proportion of old people is also increasing, so the number of households is increasing and their average size declining. The demographic structure of society is also changing with proportionately more old people, proportionately more very young (given the rising birth-rate) and therefore proportionately less in the middle age-groups.

The other social changes are concerned with the rise of mass education, including higher education. In an income-structured society, two things appear to be of paramount importance to people—education and good health. The demand for education arises from the fact that social positions are now determined by income, and education for all brings with it a demand for emancipation on the part of the housewife. In no other period of history has the housewife been subjected to so much tension. Because of the new social values, she has to keep up the home and home appearances; she is tending to have a larger family and the daily shopping—previously the excuse to get away from the sink—no longer exists with the advent of the supermarket where people buy at least half a week's supplies at a time. The housewife reacts by going out to work either part-time or full-time—and this seems to apply proportionately more to Catholic married women.

Then there are the postponement of genuine retirement, despite the more general introduction of official retiring age-limits; the development of the second job; the changing family relationships; the changing pattern of leisure pursuits and so forth. All these factors determine the changing social background in which the Church has to fulfil its pastoral mission.

II. THE CATHOLIC ECONOMIC PROFILE

In this period of change how have Catholics fared? Unfortunately, comparable statistics for the Catholic sector of the population pre-war and now do not exist. But it is clear that before the war, the Catholic economic profile was an exaggerated shape of the national profile with very much more than its average proportion in the lowest income groups, much less than average in the middle income group, but not so pronouncedly less than average in the top income group. The 1938 profile was probably something like this:

1938	*National profile % of total population*	*Catholic profile % of Catholic population*
Top income group (£1,000 and over)	2.9	1.0
Upper middle income group (£500—£999)	5.5	2.0
Lower middle income group (£250—£499)	19.3	10.0
Lower income group (under £250)	72.3	87.0
	100.0	100.0

But because Catholics were concentrated in the lowest

income groups before the war, they tended to gain proportionately more from the post-war economic and social revolution. From data compiled from national surveys conducted in 1964,[1] it is clear that the Catholic economic profile has changed quite considerably:

	Income range p.a.	*Statistical average*	*National profile % of total popn,*	*Catholic profile % of Catholic popn,*
Top income groups (higher professions and higher ranks of business)	£1,800 and above	£2,950	4	4
Middle income groups (other professions, teachers, higher clerical)	£900 to £1,800	£1,170	25	19
Lower middle income groups (manual workers, shop assistants)	£250 to £900	£565	55	61
Very poor (unemployed, old-age pensioners, etc.)	Under £250	£193	16	16
			100	100

The analysis by occupation confirms this picture. The same data show that 63 per cent of all Catholics aged sixteen and over go out to work compared with 60 per cent for the total population. Moreover, 37 per cent were engaged in manual work which is higher than the national figure of 35 per cent. The breakdown between skill and industries is interesting:

[1] ABC Television's survey 'Television and Religion' conducted by the Gallup Poll (Social Surveys) Limited.

(Based on people aged 16 and over)

Skills	*National proportion* %	*Catholic proportion* %
Skilled	20	20
Semi-skilled	7	7
Unskilled	6	10
Unclassified	2	—
Total (manual workers)	35	37
Industries		
Factory work	12	15
Transport	4	4
Building	4	6
Other	15	12
Total (manual workers)	35	37

Catholics occupy the same proportion as the national average in both skilled and semi-skilled jobs, but significantly more (even after allowing for the unclassified) in the unskilled. As regards industries, Catholics are over-represented in factory manual work and building (this is presumably reflecting immigrant Irish labour) but have the same proportion in transport. This higher concentration in factory and building might explain the higher proportion of unskilled manual work in the upper part of the table. (This picture is confirmed by other data; for example there are proportionately more trade unionists among Catholics and proportionately more Catholics are paid weekly.)

As regards non-manual work, the Catholic proportion is 26 per cent compared with the national proportion of

25 per cent with only slightly higher concentration, proportionately, in the professions, slightly less in the managerial group, the same in shops and services, and slightly more in the office and other groups:

(Based on people aged 16 and over)

	National proportion %	*Catholic proportion* %
Professional	4	5
Directors, Proprietors	7	6
Shops, Services	5	5
Office, Other	9	10
	25	26

These data provide the basis for working out the annual income of the Catholic sector, but first it is necessary to calculate the size of the total Catholic population and also the working population. From various surveys done, it seems that Catholics currently number at least 10 per cent of the total population of England and Wales and the more usual estimate is 11½ per cent. If we take 11 per cent, then the number of Catholics in 1964 was 5,200,000. This may indeed be somewhat low, even though it is 36 per cent more than the 3,827,000 total Catholic population recorded by parish priests as 'known' to them. Catholic baptisms recorded are over 15 per cent of the live births of the country and in the large cities the proportion is above 20 per cent. In the Manchester and Liverpool area it is between 33½ per cent and 50 per cent. The fact that Catholic families are larger explains most of this difference, but not all of it—certainly not in the North-west. At any rate this high proportion shows that the Catholic population is rising proportionately much faster than the total population, despite the rising birth-rate generally. But the baptism figures suggest that the Catholic population in 1964 might have been nearer 6,000,000. For our calculations, however, since we are basically concerned with evaluating income, we shall take the lower estimate of 5,200,000.

There are various ways of estimating working population and the limits of the estimates are 2,457,000 and 2,679,000. By striking an average the estimate of 2,575,000 (rounded up from 2,568,000) is obtained. The fact that this represents a smaller proportion of total population (49.5 per cent) than the country as a whole (52.2 per cent) can be explained by the larger Catholic families.

Working from the income structure of the country, the annual income of the Catholic population in 1964 was £1,850 million before tax and £1,650 million after tax. On this basis the average annual wage for a Catholic was £720 before tax and £640 after tax compared with the national average of £775 before tax and £690 after tax. This again emphasises that the Catholic population is still in the lower half of the income structure, although its relative economic position has improved considerably compared with a generation ago. Within the present generation it should certainly have caught up with the national average.

If income is calculated from average weekly or monthly earnings, a much higher total annual income is obtained—in fact nearly £2,200 million. There are statistical reasons for this figure being inflated, since the average earnings as given in the Ministry of Labour survey tend to be higher than the overall average earnings for the country. Nevertheless, the mean of these two estimates (£1,850 million and £2,200 million) is near enough £2,000 million, which is the estimate we shall use.

III. AFFLUENCE AND THE CHURCH

More Catholics are becoming affluent and more than a third of the Church's members aspire to the middle class, while over half still regard themselves as working class. Moreover, Catholics are taking on middle-class aspirations. Indeed 24 per cent classed themselves as true middle class, whereas according to income and social standards only 19 per cent were in this category.[1]

The difference covers the aspirations of those who had not yet made the grade. The top group (the well-to-do) identified themselves statistically accurately at 4 per cent. The lowest group tended to exaggerate their size: 9 per cent compared with the 8 per cent, although this difference is hardly statistically significant.

It is not so much the income people earn that is important from an economic point of view, but the income they aspire to. It is the latter that determines their pattern of expenditure, their social values and their social conduct. Catholics as a group are therefore becoming more middle class—more respectable—and Catholics are beginning to hold their own in the professions and the top managerial jobs. This is the first challenge the Church must understand.

The second relates to the Church itself. Whether it likes it or not, the Church is becoming a powerful economic force in the economy. Unfortunately, it does not publish a balance sheet, and there is no quick way of assessing the value of its tangible assets. But the value of land and property that it owns must be in the hundreds

[1] ABC Television's survey 'Television and Religion' conducted by the Gallup Poll (Social Surveys) Limited.

of million of pounds at current prices. Investments and such like probably only run into the tens of millions—if that. But the Church administration is a steward of the people of God. This wealth does not belong to the clergy but to the Church including the whole Catholic population. The clergy are merely administering it. Wealth has no absolute value; its value lies in its ability to achieve given ends. The challenge here is whether this wealth is being administered in the most effective way possible for the honour and glory of God in the guise of the spiritual betterment of the people of God—and not just for now but also for the future.

This challenge is more onerous than it may seem at first sight. Wealth has to be dominated, and clergy who have to spend most of their time and energy in administering wealth instead of in pastoral duties run a serious risk of confusion of basic values. According to press reports from the Vatican Council it seems that those prelates whose lives have been devoted to administration have argued cases for or against basic moral issues on the grounds of administrative convenience and expediency, without realising how their experience and environment had warped their outlook on fundamental problems.

If vocations were a true random selection of the total population, then it could be assumed, that proportionately just as many people endowed with administrative ability would receive vocations as not. But vocations are surely not a random selection. Nor does religious society permit, as lay society does, the natural process of selection to operate, so that the good administrators can be recognised, because the organisational structure of dioceses and orders allows the natural process of selection to operate only within a restricted group. And the chances that each limited group will have a balanced cross-section of talent must be very small, particularly as the priestly vocation is defined in terms of pastoral care. On these grounds, if the material structure of the Church is to be efficiently administered, this must involve the use of laymen. This would also conserve the scarce resources of the clergy for pastoral work, and enable the clergy to think of redefining basic Christian principles in terms of their application to the modern world and not in terms of facilitating the administration of the Church.

The fact that administratively the Catholic Church in England is divided into a number of dioceses where authority is delegated further to parish priests to varying extents does not reduce the impact of this challenge of administration. The problem of administration is not necessarily made easier by having a larger number of small units rather than a fewer number of large ones. It merely demands a greater number of clergymen with administrative ability, if it is to be effectively carried out, and the statistical chance of this happening is small. Nor can the Church (clergy and laity) reject this responsibility by presuming on the Holy Ghost to fill the gaps in their own administration.

The Church's material organisation is an administrative structure which must be designed as to make its pastoral work as effective as possible not just now but also for posterity. A generation ago—or certainly two generations ago—the hierarchy could rightly claim that its lay members did not possess the requisite professional skills to help it in these matters of organisation and administration. This, however, is no longer true and before long the Catholic proportion in the professional class might well exceed the national average. Personal prejudice and the desire for secrecy have no part here. As Christians, we live open lives in contact with everybody; we pursue a way of living based on the charity of Christ, not on a series of laws designed to make an ineffective structure effective. Admittedly, we must ensure economic viability of the spiritual mission. Hence, this question of organisation and administration of the material structure of the Church must be faced up to squarely—and professionally. And for God's sake both now and in the future, the most efficient organisation and administration must be introduced.

Many parish priests have clearly understood their function of stewardship—usually under the duress of a large debt or the need to commit themselves to large items of expenditure. They present simple income and expenditure accounts each year to their parishioners. I know of no diocese which has done the same thing, while balance sheets have probably never been thought of. Yet since parish priests and bishops are merely stewards and custodians of the Church's wealth, have they not a *moral duty* to publish at regular intervals an account of their stewardship?[1]

Whether it likes it or not, the Church at present owns a large amount of wealth which must be used to ensure the most effective pastoral mission over time. This imposes great responsibility on all members of the Church, and in particular it requires a complete reconsideration of the administrative structure of the Church. The Catholics in England are becoming wealthier every day; more and more of them are aspiring to middle class; more and more of them are acquiring university education; more and more of them are entering the professions. The laity is becoming—has become—more educated than the clergy. It is developing an inquiring mind since its professional and quasi-professional training forces it to use

[1] How often has one seen parish churches built not for the Catholic or Christian community either now or posterity, but as the personal memorial of the parish priest?

scientific method. This is the background against which the Church of the future must operate.

IV. SYSTEMATIC PLANNING

All well-run firms assume that they will live for ever, and this basic assumption determines the criteria they use for decision-taking and therefore conditions the actual decisions taken. Indeed, once this assumption is made, all the firm's decisions will tend to conform to moral law because 'living for ever' requires treating every member of the team—the consumer, manpower and capital—justly. The Church in its decision-processes must inevitably assume that it will live for ever, if only because it knows that it will.

It might be objected: why compare the Church to a well-run firm? Administratively they are both very similar. They have both clear-cut objectives—although not similar ones. They have both limited resources to achieve their objectives. They are both concerned with the present and the future. They both have to use money as a means of exchange, a unit of account and a store of value. In terms of pure administration, the comparison is even closer. Both are vitally concerned with man management—using people in teams in such a way as to increase their output in relation to effort—and with achieving an optimum combination of resources to attain their given objective. Moreover, in both cases the problems as far as administration is concerned, are essentially economic.

There are basically two ways of controlling any operation. One is to take decisions and then, if their impact is not what is required, to correct the decisions. In this system one is always looking backwards, and in a rapidly changing society, the decision-taker is always trying to catch up with himself. The other way is to forecast the impact of the decision before it is taken, so as to see if it is likely to give the required result: if not then a different decision is taken. With this method, wrong decisions are corrected even before they are taken.

In Britain with its rising standard of living and consequent rapid social changes, it is obvious that the second method is much more effective than the first. But this implies using systematic planning.

Planning must not be confused with control. It is nothing more than setting out objectives and intermediate objectives, and establishing optimum routes to achieve those objectives. It involves prediction not prophecy. It does not state what will inevitably happen, but rather establishes the probabilities of certain events occurring, given certain assumptions.

Systematic planning therefore incorporates a predictive system of one kind or another, usually mathematical. It takes conditions as they are, allows for known changes and forecasts the likely results. These are then compared to the agreed objectives, and if there is a discrepancy, new routes—or policies—are designed to reach the agreed objectives. The planning model can be used to test the various alternative policies before the final one is chosen. For a firm, it is obvious that such systematic looking-forward is essential if continued profitability is to be assured. But for the Church it is no less essential, although 'profitability' in this case is not defined in terms of pounds, shillings and pence, but in terms of the growing spirituality of God's people, measured by certain predetermined criteria. The point that cannot be over-emphasised is that since the problems are in essence similar, therefore the approach to their solution must also be similar.

Efficiency implies cutting out waste. Because the resources of the world are limited in relation to man's aspirations, resources which are wasted cause social hardship to one group or another. God so made the world as to make us all interdependent. The division of labour was part of His design. Each person is created with a distinctive personality and a separate balance of talents, but within a social context such that no one person can live alone. The quest for efficiency is therefore not a selfish objective but a social obligation. Far from the Church *not* being concerned with such materialistic concepts, it has in fact the duty and responsibility to set the correct example for the whole of society. The Church of all communities should be administratively as efficient as possible, always searching out waste and cutting it out.

V. FINANCIAL STRUCTURE OF THE CHURCH

Financially the Church should be organised like a company; it could even be registered as a company with a limited liability. The share capital would be contributed by the separate dioceses, so that there would be one investment fund for the whole Church.

Company structure has proved itself by experience to be extremely flexible and adaptable to changing environmental conditions. It can cope with both centralised and decentralised systems of control. It can be a dictatorship or a democracy—in fact, although in theory it is always a democracy. It can permit and sustain privilege and yet also provide equality of opportunity. It is, indeed, a social structure worthy of being copied.

This would achieve great economies both in administration and in the investment of the 'share capital'. The total fund would be sufficiently large to enable its composition (types of shares and other investments held) to be determined statistically, so as to ensure maximum income coupled with growth potential and minimum risk. At current price levels there would be little difficulty in achieving an annual return of over 6 per cent. Each year the 'company' would declare a dividend based on the earnings of its investment fund, and each diocese would get an income from the dividends of its 'share-holding'. The 'company' could always retain a certain proportion of its basic income to finance certain central expenditures.

The various religious orders would also be encouraged to take up 'shares' in the central 'company', so that full economies of scale can be achieved from one large investment fund. The central investment and borrowing of money would in no way impair the independence of the separate dioceses or religious orders, if that independence is wanted. All that it would mean is that the average return from their investments would be the same and most likely significantly higher than it has been.

The central organisation of finance would not only be concerned with investment, it would also cover borrowing. A large investment fund of this order could borrow both short-term and long-term finance at very favourable rates. Under these conditions, local arrangements for financial support would not be permitted except in those exceptional cases where more favourable rates can be obtained, but even then, permission would have to come from the centre.

The voting power of the shareholders would depend on just how the organisation of the 'company' would be used. If it is merely a legal method of centralising the investment and borrowing of money, then presumably each share held would carry one vote so that those dioceses that had more money invested would have more votes. But if the company structure is to be used as the basis of a proper central administration, then a two-tier shareholding system could be introduced. 'A' shares would have voting power but get no dividend, and these could be distributed either equally to each diocese and religious order so that each has equal voting power, or they could be distributed proportionately to the total Catholic population in each diocese or to mass attendance. (In a choice between the two latter sets of criteria, total Catholic population is preferable, provided it is calculated from national statistics, so as to keep to the fore the problem of the leakage.) 'B' shares would rank for dividend but have no voting rights.

The advantages of central organisation of finance are obvious. A small expert staff could deal with all the Church's investment and borrowing. It would have at its disposal, in the form of an advisory committee, the best brains available for these operations. Dioceses and religious orders would know in advance what investment income they could expect for the next few years. But the greatest advantage would be to make systematic forward planning imperative—on both the income and expenditure sides. The second most important advantage would be to provide a framework for a proper central secretariat for the Church.

The disadvantages of such a scheme are minimal, provided it is carried out properly and professionally. If the central fund were in the hands of good, honest, but inexpert Catholics (whether clerics or otherwise) then the whole Church would suffer and not just one diocese. Two other problems are first, how would parishes fit into this—and this question is discussed later on—and secondly, income from investment must represent only a small proportion of the Church's annual income. How then are weekly offerings handled? This, too, is discussed later on. Because investment income must represent a small proportion of total annual income, this financial scheme is really only worth while if it is to be the basis of a central secretariat.

VI. A CENTRAL SECRETARIAT

Two factors alone make a central secretariat essential. The first is the dramatic speed-up in communications which is reducing the physical size of the world so that it is becoming more like a single country. With the speed-up in communications, units have to become larger to achieve economies of scale. The second is the scarcity and growing scarcity of manpower (and in particular expertise) in relation to demand. In other words, manpower and more particularly expert manpower (especially administrators) must be economised. The proliferation of small independent or quasi-independent units of control involves a waste of scarce resources.

Admittedly the Catholic population is not spread uniformly over the country and it also tends to be concentrated much more in the larger towns. Liverpool and Manchester still have proportionately many more Catholics than elsewhere followed by London, Newcastle and Birmingham. Moreover, the northern half of England and Wales has a lower standard of living than the southern half, and on social values it is some five years behind the South. But despite this, the need for a central administration for the Church is paramount, first because of the scarcity of skilled people and secondly because, given this division of the country, the northern half can learn from the lessons of the southern half. This may sound strange to those who still regard the North-west as the cradle of Catholicism. But the Church's mission is to live in the world, to embrace it, to show how the Christian life can dominate material wealth and affluence and use it to the betterment of all mankind for the honour and glory of God. The Church is still grappling with the problem of how to apply Christianity to the affluent society, and its area of experimentation in England will be the South rather than the North. Society's evolution is in the last analysis determined by economic factors. And just as the United States leads Britain in the development of social values, because the United States has a higher standard of living, so the southern half of England and Wales leads the northern half. With the speed-up of communications, it is possible that within the present generation the northern half may catch up, but there are no economic reasons at the moment for regarding this as probable, although the discovery of natural gas and petroleum in large quantities under the North Sea will certainly make the North-east much more prosperous.

Two other matters also make a central secretariat essential. The first is education, and the experience of recent years has forced the Church to deal with this nationally. Education is one of the social developments that assumes priority in an affluent society, but it is also an area (like mass culture) where society has not decided what it really wants; it is not clear about its objectives. For this reason, education is likely to be an area of discussion and experimentation, even an area of turmoil, for many years to come, and a central education council alone will not be sufficient to guide the Church through this difficult period, precisely because education is so fundamental and so all-embracing.

The second matter is coupled to education—at least higher education—the need for the Church to create effective national institutions for research and learning. These would have to be centrally financed, centrally organised and centrally directed, even though they may have regional locations. If the Church is to carry out its mission in the modern world, it must understand the modern world. It therefore needs to do some good basic research into sociology and particularly religious sociology. There is also a need for a research institute in demography with particular reference to the Catholic sector, now that the Newman Demographic Survey no longer exists. There may even be a need for a specific research institute to study the family under the impact of the present and future social revolution, if this cannot be adequately covered by the institute of religious sociology. Then there is the need for research institutes on biblical theology and so forth. It is unfortunately outside the scope of this chapter to examine these different particular needs. These few have been mentioned not so much because they seem to be the more important ones, but rather to show the need that exists for national institutions which would have to be centrally directed and centrally financed.

With the limited resources available to the Church, only a central body would be in the position to examine and decide on how best those resources could be used in the general education scheme. Should the Church concentrate on primary education, secondary education or university education? Or should it achieve a balance of these three? The experience of the Catholic universities in the United States is adequate warning to those who want to establish Catholic universities elsewhere. Catholics must go out into the world and a Catholic university cannot by definition be a microcosm of the world. But there is a place for specific research institutes dealing with matters relating to the Church in the modern world, within or attached to universities. But if there is no case for Catholic universities, is there still a case for Catholic secondary schools? If so, should there not also be Catholic technical schools? Or should not the Catholic effort be reserved entirely for primary schools, with the family and the parish[1] safeguarding the children's faith until they reach eighteen. The family alone cannot do this, since communal values become dominant for the adolescent, but the family working in close harmony with the parish might be able to. These big and important issues must be properly studied and at some stage decided upon. Hence the need for a central secretariat, even if its functions are limited more to co-ordination than to control.

How then would this central secretariat be organised? A structure cannot be designed without a detailed study, but there are certain functions that it must cover. The first and obvious one is pastoral work; the second is manpower, including their training; the third is education, from primary school to universities, including existing and new national institutions. This latter division would link with the manpower division on the question of seminaries and the training of priests and nuns. The fourth would be concerned with buildings and equipment such as churches, schools, halls, etc. This is not intended to imply that the central secretariat would have its own resident architects. But the planning and siting of churches and schools should not be left to parish priests alone, particularly as regional mobility is increasing. The fifth division would cover finance and administration. There could possibly be a sixth division covering regional co-ordination, although regional differences would also have to be taken into consideration in the separate divisions.

How much power the centre would have is a separate question, and it depends to a large extent on the number

[1] A brief discussion of the parish of the future is given on page 214.

and calibre of people available. The golden rule is to delegate responsibility as much as possible but to ensure full co-ordination in the centre. The centre would also have to lay down the broad policies and determine the limits of delegation as well as the criteria by which decision implementation is judged.

VII. PLANNING INCOME

One important task of the central finance division would be to plan income and to devise means of increasing it. Unfortunately, the annual income from the weekly offertories is not known, but it would seem (according to parish priests) that the laity are not contributing enough. Indeed it is quite possible that the laity are contributing a significantly smaller proportion of their income now than they did before the war. In other words, incomes have risen proportionately much more than church offerings. It is generally estimated that the average weekly offering is 2s. per mass attender per week, *plus* another 2s. from other revenue sources. From what scanty information exists about parish finances—and probably not more than fifty parishes out of a total of 2,360 publish any form of accounts for their parishioners—these figures seem reasonable. Rounded off, this means that each mass attender contributes £10 a year to the Church—£5 in direct offerings and £5 indirectly. In 1964 mass attendance is estimated at 2,125,000. (This figure was calculated independently, but it represents 40 per cent of the total Catholic population and 55 per cent of the Catholic population 'known' to parish priests.) This means that the total annual income to the Church in 1964 was about £21,250,000. It was made up approximately as follows:

	£
Direct offertories	10,625,000
Fêtes, Bingo, Pools	5,500,000
Covenant refunds	1,250,000
Other	3,875,000
	21,250,000

The total annual income of the Catholic population was estimated above at £2,000 million, which after tax is reduced to £1,775 million. But not all Catholics are churchgoers. The estimates of the 'leakage', however, vary considerably. According to the 'official' Church statistics, the leakage is put at between 45 and 50 per cent. The Newman Demographic Survey, on the other hand, put it between 60 and 65 per cent. The recent television survey[1] stated that 59 per cent of the Catholics interviewed claimed that they go to church most Sundays. But in answer to the question of whether they went to church *last* Sunday only 23 per cent replied in the affirmative!

For the purpose of trying to estimate what annual income the Church could expect from offertories the lapsing rate will be taken as 60 per cent ranging from 45 per cent to 65 per cent. On this basis the total annual after-tax income of Catholic churchgoers is £710 million with a minimum of £625 million and a maximum of £975 million.

The annual total offerings of £21¼ million therefore represent 3 per cent of the mass attenders' annual after-tax income. In fact it is likely to represent slightly less

[1] ABC Television's 'Television and Religion' conducted by the Gallup Poll (Social Surveys) Limited.

than this. From information from surveys[1] and from parish priests' experience, the lapsing seems to be greater among the lower income groups than the higher, so that the total annual after-tax income of the regular churchgoers is likely to be nearer £900 million than the £710 million stated above. On this basis the annual contribution to the Church represents under 2½ per cent of after-tax income. This is still a high figure.

But if the annual income to the Church is to be increased, the proportion must be raised to at least 5 per cent. This would yield £45 million a year on the basis of 1964 mass attendance with a range of from a minimum of £31¼ million to a maximum of £48¾ million. (The 'statistical mean' would be £35½ million.) On this basis the cost per mass attender would be over £21 a year or 8s. a week—double what it is at present. This seems a heavy burden, but is it?

The number of Catholic households is estimated at 1,372,000 giving an average of 3.8 persons per household compared with the national average of 3.4, and 1.88 earners per household against the national average of 1.81. The average after-tax income per household is £1,300 a year and for churchgoing households (weighting the leakage in the lower income groups) it is nearly £1,650 a year. The present total annual offering to the Church is £38 15s. per churchgoing household—or 15s. a week. In terms of wage-earners per household it represents 8s. a week. Five per cent of after-tax income to the Church would mean raising the annual contribution of the churchgoing household to £82 10s.—or to 32s. a week. This works out at 17s. per wage-earner. In other

[1] The richest 25 per cent of the Catholic population has a lapsing rate of only 50 per cent (based on national statistics), while the poorer 75 per cent have a lapsing rate of 62 per cent. The overall lapsing rate on these figures comes to 59 per cent.

words, this extra contribution would mean every churchgoing Catholic wage-earner sacrificing the equivalent of forty cigarettes a week and giving it to the Church.

Once upon a time the basis of church offerings was one-tenth of annual income!

This whole question of offerings is difficult. It must be given in charity by the churchgoer and not extracted as a levy. Yet charity does not seem to provide the Church with the income that it deserves and needs. But the Church's income cannot be left to chance. It has much too important work to do for that. What then can be done to bridge the gap between the Church's financial needs and its present annual income, without destroying the concept of 'free-giving'?

Three avenues seem to be open. One is the use of mass media within the Church—letting the laity know the financial situation, their responsibility to meet it and how far they are falling short. This would not be just another plea for more money. It would be a businesslike approach, informing people with a subtle touch of persuasion. This would also be coupled to the development and extension of the covenant scheme. Catholics currently pay something like £225 million a year in income tax. The Church should therefore think in terms of getting something like £10 to £20 million a year tax refund—not just £1 million. If this were properly organised from the centre, the present level of tax refund could be substantially increased. The laity must be made to feel responsible for the Church—and not just to be the providers of finance. They must be shown how the money is spent and given the opportunity to voice their opinions.

The other avenue is what has become known as 'planned giving'. With a central secretariat the Church would be large enough to have its own 'planned giving' organisation which would have a continuing responsibility for the income, not just an initial one. The day-to-day work would still have to be done in the parishes, but the know-how, the direction and the inspiration would come from the centre. The target would be to 'guarantee' the Church an annual income from offerings of at least £50 million a year. The offerings would not go to the centre. They would remain initially in the parish but the parish must be made to realise that it is but one small unit of the Catholic Church in England and that it, too, is responsible for the financial viability of the Church as a whole.

The third avenue is to tap outside resources, particularly the lapsed Catholics. It does not seem appropriate for the Church to be dependent upon 'Bingo', football pools, whist drives, and such-like, but if these 'entertainments' are the means of getting people together socially and of providing an innocent flutter, while at the same time gaining money for the Church, then let them be retained. This whole question of tapping willing outside resources is one worthy of serious study and it could be done very effectively by a central organisation. Indeed football pools and similar legal lotteries could be organised by the centre on a national scale. If a 5 per cent of after-tax income from churchgoers is considered too heavy a burden, then outside sources of revenue must be exploited to the full.

VIII. PLANNING EXPENDITURE

For too long we have identified the Church as our parish. Only occasionally, when there is a special collection for the diocese or the missions do we realise that we belong to a much larger family—a national family and an international one. How many rich parishes which have no churches or schools to build, still continue to contribute as much as they did when they were heavily burdened with debt, and pass their surplus on to other parishes that are currently struggling financially? Do we honestly believe, and live as if we believe, that we are really our brother's keeper? A central organisation would be in a position to even out the riches and poverty that presently exist as between one parish and another.

But what is perhaps even more important is to vet and sanction such capital investment projects as building churches, schools and parish halls. Any vetting that is currently done is presumably at diocesan level, and that is probably only permissive—that parish A has to show a need for a new church or school and an ability to pay for it. But, in fact should parish A go ahead with its project, even if it has the money? Parish B might have an even greater need and no money. If it is in the same diocese as A its need might be compared with that of A, but if it is in another diocese the claims of the two will not be considered. Since the regional pattern of the Catholic population is changing, because of regional differences in the birth-rate, migration between different regions and the incidence of immigration, the Church's mission can be effectively accomplished now and in the future, only if there is central direction and even control of investment in churches, schools and halls so that decisions are made in terms of national needs and priorities. Moreover only the centre would be able to study the relative needs in relation to future developments, particularly demographic changes—and presumably these buildings are intended to last many decades, so that decisions concerning them must clearly be based on accurate forecasts. The central secretariat would therefore be able to employ scarce capital resources much more effectively from a national point of view than the separate individual judgments of bishops or parish priests.

The central secretariat would also know approximately how much money it could commit in a particular year on building projects. In addition it would have all the requests from individual parishes and it would have to assess the degree of priority, given present conditions and how conditions are likely to change during the next five to ten years. In this way it could allocate its scarce finance rationally, so as to provide the greatest material support for the pastoral effort.

The basic concept of this central organisation is that the Church administratively should be run like an efficient company. This means that both income and expenditure must be planned and sanctioned, and capital expenditure is the most important since it helps to determine the effectiveness of pastoral effort in the years to come. But other items of expenditure must also be planned. All clergy should have agreed salary scales, and they should be adequate. Whether they retain their personal salaries or donate them to their parish is their own private concern. The accounts, however, should show the true cost of the pastoral effort. In the same way there should be some standard scale for housekeeping and other ancillary expenditures. These are not fixed by the centre, but standards are laid down according to region, density of population, type of pastoral work and so forth, to act as guide lines.

IX. HOW MUCH LOCAL AUTONOMY?

In this discussion the present parish structure has been taken as given, and the central organisation as proposed here could work just as effectively with the present parish system or with some alternative. But any discussion of the organisational structure at the top will inevitably raise the question of whether the present system of geographical parishes is appropriate for the changing social conditions of Britain.

The basic problem is that parishes are becoming too large from the point of view of 'get-togetherness' but too small to support the necessary administrative structure if pastoral effort is to be effective. If regional parishes are to be retained then the administrative unit will have to be the deanery, which would also provide accommodation, secretarial and other services for the various parish priests. With mechanised transport, the parish priest would be no further away from his flock than he was, on foot, say, ten years ago. But the concentration of living quarters and office work could provide considerable economies. Instead of the present empirical, makeshift pastoral work, the priest's scarce time could be allocated more fruitfully given a proper demographic, sociological, economic and pastoral information system, kept up to date by help from a central service. Anybody who has had anything to do with a parish census will realise how out of date current parish information is about parishioners. And how can pastoral work be carried out properly without up-to-date information, quite apart from proper secretarial services?

Parish priests may well object to this idea because they will lose their feeling of being 'lord of the manor' or 'father of the flock'. Admittedly, without mechanised transport, the parish priest would tend to lose contact with his parishioners. But even nowadays when he visits them, or when they visit him, both no doubt use some form of mechanised transport, in which case to travel a further two or three miles is no burden and therefore unlikely to be a barrier to either communications or contacts.

But the real question is whether parishes should continue to be organised primarily geographically. With the increase in education and the professionalisation of labour, society is being split into smaller 'social-professional' groups rather than geographical levels. This has always been true in the so-called rich parishes, who have always found it difficult to make parishioners cohere into a group. As the standard of living rises, more parishes will come into the 'rich' category and therefore face the same type of problem. With the larger parish concept based on the deanery, priests could be allocated according to social-professional groupings rather than districts. Fewer churches may be required but many more mass centres—even in people's homes, if a group were small enough. Such an approach is worthy of serious study, but it lies outside the technical scope of this chapter. It is raised here merely to show that the proposed central organisation could accommodate such changes in parochial structure. Indeed such changes could not be made really effective without a professional top structure at the centre.

Whatever is done to the parish organisation one thing is clear. The priest of the future (as well indeed as the priest of the present) must be trained to be a true leader of men. It could almost be said that he must be trained to be a first-rate manager. It is presumptuous to rely on the Holy Ghost to inspire a priest with leadership when he is given Holy Orders, when in fact he could be trained into a leader quite effectively in the seminary—provided the present training system is amended. Industry knows that it requires many more managers over and above those naturally endowed with those specific talents. Hence it has had to get down to the task of being able to teach and train ordinary people so that they can become effective leaders of men. The education system faced the same problem ten years ago. The Church could learn much from industry and indeed the Services in this question of training student priests to become leaders.

X. THE ADMINISTRATIVE STRUCTURE

It is somewhat unwise to suggest even an outline administrative structure before the problem has been properly investigated. But the ideas put forward here are in the nature of a cock-shy, as a basis for a constructive discussion from which may evolve an organisation, which could help the Church fulfil its pastoral mission even more effectively.

An organisation is not designed just to make things neat and tidy. It is in fact a system of defining and interrelating different areas of responsibility. In this way it acts as a scaffolding to management. Indeed the real purpose of organisation is to enable (or make) people operate more effectively than they would have done without it. If everybody were perfect, there would be no need for organisation.

It has already been suggested that the new central organisation of the Church should have five or perhaps six main divisions. The first is the pastoral division, which would be staffed mainly but not entirely by clerics. One could imagine it being divided into four departments: one to co-ordinate 'social-professional' groupings in the Church; another for geographical groupings; the third for missionary work within England and Wales; the fourth to co-ordinate special activities.

The manpower division would be concerned with projecting the Church's requirements and the likely supply. This, too, is likely to be divided into four main departments. One would be concerned with vocations, another with formation (i.e., seminary training and other specialist training and even re-training—this department would have to work closely with the education division) and another with employment—to ensure that a priest's particular talents are employed to their best advantage for the honour and glory of God. The fourth department would be concerned with 'management' development—ensuring an adequate succession of competent and well qualified bishops and 'specialist' priests.

The education division would be subdivided into six or possibly seven departments (even if there are no Catholic schools): one for primary education, another for secondary, the third for technical, the fourth for university, the fifth for teachers' training and other for professional training. The sixth would cover specialist research institutes and other special institutions—or this could be a sub-branch of the university department. The seventh would cover 'special' schools.

The buildings and equipment division would be organised as a vetting department capable of carrying out special studies to enable the 'board of directors' to assess priorities correctly. It would cover 'design costing' similar to that done by the Government for school buildings so as to reduce the cost of buildings. They would also vet architects' plans and designs.

The finance and administration division would be concerned with the central investment fund, with forward planning, with development of income, with organising extra capital and with general administrative services not just for the centre but also for the dioceses and religious orders. They would advise on organisation and administrative procedures so as to reduce the burden (and therefore the cost) of administration.

If a regional division were set up, this would presumably be organised in geographical areas.

This may sound a massive organisation involving thousands of people but that is not the intention. If the quality of staff is good, then the numbers involved would not be large. The whole central organisation should not employ more than, say, a hundred people, while at the same time it would permit a drastic reduction in administrative effort at metropolitan and diocesan levels. It may not in fact reduce the total number of people currently employed in administration, but it would certainly provide much more accurate and better data for defining policies to improve and extend the Church's pastoral effort. The whole purpose of good administration is to provide a greater 'output' of pastoral effort for the same input or even a smaller input. It should help to economise on those resources that are particularly scarce. Indeed if it does not do that, then by definition it is not a good organisation.

Perhaps the most important point in favour of a central secretariat as suggested here, is that it enables modern techniques and methods to be used to reduce the 'chore' content of the logistics infrastructure that any large organisation like the Church must have, if it is to operate efficiently.

XI. THE PLACE OF THE LAITY

In dealing with finance it has already been said that the laity must be made to feel responsible for the Church. It is of little use preaching to them that they must be apostles of the faith, when the Church refuses to take them into its own confidence as regards matters both spiritual and material. For the first time for nearly two thousand years, the clergy is having to preach to and lead a laity that is more educated, more knowledgeable and more experienced than itself. Little wonder that when the Church continues to be reticent about its financial and administrative affairs, the laity are apt to put it down to petty or even selfish motives.

The modern world is so complex and the rate of change so fast, that it is virtually statistically impossible for a relatively small group like the clergy to have a valid practical experience of its different facets unless the incidence of vocations is purely random—which it is not. This means that the teachings of Christ as applied to the modern world must be worked out in dialogue with the laity. What is true of the spiritual side is even more true of the material side. Decisions affecting the material side of the Church should also be taken in dialogue with the laity. The only problem here is how to get effective representation of the laity.

The days are past when the laity will be satisfied just to go to Church and to pay their dues. Already twelve-year-olds are complaining of being brain-washed. The modern education system is rightly training pupils to inquire into things and not just to accept things passively. God has endowed us with intellects to use and to use for Him. Too long have certain sections of the Church pretended that the one area where the intellect may not be used is in Church matters. If people are to become active Christians—active Catholics—they must be given responsibility and this in turn means they must be given power.

If the layman is to become responsible for the Church and not just a passive underwriter for its debts, he must be given adequate and appropriate information—if only to give him confidence that his offerings are not being wasted. A start can be made by seeing that all parish priests and every bishop present annual income and expenditure accounts and a simple balance sheet. Neither of these need be elaborate. If possible, both the income and expenditure account and the balance sheet should be standardised in concept and uniform for the whole country. This would take only a few hours to design. But if that proves too much, non-standardised accounts and balance sheets should be published each year. In this way the bishops and priests would emphasise the fact that they are stewards and so give a practical example of making the laity responsible.

The Church's plan for the future must also be designed in conjunction with the laity, who would then feel committed to find the necessary money. Indeed, the forward plan could be a convenient method of getting the laity's co-operation in the first place.

There is a shortage of priests in England and Wales, and yet a number of them are still engaged in teaching and administrative jobs, for which able laymen exist. To argue that priests cost less is irrelevant. The Church must be based on a sound economic footing. People must be paid their true economic value. If priests are used for these jobs, the true costs must be shown in the accounts; if they do not accept their salaries, then the salaries are put in on the income side as charitable donations. But vocations are always likely to remain scarce in relation to pastoral needs, even though with the superfluity of young men there will be more enforced bachelorhood. Given an effective central organisation, much of the non-pastoral work which is at present done by priests could be performed by skilled laymen on a professional basis. There is certainly enough talent in the Church for that.

The hierarchy would be like a board of directors laying down broad policy. Laymen and some clergy would form the executive staff. They would put policy papers up to the 'board'; they would see that the 'board's' decisions are carried out. In the same way, the requests for new churches, schools and halls would be processed by the executive staff and amplified by background studies and scientifically designed forecasts. But the final decision would rest with the 'board of directors' —the hierarchy.

The Church in England has always seemed loath to use lay experts; this is often said to be because of unfortunate experiences in the past. That may well have been. It is only in recent years that Catholics can claim to hold their own, proportionately, in the various professions—in some of them more than their own. In many professions, Catholics are at the top and accepted as such by their professional colleagues. Why all this talent and skill cannot be used more directly for the benefit of the Church is incomprehensible. Part of the reason may be that the hierarchy lacks confidence in its judgment of selecting good professional people. In that case there are a number of organisations willing to cope with the advertising and initial interviewing and to provide a short list of competent people meeting the specified requirements. Hitherto, professional skill was usually judged by mass attendance and going to the sacraments. A good church going Catholic was automatically regarded as a good doctor, or a good accountant or a good economist, even though no causal correlation between the two existed.

If a professional job is to be done properly, then a competent professional man must be employed. But good professional people will not accept jobs if they are going to be treated like office boys or clerks. They will require properly defined areas of responsibility, an adequate degree of intellectual freedom and a confidence that their professional talents will be properly used. The real problem here is that first-rate men often look 'dangerous', in that they can usually see farther ahead than most people. They tend to sense the long-term trends of change and try to accommodate themselves to those trends rather than fight against them. For this reason they tend to be more liberal than conservative. On the other hand there are the pseudo-professionals who in order to look good, always accept new trends without distinguishing between the short-term and the long-term. Good selection procedures can seek out the sheep from the goats.

But the laity also has a contribution to make at lower levels. Here, too, strict 'professional' standards must be maintained if efficiency is to be achieved. This does not mean that an efficient organisation has no room for charity. Indeed it has; the more efficient an organisation the greater the scope for charity. But the efficient organisation does not confuse charity with indifferent selection, lackadaisical control or bad management. It can afford to give more charity, and it knows the difference between charity and inefficiency. In such an organisation, priests should be used only where laymen cannot be, since priests have a special vocation in life and are always likely to be scarcest of the resources at the disposal of the Church.

XII. SUMMARY

Britain is undergoing a social and economic revolution and if the Church is to play its true part in influencing and directing the lives of the people of God, its material structure must be organised not just to cope with the change and the increasing rate of change, but to use the new conditions in a positive way to extend its own pastoral work.

Since company organisation has proved itself to be particularly effective in adapting itself to change and using change for its own advantage, the Church should adopt such a form of organisation for its own ends. There should be a central organisation covering the whole Church in England and Wales with a central investment fund, the shares of which should be held by the different dioceses and religious orders. This would mean a central secretariat, co-ordinating the pastoral work, manpower, education (in its widest sense), capital expenditure and finance and administration. It should have as one of its functions planning the operations of the Church some five to ten years hence, ensuring it an adequate annual income and providing a system for vetting capital expenditure so that the most urgent needs are met first. It should be staffed mainly by competent laymen and it should publish its accounts each year for the scrutiny of the faithful.

Liberal Catholicism in America

DANIEL CALLAHAN

I

LET me make a flat assertion, one which I hope will not seem unduly chauvinistic. The numerical, financial and social development of Catholicism in the United States within the past two centuries has been one of the most remarkable features of modern Roman Catholic history. Note that I say 'the numerical, financial and social development' and not, for instance, the 'spiritual, intellectual and theological development'. These latter have been impressive in their own way, but hardly such that one could speak of them as remarkable. On the contrary, one of the striking features of American Catholicism is that its interior development has not kept pace with its exterior growth. In these respects, it is characteristically American. Very much like the Protestant churches, its genius has been in building, expanding, adding, moving horizontally rather than vertically.

The result is a rich, huge, materially dynamic and financially sound Church. If at one time the American Church was something of a pariah in American life, the election of John F. Kennedy in 1960 signalled the end of that era. Not only is the Church rich, then, it is now also respectable. Yet as often happens with rich and respectable men, much of its thinking has been derivative, unimaginative and prone to remain attached to tried and proven ways. With only occasional exceptions, it is a Church which has not caused much trouble in the community. Excluding a few select areas—most notably, sexual morality—the American Catholic hierarchy and the great mass of people whom they serve are indistinguishable from other people. They have been good, solid citizens who can be counted on to lend support to the prevailing social, political and economic consensus. One can go a step further. American Catholics are so well assimilated into American life that some are now beginning to be found, for the first time, at the fringes; they are beginning to contribute a small share to radical liberal movements at odds with the national consensus. That share, however, is just enough to emphasise the fact that the overwhelming majority of American Catholics stand squarely in the middle road.

Taken together, these dominant traits of American Catholicism can be both a source of hope and of distress. To take the distress first, it often strikes many Catholics—particularly those who could be called political and theological progressives—as perfectly appalling that such a rich and now secure Church should provide so little national and international leadership. Its theologians of international stature can be counted on the fingers of one hand. Its scholars fare little better, either nationally or internationally. Its visionary political leaders, its prophetic social thinkers, its creative economic planners are no less scarce. This litany of complaints could be continued almost indefinitely, but that would be unwise. Boredom with the complaints set in long ago and it would be tedious to repeat them here (which is hardly to say they are no longer valid).

It would be more useful, and certainly fresher, to indicate the solid grounds for hope. The standard explanation for American Catholic deficiencies has for decades been based on its immigrant origins: the long-time hostility of Protestant Americans; its initial poverty; the early dearth of a theological and intellectual culture; the need to create buildings and facilities first, and so on. On the whole, this is a valid enough explanation, deficient only in speculating whether the type of theology and spirituality available during the nineteenth and early twentieth centuries was of a nature to breed a temptation towards external power, ecclesiastical materialism and a defensive, individualistic piety. However that may be, the very material strength and security of American Catholicism should now provide a solid base from which to begin a development in richer directions. For that is the other side of the immigrant-origin theory: once Catholics established themselves, they could begin exploring those dimensions of life, thought and society which had to be slighted by earlier generations. That day has arrived, and the theory can now be tested. Is it likely that a significant breakthrough will take place?

Before trying to answer that question directly, it would be useful to take a brief look at some of the main patterns which have marked the history of American Catholicism. They have set the stage for whatever the future will bring and, in addition, provide some useful clues about the direction it could take.

Prior to the American Revolution, the Catholic was in a notably awkward position. There were only a handful of priests, hardly any churches and nothing at all in the way of an organised ecclesiastical structure. In addition, Catholics suffered many legal penalties and this, together with their dearth of numbers, tended to keep them quiet and unobtrusive. The one thing which helped lighten their burdens was the fact that they spoke the same language as their Protestant neighbours, came from much the same kind of English social background and shared the values common to propertied classes with an interest in economic prosperity and stability. Their only shortcoming was their religion, and for this they had to pay a price.

But it was not an unbearable price after the middle of the eighteenth century and by the time of the Revolution Catholics were reasonably well accepted. The Revolution solidified their position, and what their loyalty during the war could not by itself accomplish the Constitution could. The guarantee in the first two articles of the First Amendment to the Constitution of a separation of Church and State meant that religious freedom was as much their right as that of any other American.

Historians have often referred to the period just after the Revolution and prior to the onslaught of massive waves of immigrants beginning in the 1830s as a time in which the Church could 'catch its breath'. The expression is apt. Beginning in 1789, the Church was able to accelerate its material development in many important ways. In that year the first bishop, John Carroll, was appointed, the first Catholic college was founded, a seminary was established, and a start was made towards organising the clergy. The fact that the Church continued, for some decades, to be primarily English in its ethnic roots was of no small social help, though the presence of a number of émigré French priests created some internal difficulties. By and large, the laity were helpful to the clergy and to the newly formed and rapidly expanding hierarchy. The only major source of friction came in the numerous trustee controversies, most of which turned on the question of the right of laymen to control the spiritual destinies of parishes along with their legal control of parish finances. It is not hard to guess how those struggles came out and it was only a matter of time until the bishops managed to put an end to trusteeism and have all church property placed in their name.

The trustee disputes, however, were to leave an enduring suspicion among the clergy and hierarchy of presumptuous laymen; laymen, that is, who let the spirit of American democracy go to their heads and demand something of the same freedom within the Church which they experience in society. Herein lies one important element of what has been an enduring tension in American Catholicism. From the outset of the Republic, American Catholics have been noteworthy for their unbounded patriotism. No protestations of fidelity to the flag, no rhetorical pledges of civic devotion, have ever seemed excessive. No doubt, part of this spirit can be explained by the need of Catholics to defend themselves against those who believed that Catholicism and democracy are intrinsically incompatible. But that is only part of the explanation, and just as important a part would have to be credited to the genuine enthusiasm felt by all Americans for the system of liberty guaranteed by the Constitution. Yet it was the kind of enthusiasm, and still continues as such, which was bound to place the quite different system of Catholic obedience and discipline in a harsh light. No wonder, as in the instance of trusteeism, that conflicts between bishops and priests, bishops and laymen, and priests and laymen would inevitably break out now and then. Nor is it any less surprising that Church authorities would from time to time have second thoughts about the spirit of American freedom when they felt its force among their flocks; as an antidote they sought, and got, a tightly organised structure.

Rebellion, or simply vocal dissatisfaction, requires self-confidence, an articulated sense of values different from that of the ecclesiastical establishment, and a reasonably high degree of education and purpose. After the suppression of trusteeism in the early decades of the nineteenth century, there was little chance for these characteristics to develop among the laity or the lower clergy. Once the immigrants from Ireland, and then Germany, began to arrive in large numbers, the situation of Catholicism changed in many drastic ways. The early social and intellectual leadership of the Anglo-American group shifted to immigrant hands. The clergy and hierarchy, by dint of a superior (though hardly good) education became the natural leaders of the immigrants, taking up the same rôle of dominance they usually had in the old country. If these immigrants were Irish, as they were most apt to be, they were also docile and fearful, gladly willing to be protected and led by their spiritual betters, especially when this promised them some significant help in adjusting to the strange ways of a new and not always friendly land. It was, on the face of it, a good exchange, but it meant that independence, initiative and imagination had little chance of developing. The main job at hand, for no one seriously proposed any other, was the development of the material, political and social strength of the Church and of the Catholic community.

If the success of this growth was in many ways praiseworthy, and all the more so in the light of frequent outbursts of violent anti-Catholicism, there were drawbacks as well. One of the most notable, especially in terms of later consequences, was the absence of any developed sense of social justice among Catholics. This was painfully the case with the Abolition movement preceding the Civil War. As seems to happen so often with rising minority groups, the persecutions and injustices suffered by those on a still lower rung of the social ladder are a matter of only faint interest to them. So it was with Catholics in the face of Negro slavery. Not only were they generally opposed to the movement to free the slaves, but they were able to supply, for good measure, some theological arguments of their own to support the retention of slavery. The principal argument against the abolitionists was that the sudden freeing of the slaves could produce widespread social disturbances. While it would be desirable in the long run for the slaves to have freedom, the best way to bring this about was by gentle, patient moral persuasion. This line of argument is a familiar one.

There were also other influences at work in shaping the Catholic attitude towards slavery. One of these was the still-high concentration of Catholics below the Mason–Dixon line whose orientation was primarily Southern. Another was the pronounced inclination of Catholics to vote with the Democratic Party—a party which, while it was receptive to the Catholic immigrant, was also dominated by Southern interests. Still another influence was Catholic hostility to almost everything 'Yankee', including, very prominently, hostility towards the kind of moral crusading which was a mark of New England and Northern Protestantism. This last point has a special importance, for it was from 'Yankee' circles that the genesis of American social and political liberalism occurred. By decisively cutting themselves off from this group—the antipathy, it must be said, was mutual—Catholics were for decades doomed to be outsiders to

American liberal thought. Only when there were questions of the rights of the working class were ideological *détentes* possible, but then only sporadically and more as parallel streams of social concern than as a genuine alliance. The failure of Catholics for many decades to enlist in the cause of systematic social reform, a failure abetted by a persistent suspicion of government reform efforts, meant that Catholic social liberalism had to develop its own private rationale and justification. To this I shall return.

As it happened, the publication of Pope Leo XIII's encyclical *Rerum Novarum* in 1891 provided just the rationale that was needed, and it came at a timely moment. During the last few decades of the nineteenth century, a small liberal voice began to be heard in the Church, centering especially around a number of articulate and thoughtful laymen. A lay congress in Baltimore in 1889 marked the full flowering of this group, and the publication of *Rerum Novarum* two years later meant that their social liberalism now had firm theological backing. They made the most of this support, and a major theme of a second lay congress, held in Chicago in 1893 in conjunction with the Columbian Exposition, was the need for social justice, peace between labour and capital, the evils of unchecked capitalism and the value of Catholic co-operation with non-Catholics in matters concerning the common good. While no noticeable reconciliation between Catholics and secular liberals took place, Catholic liberals now had the kind of authoritative support they needed to begin their own development.

Unfortunately, the burst of vitality which marked the end of the nineteenth century was doomed to flag with the arrival of the twentieth. The condemnation by Leo XIII in 1898 of 'Americanism' and the Modernist crisis shortly thereafter called a temporary halt to the emergence of liberalism. For at least two decades thereafter, Catholic intellectual and cultural life was overshadowed by a nervous conservatism, which hampered the attempts both to adapt Catholicism to American democratic ideals and to create a strong theological culture within the Church. One of the few bright spots during these dismal decades was the work of a handful of social thinkers, most notably Father John A. Ryan at the Catholic University of America in Washington. They continued to explore some of the openings provided by *Rerum Novarum* and, of equal importance, trained and inspired a number of priests towards increasingly bold thinking and action on the political and economic front. This was in turn passed on to a growing body of socially sensitive laymen.

A major breakthrough, however, only came in the aftermath of World War I. An important stimulus was a document with the formidable title 'Social Reconstruction: A General Review of the Problems and Survey of Remedies', published in 1919 and signed by a committee of bishops. This document, which came to be known as the 'Bishops' Programme', urged immediate reforms to bring about a living family wage and looked forward to the day when the majority of workers would at least own part of the instruments of production. The ground was thus well laid for further advances and consolidation, at least so far as official sanction was concerned.

The only missing element, the social confidence and milieu necessary for liberal development, was soon supplied. Catholic service during World War I, the prosperity of the twenties, and the fact of an almost complete cultural assimilation, quickly swept away the fog which lingered on after the Americanist and Modernist upheavals. Though Catholic theology in America was far from being creative, and the earlier emphasis on material development continued, the twenties saw the appearance of a fresh cultural and intellectual life. My own journal, *Commonweal*, began publication in 1924, the first serious Catholic lay publication since *Brownson's Quarterly Review* in the middle of the nineteenth century. Catholic historical and philosophical associations were also formed and there were expressions of concern from many quarters about the failure of Catholics to make any significant contribution to American intellectual life.

But it was not until the thirties that this renascence began to have some bite. As had happened with *Rerum Novarum* forty years earlier, Pius XI's encyclical 'On the Reconstruction of the Social Order' in 1931 provided a major prod to American Catholic social thought. The National Catholic Welfare Conference took the lead on the official level in stimulating 'Catholic action' and in bringing before the public issues of political and economic justice. No less important, the thirties saw the founding of the Catholic Worker Movement, led by Dorothy Day and Peter Maurin, and a consequent acceleration of Catholic radicalism. Though the Catholic Worker group was comparatively small in numbers, it served as a rallying point for a new generation of Catholics who saw in the Great Depression solid evidence that laissez-faire capitalism was unjust and economically destructive. Only a lingering alienation from secular and Protestant liberalism, as well as pervasive fears of being labelled a 'pinko' or 'commie', kept the new Catholic liberal from forging strong bonds with other liberal and radical movements in America. In the years following World War II, however, American Catholic liberalism became a well-established reality, needing only the work of Vatican II to insure its permanent strength.

This brief sketch is necessarily incomplete. It makes no mention of the growth of Catholic education, of the rising level of Catholic participation in national politics, of the Catholic political domination of most of the major cities of the Eastern seaboard, of the response to urban life by immigrants from a predominantly rural background. All of these elements would have to enter into a full history of American Catholic liberalism. One could hardly afford to neglect, for instance, the lamentable fact that Catholic political power in Eastern cities was not matched by a corresponding zeal for urban reform; indeed, civic corruption among Catholics seemed almost a way of life in cities like Boston and New York. But that is a story which cannot be gone into here.

II

Yet enough has been said, I trust, to provide a tentative answer to the question raised earlier: is a significant breakthrough in Catholic thought, especially Catholic liberal thought, now likely? The answer, I believe, has to be yes. More than that, the breakthrough has already taken place and what remains is to see how far it can and will go. The present situation of the Church in America is one of the unprecedented vitality, and this vitality is being experienced on a wide variety of fronts.

Easily the most important sign is to be found in the steady and increasingly deep self-criticism which has been a mark of the Church for the past decade or so. Hardly anything has been spared: Catholic education, the hierarchy and clergy, the laity, and on and on.

Though many have complained about the self-criticism, calling for 'moratoriums' on 'breast-beating' and 'masochism', 'less negativism' and more 'positive thinking', their words have had little effect. Where in earlier days Catholic liberals were given to complaining about a conservative domination of the Catholic press and intellectual life, it is now the conservative who is likely to complain about a 'liberal conspiracy'. Naturally, complaints of this kind lay a heavy stress on the 'few' and 'unrepresentative' people who, by a sleight of hand, manage to convince an 'uninformed' public that their views represent those of the majority. To a certain extent this is no doubt true. Very few conservative Catholic thinkers have managed to achieve any special distinction or to gain a public following; thus one hears very little about them or from them. At the same time, as Catholic liberal thought has gained a public ascendancy and continued to expand the range of its thought and criticism, signs of a back-lash have begun to appear. This can be seen in a number of statements issued by individual bishops within the last two years deploring 'arrogant' laymen, a dangerous spirit of disrespect for authority, and the tendency to extend self-criticism into the very heart of theology and doctrine itself. Other signs can be found in many diocesan papers, where both editorial writers and letters-to-the-editor display considerable uneasiness about the advance of liberal thought; in a small movement like that of the 'Traditionalist Society', established to combat a 'protestantising' of the Church; and in the reluctance of many bishops and priests to do more than minimally observe the spirit of Vatican II.

But it is important to distinguish between a back-lash and the broad direction of the Church. As in the Negro civil rights movement, a back-lash is itself persuasive evidence of where the major winds are blowing. It can hurt and slow down progressive trends, but only rarely does it make a decisive difference to the movement forward. At any rate, there is no evidence yet that the growing conservative episcopal, clerical and lay worries are about to effect a major reversal of the fortunes of Catholic liberalism. There have been very few successful attempts on the part of conservatives to silence the liberal critics and reformers; indeed, comparatively few attempts have been made.

The more dramatic instances of stress and strain do not, however, provide the only clues to the future of Catholic liberalism. There are at least three other important trends with a very important bearing on the question.

The first of these is the entrance of the layman into the thickets of theology. Until less than ten years ago, American theology was exclusively in the hands of the clergy, and then only a handful of priests at that. Moreover, the quality of American theology was third-rate, Roman and legalistic in its orientation, derivative in its speculations and almost wholly lacking in any special character or genius. The Catholic University of America, which might be a central source of theological creativity, has never been a major university. With the exception of the Jesuit quarterly *Theological Studies*, there have been no recognised theological journals. Only John Courtney Murray, S.J., has achieved any kind of international standing. Though they might have been expected to do so, the Catholic colleges and universities have produced nothing in the way of distinguished theological scholarship; until very recently they only aped the methods and preoccupations of seminary theology.

The entrance of laymen into theology promises to help change the situation. Within the past decade, graduate programmes in theology have been started in a number of Catholic universities; a number of Catholic colleges have begun hiring laymen to teach theology; in the bloom of ecumenism, a sizeable group of secular universities has invited Catholics to teach in religion and religious studies departments; and the influx of Catholic faculty members has been far exceeded by the number of Catholic students who have undertaken graduate work in theology and religion at secular universities, even Protestant divinity schools.

The significance of this trend is likely to be two-fold. First of all, it should help broaden the base of theological education and the number affected by it. This will help break the grip of the seminaries and assist in the creation of a theology which is integrated into the mainstream of American higher education. Second, it should help create a body of theologians far more relaxed and far more independent of ecclesiastical bureaucracy and timidity than was possible for priest-theologians under the watchful eye of bishops and religious superiors. Doubtless this will mean from time to time some aberrant if not heterodox lay theologians writing and teaching, but these will probably be only a small minority. What the majority could succeed in doing is not necessarily to produce better theological work than that of priests, but a theology which springs from a different situation in, and perspective on, the world. The greater freedom of the layman, together with his different perspectives, should in turn serve as a healthy stimulus to the work being done by priests.

Quite apart from the professional work done by academic theologians, clerical or lay, there should also be a greater boldness on the part of broadly educated and informed laymen to venture opinions on theological questions. Already a small number of lay publications do not hesitate to comment critically on issues dealing with the inner life and structure of the Church, theological disputes and the pronouncements of Church authorities. In an earlier generation, even highly educated laymen rarely spoke on such matters, though they would have felt no hesitation in speaking on other issues which went beyond their academic or professional training. The notion, once revered, that a Catholic could not claim responsibility for beliefs and practices imposed upon him by the Church, that his only duty was docility and trust, finds fewer and fewer adherents.

A second important trend might best be characterised as a new willingness of Catholic liberals to take their opinions, grievances and crusades 'into the streets'. Prior to the last few years, very few Catholic intellectuals or social action advocates were prone to take strong and public stands on their convictions and positions. They were careful, timid, and given to delicately couched opinions; rarely would they make known either to the Catholic or the non-Catholic public how they really felt about various problems within the Church. Much of this has now changed. The presence of numerous priests, nuns and laymen in civil rights demonstrations; the frequent circulation of petitions directed to one or more members of the hierarchy; public protests of abuses within the Church; blunt articles in Catholic newspapers and magazines—all of these things signal a new spirit, one marked by an absence of timidity in the face of authority and a drive towards open discussion and argument. Despite a number of episcopal admonitions, the problem of birth control has been vented from all viewpoints, with very few reluctant to express their uneasiness about the teaching of Pius XII. On other fronts, lay groups have picketed chancery offices, priests have risked censure to take part in racial protests and hardly any lay writers now seek an *imprimatur* for their writings. For those of a more traditional cast of mind, none of these changes are happy omens. But for those committed to a deepening of Catholic liberalism, they are minimal conditions for an effective Christian witness and dialogue.

A third important trend is the significant extent to which non-Catholic thought, both religious and secular, is drawn upon in matters theological as well as secular. Closely related to this is a genuine breaking down of many of the barriers which kept Protestants and Cathlics, and Catholic liberals and secular liberals, alienated from each other. Ecumenism in America has become a living force within the Church, if not always on the popular level, at least very much so in academic and intellectual circles. This has meant a serious attention by Catholics to Protestant thought and scholarship. References to Karl Barth, Rudolf Bultmann and Dietrich Bonhoeffer are almost as common now in American Catholic writing as references to Karl Rahner, Hans Küng and John Courtney Murray. Since so many Catholics are now studying theology under Protestant auspices, the impact of ecumenism is bound to be even greater in the years to come.

If the alienation which kept Catholic and secular liberals apart for so long is disappearing in a less noticeable fashion, it is, none the less, giving way to a new relationship. The civil rights movement and the gradually more active participation of Catholics has been one solvent. Catholic participation in demonstrations against nuclear weapons and the Vietnamese war, though involving very few people, has been still another. It is not difficult now to find Catholics openly willing to call themselves socialists, to commend the welfare state, and to express agreement with many aspects of Marxism. The liberal élan of John F. Kennedy, as well as that of some of his Catholic advisers and assistants, did much to suggest to secular liberals that the Catholic could be a potential ally. That the overwhelming majority of Catholics voted for Lyndon B. Johnson in 1964 (over 70 per cent) rather than Barry Goldwater was further evidence that the Catholic community has no special predilection for right-wing politics. The hysteria in many Catholic quarters during the McCarthy era of the early fifties was no permanent index of an innate conservatism.

I have dwelled very much on the hopeful side of the picture, but only because, for one who has seen many dark days in years past, the present ferment is exciting beyond description. At the moment, it seems fully vigorous enough to withstand any immediately foreseeable back-lash, any let-down in Rome after the Council, or even any failure of the American bishops to extend the frontiers provided by the Council. Yet much is still missing and it is easy to conceive of circumstances which could alter the present direction. The most noticeable soft spot is the American hierarchy. As a group the American bishops are hard workers, full of good will, little given to suppressions and relatively innocent of the kinds of machiavellianism which mark some episcopal groups. But like their predecessors they remain primarily administrators, little alive to the newer currents of theological thought or to the currents which move through American intellectual life. There is only a handful who have ever written a serious book or article and their speeches, sermons and statements give little indication that they even read such books or articles. Though it is true that the American bishops quickly became identified with the progressive majority at the Council, it is not easy to resist the belief that they did so more out of conformity with the rest of the bishops—because that was the way the wind was blowing—than out of personally achieved thought and conviction. On the whole, they have gone no further in implementing reforms in America than those minimally required by the conciliar constitutions and statements. One is bound to wonder whether, should the winds from Rome shift in any significant way, the American bishops would quietly and quickly shift without a murmur—that has been their tradition in the past. There is no way of telling, but it is far less certain that the American hierarchy would show a respectful independence than, say, the German or Dutch hierarchy.

What seems most likely is that Catholic liberalism will have to get along without enthusiastic and imaginative support from the hierarchy. But there are many mitigating circumstances. Despite their many qualms, the bishops as a group remain permissive. That is a tremendous asset, as helpful a virtue as any reformer or experimenter can realistically ask for. It is a virtue far less frequently found in American chancery offices. For it is in those offices, rather than in episcopal palaces, that narrowness, bureaucracy and timidity reach full bloom. The wise priest in America discovers at an early age that he should not ask permission from a chancery functionary to do anything faintly novel unless he absolutely cannot avoid it. The same can be said, though less harshly, of diocesan officials, organisation supervisors, superintendents of this institution or that. As much as anything, however, they are victims of an ecclesiastical system which is cumbersomely large, forced in the direction of bureaucratic impersonality, and too harassed to have much time for sensitive human relationships. However great the penetration of liberal ideas may be in other quarters of the Church, they have made few inroads into the machinery of administration, fund-raising, and economic planning. For it is not ideas which are threatened here so much as empires; they are proving durable and hardy.

The parochial school system is a special case in point. Despite the publication in 1964 of a widely discussed book by Mary Perkins Ryan, *Are Parochial Schools the Answer?* (which concluded: not necessarily); despite the results of some studies showing that the schools have not achieved results in proportion to the time, money and single-minded zeal which have gone into them; despite the presence of much dissatisfaction with the way in which the American parish, financially and spiritually, has almost become an appendage of the school—despite all these things, resistance to discussion, experimentation and the consideration of other methods of religious education still continues to be the rule in official quarters. (The only point that seems to make any difference is the financial troubles of the schools; they can galvanise bishops and school superintendents to act imaginatively where no other considerations have any influence at all.) There is a faith in the schools, and a zeal for their welfare, which is proof against any statistics, questions and alternative suggestions. So much is this the case that the bishops have not hesitated to throw their weight against urgent federal education bills if the funds involved did not also benefit the parochial schools. This intransigence has not been wholly ineffective as a strategy. The American public is more willing now to consider providing some money for aspects of the religious schools than at any time in the past. But it has also meant the forcing of Catholics back into the mould of ghetto isolation and self-centredness, fighting for their own rights at the expense of the improvement of public education.

Problems like this wax and wane in the Catholic community, but they usually serve to drive a wedge between those Catholics committed to broadening the concerns of the Church beyond matters of immediate self-interest, and those who seem to believe that what benefits Catholics must necessarily benefit the whole nation. Some of the sharpest conflicts between the ecclesiastical establishment and Catholic liberals come when the latter judge the duties of the Church in the light of national needs rather than in terms of institutional Church needs. Many Southern parochial schools, for instance, were very reluctantly and slowly integrated, and the main argument of those responsible for establishing policy was that the schools would suffer financially, that it was not their duty to provide leadership, and that community sentiment would be hostile towards the Church as a result. The legitimacy of arguments like this, which placed the physical survival of the schools and their financial solvency before all other considerations, was violently rejected by Catholic liberals. In turn, the liberals were criticised for their supposed insensitivity to local problems, their willingness to sacrifice long-established institutions for the sake of problematical results, and so on.

What is at stake in an argument like this goes well beyond the practical issues involved. It involves the very broad question of the way in which the American Catholic should relate his religion to the society in which he lives. Let it be granted that, once upon a time, Catholics had little choice but to seek first the consolidation and strengthening of their own social and financial condition. Their weak, struggling position left them few options; and the hostility of Protestants was enough to deprive them of the chance to make constructive contributions to the national good. But this has now changed, and any further excuses in this respect will carry no weight.

The American Catholic liberal is now in a position to do at least three vital things. First, he should feel fully free to enter into working alliances with non-Catholics for social and political reform. If he does so, then the parallel liberal movements which so often existed in the past should now be able to unite, resulting in the enrichment of both. Second, the stage is well set for a renewed attempt to work out the theological dimensions of the American experience. This task was aborted by the condemnation of 'Americanism', but has since taken on a new life because of the work of John Courtney Murray. Yet he has only scratched the surface, and much remains to be done. This task would inevitably carry with it the need to create an American theological idiom, which could draw on native resources and cease to be so dependent upon European leadership. Third, the Catholic liberal can take full advantage of the renewal taking place in the whole Church. Now is the time to press long-delayed questions. Now is the time to try new things. Now is the time to bring everything out into the open. It might well happen that a serious reaction could set in after the Council—such seems to be the common rhythm of movements in the Church. With this possibility in mind, however remote at the moment, the liberal could at least ensure that, whatever his fate, posterity would have some fruitful questions, suggestions and ideas to work with. The advice of the tradition to reformers is finesse, patience and diplomacy. The lesson of Vatican II is that bluntness, boldness and impatience can be even more productive.

Yet to suggest the possibilities and opportunities open to Catholic liberalism is by no means to say that they will be realised. On the whole, there is bound to be some progress in the years to come. Even those who at one time were dubious about many things dear to the hearts of liberals have now swung over. There are no serious doubts any longer about the necessity for a more vigorous theology, or better Catholic universities, or the need for an atmosphere of freedom in the Church. Nor are there doubts about the need for an effective social witness, some structural reforms at the diocesan and parish level, better seminary education and a greater reliance on the layman. Even with some degree of reaction against those who press for rapid reforms, who continue to find new aspects of Catholic life to criticise, the momentum is likely to continue in a forward direction.

None the less, there are the ingredients of a serious crisis lurking just below the surface. These ingredients are not easy to describe, for they are as yet inchoate, but they have certain things in common. Perhaps the most important is that they each involve a very radical questioning of some central point of Christian and Catholic belief. One does not, for instance, have to search very hard to find some who wonder about the contemporary validity of the 'supernatural'; they have taken to heart the enterprise of demythologising Scripture and Christian doctrine. Nor does one have to look far to find some who wonder whether the idea of the Church as a hierarchical society has had its day; or whether the Church can, without falling into idolatry, claim any binding authority; or whether the doctrine of papal infallibility was simply a very bad mistake on the part of the Church.

Speculations of this kind do not appear in print, for reasons both obvious and subtle. The obvious reasons are the certainty of a major explosion should anyone dare express such questions openly, and the practical impossibility of finding Catholic journals which would tolerate their publication. But the subtle reasons are probably more important: an awareness on the part of those with such problems that they are, even by the most liberal standards, skirting the edge of serious heresy. That recognition, taken alone, would probably be tolerable, the price that has to be paid for a deeper penetration of the Gospel. But there is an even deeper perception that outright heresy is too costly to the Church, that the price paid for progress of that kind is too high—the price of disunity, of the hardening of factions, of bitter and harmful acrimony. Of equal importance, those who raise such questions do so in a speculative way, not in the manner of determined revisionists fully equipped with alternative theologies, but rather because a full attempt at renewal seems to entail a radical willingness to investigate afresh the traditional fundamentals of Christian belief. The result is, to say the least, a very complicated stance, both theologically and psychologically. With equal vigour it affirms the necessity of a common creed and the necessity of a free investigation of the validity of that creed.

Let it be said, at this point, that I am offering an interpretation of the thought of some Catholic liberals; no one has quite put the matter this way. Indeed, most liberals would publicly repudiate the suggestion that they have any difficulties with basic doctrines. But I want to assert that they do, and that a close reader of the printed word and a careful listener in the small hours of the morning can find many clues to support this judgment. No doubt many of the bishops sense what is happening. Though they are easily refuted when they try to argue that some given book or line of criticism *proves* the bad faith of those they attack, their instinct for danger is reasonably accurate. The authority of the magisterium *is* being challenged, though not always or even most of the time in the ways in which the bishops think it is. Quite correctly, however, they have discerned that the effect on some Catholics of the Church's effort at reform has been to throw almost everything into question.

Hence, if one is to ask about the future of Catholic

liberalism, one has to ask what the consequences of this drive for a total re-examination of Christianity and the Church are likely to be. My own guess is that some serious struggles are bound to take place, quietly at first but eventually on the public stage. They will not be struggles in the old style, between those who want the Church to stand perfectly still and those who want it to make some vigorous efforts towards renewal. On the contrary, they are likely to take place within the liberal camp, between those who feel that the Church can and should change—as long as nothing fundamental is called into doubt; and those who feel that partial renewal is self-defeating—that only the most courageous and total questioning will suffice to insure a meaningful change. Since it will not be easy to reconcile these two positions, open conflict seems inevitable.

The severity of the conflict will depend upon two things, the continuing possibility of expressing and developing radical lines of thought in public; and whether those who want to do so persist in abiding by the traditional rules of the game. There is no special reason to suppose that the first condition will not continue to prevail. If it is not yet possible in America for every conceivable issue to be discussed fully in print, it is possible at least to touch on everything—provided this be done in a circumspect way, with a plentiful number of scriptural and theological citations and in a tone which is that of respectful speculation and mild wonderment.

As for the second condition, the question here is whether the radical speculators and questioners will continue to observe the *de facto* etiquette which normally sets rough norms or standards for the pressing of new issues in the Church. At present this etiquette demands—if I interpret it correctly, for it is of course more implicit than explicit—that one proceed cautiously, in a tentative way, expressing frequent words of humility, docility to authority and a willingness to let one's work be judged by those more competent than oneself. Moreover, the etiquette demands that one keep one's radical speculations from the public eye, submitting them first to other professionals and ecclesiastical authority, and only if they have met approval there taking them into the public domain. As part of this same constellation, the etiquette requires that, if rebuffed by the professionals or by authority, one retreat into silence, mulling over one's mis-steps and, perhaps, attempting to recast one's thoughts in a more acceptable fashion. Such, I take it, has been the pattern adhered to by most Anglo-Saxon theologians for many decades now.

Yet there is a real possibility that this pattern will break down; it has already to a great extent. A fair number of Catholic writers have discovered that some Protestant journals are open to articles by Catholics on Catholicism which might not, because of the line they take, be accepted by Catholic journals. Again, since most lay writers no longer seek *imprimaturs*, the possibility of totally circumventing the censorship system is now a full reality. Finally, the new public interest in matters Catholic, stimulated by the Council, means that Catholic writers can place their articles in secular papers and journals; hence, there will be even fewer restraints on the Catholic who wants to voice opinions which would be unacceptable to the Catholic community as a whole or to the episcopacy. I am, myself, glad that these possibilities are now available (and I have made use of them myself). At the same time I think it necessary to recognise that developments of this kind—making possible a totally unfettered criticism and speculation—are likely to make the bishops increasingly nervous (for there will be no easy means of control available to them); are likely to encourage at least some to develop their thought quite independent of and indifferent to ecclesiastical authority and judgment; are likely to stimulate, and lend credence to, those who feel that the new spirit of freedom in the Church has opened a Pandora's box. The possibilities for instability, serious crises, and open struggles in this kind of situation should be obvious. That they will come I do not doubt. How they are handled will, more than anything else, determine the future of Catholic liberalism in the immediate years to come.

Quaker Marriage

A Dialogue between Conscience and Coercion

ARCHBISHOP ROBERTS, S.J.

A LITTLE girl, taken by her mother to Mass for the first time, was talking loudly: 'Hush, darling,' said her mother, 'the people are going to say their prayers.' 'But, Mummy,' was the plaintive protest, 'they haven't taken their clothes off yet.' The child's picture of intimacy with God is her dialogue at bedtime with God and parents. Her mother would be just as shocked if the priest did not have many and all the proper clothes—if he were a bishop on a great occasion, she might expect five varieties of hats, two of them on together (note the wisdom of Rome with women old and young)!

Important as is the body's vesture, our concern here is with the state of our mind in the approach to God. There is less difference between the attitude of Quaker and of papal prelate to a five-hour function in Rome than between the Quaker and the typical Roman Catholic mental approach to God. The difference is chiefly in the demarcation of frontiers between conscience and authority. Because this is also, I believe, what Vatican II was about, I propose to sketch a wholly imaginary marriage between Adam, a devout Quaker, and Eve, a devout Catholic. The nicknames were Adam's, chosen in a trying moment to emphasise at least their common origin.

Eve had a very difficult time carrying her first baby. Both nearly died. Advised by her doctors never to risk another pregnancy, Adam makes up his mind. Rather than put the remotest pressure on her conscience or involve her in the disputes of her Catholic friends over their safe-period babies, Adam decides on total abstention. He believes that love should operate (even on a level to him unnatural) as powerfully as the fear of Hell for her, of punishment for 'mortal sin against the natural law' interpreted by Catholic authority.

Eve's belief, unknown to herself, goes back to Aristotle on natural functions. Augustine followed him, dotting all the i's and crossing the t's. Thus it became established in the Catholic Church as nearly all the theologians held that the only marital intercourse not sinful was intercourse that might lead to procreation.

Eve's parish priest and confessor receives from Adam the nickname of Msgr. Conrad. This is to mark his spiritual descent from Conrad of Magdeburg. The latter was a very fierce inquisitor who received from the pope of his day the spiritual charge of St Elizabeth of Hungary. Widowed and bereft of crown, land, friends, and money, Elizabeth submitted to a regimen of guided 'mortification', rare even in the Middle Ages—no friendships with women (these apt to become 'Particular'), rigorous fasting, and severe corporal punishment inflicted to kill pride as well as fleshly desire. Eventually Conrad, Elizabeth's spiritual mentor, was killed by heretics who shared his belief that 'error has no rights'.

Eve's Conrad is absolutely uncompromising on the teaching which has been drummed into her throughout her Catholic life. His reply to a hint that the Vatican Council might reconsider the matter of contraception is that the Church is free to revise her own laws, but has no power of any kind to alter the laws of God. He quotes Pius XI and Pius XII, who claimed that the present discipline is not a precept of human law, but rather 'the expression of a law which is natural and divine'. Conrad frequently quotes as decisive the case of Onan. Conrad takes no notice of the interpretation of biblical scholars, Protestant or Catholic; if they differ from the teaching of Pius XI in his letter on marriage, *Casti Conubii*, well, Rome has spoken and the subject is closed. Any practice contrary to the traditional one is a 'pagan solution'. Any husband or wife troubled in conscience must recall that the Church is an infallible guide in the matter of faith and morals.

Another reason that reconciles Adam to having no more than this one son is that he has now come to realise the full implications of his promises given as the condition for a valid Catholic marriage, namely that his children must be educated as Catholics. Like many Protestants, he has studied, for the formation of his own conscience, the debates and statements of different Lambeth Conferences over the years. Not unreasonably, he has also hoped that such prayerful and scholarly thought, built on married experience in the light of growing modern understanding, would also be studied by Catholics. Is it not the essence of the Catholic position to discover what the 'natural law' prescribes? What more relevant than to work in union with other Christians similarly engaged? He ventures to express this thought to Conrad who sees no reason for the True Church to have any truck with false religions.

Here is the 115th resolution of the Lambeth Conference in 1958 (Adam was later to find marked similarity between this resolution of the Anglican Church and the wording of the schema at Vatican II on *The Church in the Modern World*—the conclusions, of course, of the Schema, were reserved by the Pope on the setting up of his advisory commission):

> 'It has long been held that a primary obligation in Christian marriage is that children may be born within the supporting framework of parental love and family concern with the right to the opportunity for full and spiritually wholesome life.... Yet we believe that the procreation of children is not the sole purpose of Christian marriage. Implicit within the bond between husband and wife is the relationship of love with its sacramental expression in physical union. Because these two great purposes of Christian marriage illuminate each other and form the focal points of constructive home life, we believe that family planning in such ways as are mutually acceptable to husband and wife in Christian conscience, and free from the corruptions of sensuality and selfishness, is a right and important factor in Christian family life.... Such responsible parenthood, based on obedience to all the duties of marriage, requires a wise stewardship of all the resources and abilities of the family, as well as a thoughtful consideration of the varying population needs and problems of society, and the claims of future generations.'

It seems to Adam that Eve's Catholic education has

driven out by *fear* much of the love for which her character thirsts. Her every Act of Contrition in her prayers mentions 'the pains of Hell' in the formula learned as a little girl from her American convent-educated mother. The *Hail Mary* in her rosary repeats the same thought, as enjoined, indeed, by Our Lady of Fatima in the revelations attributed to her. Conrad, moreover, has quoted to her the severe warnings of the Holy Office (given not so very long ago) against the dangerous view that the fires of Hell were not 'real'. Pious books and saints' lives, conferences and sermons, and novenas, like St Francis Xavier's, tell of Hell 'daily filling with pagans', and with Catholics, even children, guilty of 'bad thoughts'. The latter were nearly always in violation of 'THE holy virtue of chastity'. Even as a child Eve had been taught to examine her conscience for mortal sins which, not confessed, merited Hell. Not only was mortal sin possible against any of God's Ten Commandments; there were also numerous prescriptions of positive law, chiefly the six Commandments of the Church, about which theologians were very grim: missing Mass on Sunday or a day of obligation, being late for Mass (how late to avoid a mortal?), eating meat on Friday (a very paradise for the casuist), fasting during Lent—a law much complicated by local variety of episcopal rulings. Would it be a mortal sin if Eve sent her children to a non-Catholic school without the bishop's permission? Would he give it? How would he receive her comment that her own school had been more Catholic than Christian? Would he consider the pain to a deeply conscientious non-Catholic father, deprived of any contribution towards his son's religious development?

Conscience is the crucial issue. And it is at this point Adam receives more than a ray of hope from Monsignor

Conrad's new curate, Father Agnellus (nicknamed Agnellus for 'the lamb that roars'). Agnellus is deeply versed in the Second Vatican Council summoned by Pope John. Educated in France, he tells of the theological ferment there, a ferment familiar to Roncalli—later Pope John—when he was Papal Nuncio in Paris.

Even in 1950, Roncalli had read statements by the French episcopate even more direct and uncompromising in their condemnation of all indiscriminate killing—nuclear or not—than his own *Pacem in Terris* letter to 'Everyman' a dozen years later. No other hierarchy had dared to use such language in modern times. Issued only five years after the end of World War II it was acceptable to French public opinion as condemning bombs they had not then got, German bombs used to enslave them, and American and British bombs, used on their towns to liberate them. Later, the bishops' statement was muted by the rattle of Catholic de Gaulle's weaponry, by the cheers of those greeting the end of their humiliating dependence on Anglo-Saxon power and greeting the dawn of a flourishing French armaments industry.

But the French bishops' manifesto was not dead. It lived on in the continued dialogue between bishop, priest, and layman. It spoke through a few other bishops, not politically committed. It cried like a trumpet in *Pacem in Terris* and in the final Conciliar speeches of a Lienart, a Martin, a Boillon, an Ancel, and others.

To Adam the Quaker, such news brought by Fr Agnellus is nectar. It means that his son might not in future be penalised as a Catholic bound by blind obedience, but might enjoy to the full the benefits of his country's laws. Conscientious objection, allowed by British law in 1916, largely through the strength of Quaker tradition operating even at the height of World War I, made a timid appearance in the *adnexa* of Schema XIII (denied, however, any official recognition at first) on 'The Church in the Modern World'.

This was a hideous and dangerous innovation to those brought up in the tradition that 'the Duce is always right', even when the Duce was the puppet of the Führer and ally of Nüremberg criminals. But Agnellus told Adam on good authority that the debate on Conscientious Objection in St Peter's must sooner or later register the fact that the Basilica was undeniably a monument for a Conscientious Objector to a pagan Supreme Pontiff.

Adam warms to Agnellus. He sees that devotion to conscience is really the hard core of the Catholic rock; certainly, it had been among the Church's treasures, though steadily pushed to the back of the Catholic drawer by more flashy jewels. But now here it was being rediscovered, cleaned, and polished in Pope John's studio. Soon the principle of freedom of conscience would shine forth again in the gospel message—as in the gospels themselves which are a record of the Divine Conscientious Objector to the religious and civil Caesars of His time.

Adam hopes, naturally, that Agnellus will enliven the informed conscience of Eve with the good news. They talk this policy over, and come to the conclusion that a non-violent campaign against Lord Conrad (Agnellus prefers English to Italian titles in England) will yield more lasting dividends. For a very close study of Vatican II by Agnellus had revealed the fact that many of the victories of 'liberals' (alias, in the view of the Conrads, relativists, indifferentists, rationalists, modernists, and Marxists) had been scored by the Conrads kicking the ball through their own goal. Good players avoid this habit, but some very Eminent and prominent players had scored heavily—*for their opponents.* For, in the sphere of sex, it seems now to Adam (and to most non-Catholics) and to Agnellus (and to very many Catholics) that Conrad and his team are committed to redefining natural law in whatever terms the Pope chooses to use.

That authority should *guide* the conscience is a reasonable claim to Adam, as well as to Agnellus. Adam himself deplores the loss of his right to guide his own son. Expert moral guidance has its place together with expert legal guidance.

But both feel it is another matter for Conrad to demand of Eve, in the Pope's name and under sanction of eternal flames, an obedience involving a constant threat to her health and to her marriage—an obedience impossible to understand or even discuss, much less to love as the reflection of God's love. Can a human being obey without loving, bow to commands not understood or understandable? Was not our Lord's model prayer a prayer for His Father's will to be done on earth, even as in Heaven? Did not true love cast out fear, even on earth?

Blind obedience? Surely not in Heaven. Blind obedience not to any earthly power, either, if Conscience is God's own sunbeam, and His gift is to pierce the mists obscuring the sun shining on every human being.

So when Pope Paul announced his commission to examine questions previously declared closed, Agnellus said, 'Lord Conrad has over-reached himself'. For, taking a leaf out of Lord Conrad's book, who never ceased to quote papal and episcopal documents, he had read very carefully, with emphasis on each word, the statement made by Pope Paul VI in announcing his expert commission on June 23, 1964:

'A problem which everyone talks about, is that of

birth control, as it is called, namely of population increases on the one hand, and family morality on the other. It is an extremely grave problem. It touches on the mainsprings of human life. It touches on the feelings and interests closest to the experience of man and woman. It is an extremely complex and delicate problem. The Church recognises the multiple aspects of it, that is to say, the multiple rights in the forefront of which are certainly those of married people, their freedom, their conscience, their love, their duty. But the Church must also affirm her own rights, namely that of God's law, interpreted, taught, favoured, and defended by her. And the Church will have to proclaim this law of God in the light of the scientific, social, and psychological truths which in these times have undergone new and very ample study and documentation. It is necessary to face attentively this development, both theoretical and practical, of the question. And this is in fact what the Church is doing. The question is being subjected to study, as wide and profound as possible, as grave and honest as it must be on a subject of such importance. It is under study which, we must say, we hope will soon be concluded with the co-operation of many and outstanding experts. We will therefore soon give the conclusions of it in the form which will be considered most adapted to the subject and to the aim to be achieved. But meanwhile we say frankly that up to now we do not have sufficient motive to consider out of date and therefore not binding the norms given by Pope Pius XII in this regard. Therefore they must be considered valid, at least until we feel obliged in conscience to change them. In a matter of such gravity, it seems well that Catholics should wish to follow one law, that which the Church authoritatively puts forward. And it therefore seems opportune to recommend that no one, for the present, takes it on himself to make pronouncements in terms different from the prevailing norm.'

Always in the end the human mind (which is made for truth) will reject error as the body rejects poison. But minds long conditioned to error in guise of truth will reject poison only when it tastes too bad to be retained. The Resurrection would not have been Truth fully vindicated if Error had not tortured and killed.

So Adam the Quaker and Agnellus the Priest in the pursuit of truth got down to minute study of the published speeches, press conferences, interviews of the council Fathers, then discussing religious freedom, and became involved in these deliberations.

It was a strict right of a human being—the recognition of his human dignity, ran one theme—to enjoy religious freedom. Every man, therefore, should be free from coercion, positive or negative, whether by individuals or associations. All this 'within due limits'; but what limits? Adam and Agnellus found that Vatican I had not defined these limits with sufficient clearness. A short time before that Council, Pius IX had condemned all who held that the papacy should reconcile its claims with liberty, progress, and modern civilisation. The world of that day had asked where the new steam-engine and gas fitted in. Who were the 'liberals' condemned by Pius IX? Who fixed the frontiers of authority? In the Church? In the State? What about Pope Alexander VI who had settled the problems of the New World, then being discovered, by assigning the West to Spain, the East to Portugal? St Pius V could find plenty of precedents for his excommunication and deposition of Queen Elizabeth I. Who was, then, the patriot, who the traitor? Who the true Christian? For here natural law was quoted, as well as divinely revealed law.

And these were not just academic questions to Adam and Agnellus. The experts were at loggerheads, too. In Vatican debates were the following from the Conciliar Fathers to the new propositions on religious freedom: 'It must be made more clear,' one read, 'that freedom from coercion was to seek and hold the truth, as declared by the Holy See'. On the other hand another went, 'the right to be wrong in good faith must be underlined'. 'There must be no mistake about the right to form a true conscience.'

But 'We must never allow to a false conscience the dignity we give to a true one'. And 'Since the Church can never give to a false religion what is her exclusive right, much better say nothing at all'.

Conrad's champions were making up in clamour what they were rapidly losing in numbers. 'We must place beyond all doubt,' they said, 'the right of ecclesiastical authority to coerce; to punish the faithful (spiritually); to proclaim that true religious freedom is not thereby lessened. *Item*, these propositions on freedom favoured pragmatism, indifferentism, laicism, naturalism, humanism, situational ethics, and they threatened the missionary rights of the Church. *Item*, the Schema contradicted Catholic doctrine, tradition, especially the teaching of supreme pontiffs. At most, false religions may be *tolerated* within certain limits. The Schema, under cover of freedom of conscience . . . sacrificed the divine law.'

It was clear that Conrad and Agnellus could not yet, on many points, be soul-mates! But their Church was no longer wholly monolithic. The individual was asserting his person.

As to the Church of the future, what had the meeting of the Conrads and the Agnelli in their clash and final statements brought (1) To Adam the Quaker, (2) To Eve the Catholic, (3) To Adam and Eve, two in one flesh?

First to Adam: the Sun of Conscience, which he venerated as symbol of Love's light, of Love's warmth, of Love's energy, was declared central and essential in the pursuit of all love, human and divine. Christ was the Light of the World: Him to seek in honesty was Him to find in joy.

Secondly, then to Eve: Eve could look forward to the fullness of her inheritance as wife and mother in God's own time. 'It is not good for man to be alone—a companion, bone of his bone, flesh of his flesh, heart of his heart—they shall be two in one flesh.'

Inspired scripture's *Song of Songs* had come into its own at last. And like Eve, Catholic girls might learn true marital chastity—that chastity which implies worship with the body—from their mothers, as well as from dedicated virgins, all experienced in such self-giving love as is the heart of chastity.

As for Adam and Eve no longer separated, now fully united, no doubt their favourite bed-time reading would be the Latin *Schema De Ecclesiae Habitudine ad Religiones non-Christinianas*, 'The Church and the non-Christians'. Heaven to think of the primitive animists a million years ago, of Buddhists, Muslims, Parsees, Hindus, who, having never read this *Schema*, would have steered by the same Sun, and made the same Heaven.

The Wisdom of the Spirit

A Platonist's Faith

E. I. WATKIN

'MANY great storms and tempests' rise 'in this time and thou knowest never whither to run for sorrow. Suddenly, or ever thou knowest, all is away and thou left barren in the boat, blown with blustering blasts now hither and now thither, thou knowest never where nor whither.' 'For now art thou in the ghostly' (spiritual) 'sea . . . shipping over from bodilyness into ghostliness.'[1]

This tempest with its confusion and dismay pictures the condition of the contemplative who is being withdrawn from a prayer of affections, images and concepts into a bare adherence to God beyond all images and concepts. It is a descent from the surface and letter of prayer into the depths of its spirit or, if another metaphor be preferred, an ascent to its summit. The picture

[1] *Epistle of Privy Counsel*, Ed. McCann, Chapter 12.

however fits equally well the present condition of Christianity and in particular Catholic Christianity. 'It must,' writes a Dominican theologian in comment upon the Jesuit Rahner,[1] 'be a matter of common knowledge that Catholic theology today is going through a profound upheaval. Areas of apparent stability may still be found, the hard crust which resists the volcanic eruption; but it is improbable the resistance can last much longer.' In this theological eruption many pronouncements concerning dogma and morals deemed hitherto immutable, because divinely guaranteed, are being exploded. The elaborate structure of theological and moral doctrine crumbles before our eyes. For its letter is being discredited. The question which today presses itself upon us is whether this perishing letter has contained a void or an inexhaustible substance of spiritual reality. That the latter is true is my faith which I would desire to convey to those who may be disturbed, disheartened, even reduced to despairing doubt by the collapse of the traditional presentation of doctrine and morals.

What in fact is this letter? The translation in terms of reason of the spirit's intuitions of spiritual truth, the spirit beneath and beyond the letter. In words of singular wisdom Bertrand Russell distinguishes three grades of human life and experience: instinct, mind and spirit. Mind is critical and in the last resort destructive. If accorded supremacy, or held sufficient, it desiccates the life of instinct, produces a frustrating scepticism in respect of all human values. Russell then turns to spirit. 'The life of the spirit,' he proceeds, 'centres round impersonal feeling as the life of the mind centres around impersonal thought. . . . All art belongs to the life of the spirit, though its greatness is derived from its being also intimately bound up with the life of instinct. Art starts

[1] *Catholic Herald*, March 6, 1964.

from instinct and rises into the region of the spirit; religion starts from the spirit and endeavours to dominate and inform the life of instinct. It is possible to feel the same interest in the joys and sorrows of others as in our own, to love and hate independently of all relation to ourselves, to care about the destiny of man and the development of the universe without a thought that we are personally involved. Reverence and worship, the sense of an obligation to mankind, the feeling of imperativeness and acting under orders which traditional religion has interpreted as Divine inspiration, all belong to the life of the spirit. And deeper than all these lies the sense of a mystery half revealed, of a hidden wisdom and glory, of a transfiguring vision in which common things lose their solid importance and become a thin veil behind which the ultimate truth of the world is dimly seen. It is such feelings that are the source of religion and if they were to die, most of what is best would vanish out of life.'[1] 'When thought is informed by spirit, it loses its cruel, destructive quality; it no longer promotes the death of instinct, but only its purification from insistence and ruthlessness and its emancipation from the prison walls of accidental circumstance.'[2] 'The life of the spirit . . . brings with it the joy of vision of the mystery and profundity of the world; of the contemplation of life and above all the joy of universal love. It liberates those who have it from the prison house of insistent personal passion and mundane cares. It gives freedom and breadth and beauty to men's thoughts and feelings and to all their relations with others. It brings the solution of doubts, the end of the feeling that all is vanity. . . . For those who have once entered the world of thought, it is only through spirit that happiness and

[1] *Principles of Social Reconstruction*, pp. 207–8.
[2] Ibid., p. 210.

peace can return.'[1] 'If life is to be fully human, it must serve some end, which seems, in some sense, outside human life, some end which is impersonal and above mankind such as God or truth or beauty. Those who best promote life do not have life for their purpose. They aim rather at what seems like a gradual incarnation, a bringing into our human existence of something eternal, something that appears to imagination to live in a heaven remote from strife and failure and the devouring jaws of Time. Contact with this eternal world —even if it be only a world of our imagining—brings a strength and a fundamental peace which cannot be wholly destroyed by the struggles and apparent failures of our temporal life. It is this happy contemplation of what is eternal that Spinoza calls the intellectual love of God. To those who have once known it, it is the key of wisdom.'[2] 'By contact with what is eternal, by devoting our life to bringing something of the Divine into this troubled world, we can make our own lives creative even now, even in the midst of the cruelty and strife and hatred that surround us on every hand.'[3]

The reader will note Russell's qualifications 'seems', 'in some sense', 'seems like a gradual incarnation', something 'that appears to imagination to live', 'even if this eternal world be only a world of our imagining'. For he cannot emancipate himself from an *a priori* dogma, accepted, almost, as self-evident by our self-styled empiricists; the sole objective truth attainable is truth susceptible in principle to scientific proof. Russell indeed states explicitly: 'I cannot admit any method of arriving at truth except that of science'.[4] How, we may well ask,

[1] Ibid., pp. 222–23.
[2] Ibid., pp. 245–46.
[3] Ibid., p. 246.
[4] *Religion and Science*, p. 189.

can an even possible illusion, a subjective experience with no ascertainable foundation in objective fact be, as Russell has insisted so emphatically, of greater value and potency than the certain objective truth attainable by reason working from and upon sense data? Be indeed the sole type of experience which imparts significance and positive value to human life? To support this divorce between value and fact, Russell points out that 'hunger' is not evidence 'that I shall get food'.[1] Only too true. Neither does an individual's need of God necessarily produce an *experience* of God. Hunger, however, proves the existence of the food necessary to its satisfaction. Hunger and food are biological correlates. The existence of the one implies the existence of the other. The fact of spiritual needs, and even more their satisfaction in human experience presupposes an order of objective spiritual reality. We are indeed as certain of such moral truths as the utter wickedness of Hitler's extermination of Jews, the moral value of self-sacrifice for others or the aesthetic truth that a huge block of featureless flats is ugly, St Paul's cathedral beautiful, as we are of facts scientifically demonstrable.

Einstein did not share Russell's scepticism, his conclusion that the highest values in human life may after all have no objective foundation. 'To *know*,' he writes, 'that what is impenetrable to us really exists, manifesting itself in the highest wisdom and the most radical beauty which our dull faculties can comprehend only in their primitive forms—this knowledge . . . is at the centre of true religiousness.' God is 'the illimitable superior spirit who reveals Himself in the slight details

[1] *The Philosophy of Bertrand Russell* (Library of Living Philosophers), p. 726. Russell, in fact, combines a fundamentally Platonist valuation with a positivist theory of knowledge, a combination, hardly, I think, consistent.

we are able to perceive with our frail and feeble minds'. 'The most beautiful and the most profound emotion', surely rather intuition, 'we can experience is the sensation "awareness" of the mystical. It is the source of all truth. He to whom this emotion is a stranger, who can no longer wonder and stand rapt in awe is as good as dead.'[1] 'Whoever has undergone the intense experience of successful advances in this domain of scientific thought is moved by profound reverence for the rationality made manifest in existence. By the way of understanding he achieves a far-reaching emancipation from the shackles of personal hopes and desires and thereby attains the humble attitude of mind towards the grandeur of reason incarnate in existence which in its profoundest depths is inaccessible to man. This attitude appears to me to be religion in the highest sense of the word.'[2] Reason here is clearly not the solvent and destructive reason opposed by Russell to spirit, but a manifestation and operation of spirit. This spiritual depth, this order of spirit, is grounded in that centre or apex of which mystics speak, a radical volition which springs immediately from God and where God is specially present. A Spanish mystic, Mother Cecilia of the Nativity, terms it 'the intimate part of the will, the essence of the soul; a life grounded in the very life and essence of' the 'Creator'.[3] It rises above time and space into God's eternity and immensity. It is, in short, man's entrance into God, symbolised by the door into heaven opened to the seer of Patmos.[4] This centre lies beyond the psychic

[1] Quotations by Anne Freemantle. *The Commonweal*, May 6, 1955.

[2] Quoted from Einstein, 'My Later Years', p. 168, in *Cross Currents*, Winter 1964–65.

[3] *Transformation of the Soul in God*, Stanza 1.

[4] *Apocalypse* iv. 1.

level reached and studied by psychoanalysis, despite its claim to be a depth psychology. It is distinct from the more superficial self, our normal consciousness. As Father Merton states it: 'This superficial "I" is not our real self. It is our "individuality" and our "empirical self" but it is not truly the hidden and mysterious person in whom we subsist before the eyes of God. The "I" that works in the world, thinks about itself, is not the true "I" that has been united to God in Christ. It is at best the vesture, the mask, the disguise of that unknown "self". Our external superficial self is not eternal, not spiritual. Far from it. This self is doomed to disappear as completely as smoke from a chimney. It is utterly frail and evanescent.'[1] Little wonder that contemporary secularism which recognises only the self of instinct and reasoning and dismisses the depths of spirit as illusion does not, cannot indeed, credit or even desire any survival of death.

When this empirical self whose life is sensation and reason ignores or opposes spirit, it is the 'flesh' condemned so vehemently by St Paul.

In the transforming union the subject, so St Teresa and St John of the Cross and Mary of the Incarnation bear witness, becomes aware of a sharp division between the empirical self and the spirit. The former may be occupied with the business of life or beset with cares and sufferings. The latter enjoys the peace of God.[2] According to St John of the Cross 'the higher and lower portions of the soul seem to it to be so far apart that it recognises two parts in itself, each so distinct from the

[1] *New Seeds of Contemplation*, p. 7.

[2] 'St Teresa Interior Castle VII', Ch. 1; 'St John of the Cross'; 'Dark Night of the Soul', Ch. 23; 'Life of Mary of the Incarnation', Ch. 20. These passages are collected in Père Poulain *Des Graces d'Oraison*, Ch. 19.

other that neither seems to have anything in common with the other'.[1]

The empirical self is the product and activity of the spirit in its inferior and temporary function as the soul of the human body, the principle which not only gives the body life but organises its material particles, that is to say, its subordinate energies down to its electronic constituents thereby making it what it is, a living body and a particular living body. In the language of scholastic philosophy it is its form, more accurately, I think, its informative or informing principle. Were the human spirit essentially the form of the body so that the human being is, as St Thomas taught, following Aristotle, a body-soul, survival of death would be an intrinsic impossibility. The Thomist statement that it is a subsistent form is meaningless because self-contradictory. For by its metaphysical nature a form cannot subsist apart from its matter. The spirit is in its own right an energy-object, that is a dynamic centre beyond and above its ensoulment of the body. Nor even in this life does it merely ensoul the body producing its biological functions. It also, though not without biological restriction, even in many cases resistance, inspirits the body employing its senses and organs in the service of its distinctively spiritual perception or action, as in aesthetic appreciation and creation, in moral choice, in study and scientific research and above all, because most radically, in religious communion with God present in its central depth, with Reality where created being is most real. Over the waters of man's spirit from the dawn of humanity broods the spirit of God to make them fertile and creative. Though the conceptual surface of Catholic theology may be, as now it is, tossed by winds of inevitable change the deep of spirit below is unruffled. For by

[2] 'Dark Night of the Soul II', Ch. 23 14.

whatever mutable images or conceptual formulas it may find expression, it is a region of immutable spiritual truth arising immediately from the spirit's experience of the Eternal.

The spirit's concern with sensible event or rite, conceptual statement or doctrinal formulation is only in so far as it expresses or serves its wisdom. Through language addressed to imagination and thought Scripture and Church speak to the spirit of man the things of the spirit of God, to the spirit the language of Spirit. For the spirit's truth exceeds reason's. It penetrates to a deeper level, enters another dimension, apprehends a more real reality. Though more obscure it is richer and more satisfying. It is discerned by the spirit's quiet and brooding contemplation, in the experience of a work of art, be it literature, painting, sculpture, architecture or music, in religious ritual or liturgical prayer, Scripture and ecclesiastical doctrine. Even the rites and beliefs of primitive religion, scornfully dismissed by an arrogant and superficial rationalism, are expressions, however crude and too often perverted, of profound insights of the human spirit which in higher religions and pre-eminently the Christian have found an expression progressively purer and less inadequate, though an adequate expression is impossible.[1]

Of this spirit I would understand the term, so frequent in the liturgy, '*cor*', heart. As Pascal insisted, it possesses its distinctive wisdom, that wisdom of the heart, *sapientia cordis*, for which we pray in Psalm 90 (89): 'That we may attain to the wisdom of the spirit', '*sapientiam cordis*'. Of this wisdom it is said in the Miserere: 'Thou takest delight in a sincere heart and in the depth of spirit dost teach me wisdom'. 'To Thee my heart speaketh' (Psalm 27/26). Thus the heart of

[1] See the works of Jung, Mircea Eliade, E. O. James.

Jesus is His spirit, not the purely physiological blood pump pierced by the soldier's lance which is but its symbol. Devotion to the Sacred Heart is therefore devotion to a human spirit in its most intimate union with the Divine Superspirit. Unlike rational knowledge, spiritual knowledge cannot be precisely formulated. It is a spirit perception analogous to sense perception. To this spiritual perception, not to sensible images or conceptual formulas, religious faith holds fast and bears its witness.[1] With it alone are Scripture and Church concerned for its own sake. 'It is important,' writes Père Grelot,[2] 'not to confuse the intellectual outlook, the mentality which at every stage of revelation condition its literary expression—with the Absolute Truth of God's Word of which the former is the envelope.' We must not, that is to say, attribute to the human letter the truth of the Divine Spirit divinely revealed which it strives so fallibly to express.

'The letter,' wrote St Paul, 'kills but the spirit gives life.'[3] The letter indeed is inevitable and indispensable and therefore good. For it is the necessary translation and expression of the spirit in the imaginative and conceptual orders, in a particular environment or climate of opinion, in relation to scientific knowledge, political or social organisation. To neglect or despise it is folly. If however it is made an end in itself or regarded as immutable, infallible and divinely revealed, when in

[1] Those Quietists confused these levels of the human psyche who mistakenly concluded from the truth that 'one act' of the spirit's loving union with God persists until or unless it is revoked by deliberate and serious sin; that there is therefore no need to express and intensify this abiding orientation of the spirit by acts of love and devotion exercised on more superficial levels of emotion and reason.

[2] *Nouvelle Revue Théologique,* Sept.-Oct. 1963.

[3] II Corinthians iii. 6.

process of time it becomes a servitude or incredible, it kills and is doomed to death. The letter of religious doctrine, that is to say, is but human and therefore mortal, the spirit divine and therefore immortal. Scriptural statements consequently are human and fallible translations of spiritual insights into conceptual terms or their presentation in and through imagery, poetical and often mythical. And doctrinal affirmations are conceptual translations of spiritual truth.

The Church exists, and this is the fundamental fact about her, for prayer—to unite men to God and unite them as intimately as possible, in this life, here and now. And it is prayer that discerns the spiritual truth which is the veritable deposit of faith. That Christian doctrines represent insighıs of contemplative prayer and derive from them was recognised by Father Augustine Baker, when he wrote: 'The first knowledge of our mysteries of Christian religion came in and by contemplations . . . to which God called the holy apostles, doctors and other principal members and beginners of the Church and to them in the said contemplations revealed the said mysteries, and by them hath communicated and imparted the same to other Christians who took it by tradition from those contemplators who *saw and felt* the truth of those mysteries'.[1] Underlying and upholding the apostolic succession of official teachers and liturgical ministers there has been a charismatic succession of contemplatives. The conceptualisation and imaginative presentation of their spiritual intuitions were however conditioned by the recipients' theological and psychological milieux. According to the adage of the Schools: 'Whatsoever is received, is received after the fashion of the recipient'.

[1] *Secretum.* Excerpted in *The Confessions of Father Baker,* McCann, pp. 71–72.

The necessity of such translation of Divine Truth into human language was most beautifully and powerfully expressed by the Cambridge Platonist John Smith. 'Divine Truth hath its humiliation and exinanition as well as its exaltation. Divine Truth becomes many times in Scripture incarnate, debasing itself to assume our rude conceptions, that so it might converse more freely with us, and infuse its own divinity into us. . . . If "God" should speak in the language of eternity, who could understand Him or interpret His meaning? Or if He should have declared His truth to us only in a way of the purest abstraction that human souls are capable of, how should then the more rude and illiterate sort of men have been able to apprehend it? Truth is content when it comes into the world to wear our mantles, to learn our language, to conform itself, as it were, to our dress and fashions. . . . It speaks with the most idiotical' (simple) 'sort of men in the most idiotical way, and becomes all things to all men, as every son of truth should do, for their good. Which was well observed in that old Cabbalistical axiom among the Jews: Lumen supernum nunquam descendit sine indumento.' The heavenly light never descends to earth naked.[1] I salute Platonism's authentic speech. For Plato long since knew that myth is the most fitting statement of ultimate spiritual truth.

At this point I declare myself a Platonist, a Christian and a Catholic Platonist, according however to the spirit rather than the letter of Catholic Christianity. For the prophet's word: 'Truly God is hidden in thee',[2] His Jewish people, has been fulfilled in the Catholic Church,

[1] *John Smith's Select Discourses*. 'Of Prophesie', Ch. 1, ed. 1660, pp. 171–72.

[2] Placed in the mouth of converted pagans. Isaiah xlv. 15. Translation of the *Bible de Jérusalem*.

where God is supremely, indeed uniquely, present, concealed beneath the letter, revealed by and to the spirit. That is to say I adhere, unfashionable though it may be, to the fundamental principles of the Platonic Aristotelian philosophy, as it has been developed from Plato onward to the Schoolmen but with emphasis rather on the Platonic than on the Aristotelian constituent. There were indeed Aristotelian components in the Neo-Platonism of Plotinus and his successors.

Two philosophies contest the favour of contemporary philosophers, linguistic analysis and existentialism. The former is no more than a valuable technique without claim to be a metaphysic, which it rejects as meaningless, a prolegomenon therefore to philosophy, not philosophy. The latter exalts the existential factor of created being, material or spiritual, its existence, above and at the cost of its essential factor, the form, the nature, the essence of an existent by which a potential energy, the matter, is informed and made the actual energy which is an object of a particular form or nature. Up and down the scale of being the energy-object is constituted what it is, by its form, its distinctive nature specific and individual.

Reality is indeed throughout dynamic, the truth existentialism perceives. But this dynamism is determined by form, by the essence, the nature of the energy-object. Everywhere energy is formed energy. Pure activity, energy wholly fulfilled in itself, is beyond change, a coincidence of rest and energy. And this is God at once pure act and unmoved mover. That our direct knowledge of God in this life is existential not essential, knowledge that He is, not what He is, is but the infirmity of human understanding. To comprehend is fuller knowledge than to apprehend.

Existentialism which reverses this order of form and

energy opens the door to irrationalism, to unintelligibility, therefore to intellectual suicide. In the concrete an existential philosophy tends to become an ideology of instinct, the affirmation of instinct at the expense of reason and spirit alike, whether individually in D. H. Lawrence's cult of sex, Nietzsche's cult of the superman, or socially in the ideology of National Socialism.

That our scientific knowledge exceeds immeasurably the science of past ages and is advancing with giant strides imparts no sanction to contemporary philosophy. Metaphysics is concerned with facts outside the sphere of scientific investigation.

Science therefore cannot refute Platonism, rooted as it is in the profound insights of spirit. Platonism is the inherent philosophy of art. It was a Platonist aesthetic of mathematical proportion, of harmony and light which presided over the birth of Gothic architecture and the glories of Chartres. What comparable artistic creation has been inspired by linguistic analysis or existentialism? The union between Platonism and religion has always been intimate. Plotinus was a mystic. Platonism was the earliest Christian philosophy.

In flat contradiction of contemporary materialism for which a science founded on sense perception is the sole criterion of objective truth, the Platonist sees Ultimate Reality, Pure and Complete Being as superspiritual. All orders of limited and dependent being are communications of this Perfect Being, increasingly unreal to the degree of their limitation. Created spirit therefore is more real than matter, closer and more like to the creative Godhead, though paradoxically always more remote than near, more unlike than like. Its wisdom accordingly is truer, though less clear, than the scientific knowledge of material objects derived, as it is, from perceptions of the bodily senses. Spirit is a brighter reflection, a less insubstantial shadow than matter of incomprehensible Divine Being, the material universe spirit's reflection or shadow.

The Platonist can agree with the materialist that the difference between matter and mind, physical and spiritual energy is not absolute but a distinction of degree. But he reverses the materialist's estimate of their respective value and reality. For the materialist spiritual energy is a product and manifestation of corporeal, less real therefore. For the Platonist it is fuller being, more real.

Thus we inhabit a half-world poised between Being and nothing. If foolish, we shall accept our half-world as sufficient and be content with its prison. If wise, though accepting it as our inevitable lot on earth, we shall escape from it in the freedom, rise above it in the ascent, of our spirit.

The Platonist is less impressed by the corporeal immensities discovered by the astronomer than by the astronomer's mind which can measure these unimaginable distances, determine the composition of remotest nebulae, investigate the laws of their formation.

Nor is he the slave of time concerned with fashions of thought. For his philosophy is contemplative 'of all time and all existence'.[1] To the Platonist the labels 'reactionary' and 'progressive' are insignificant. Truth is no less true, because it was known to our forbears, no truer, because recently discovered. Metaphysics is speculation of the eternal, mysticism its experience. Light years flash by, galaxies form and fade, evolution and dissolution follow each other in rhythmic sequence. But God is Now, eternity His instant.

A spirit possessed by this wisdom, Platonic and Christian, is in peace, though tempests may toss or mists over-

[1] *Republic*, VI, p. 486, in Jowett's translation.

cloud the zone in which the spirit ensouling the body is subject to psycho-physical disturbance. Its peace however is not slumber but a concentrated life, an identity of action and repose in which it displays its affinity with the God with whom it communes. The Unmoved Mover is no mere conceit of Aristotle's philosophy, but the mystic's twofold experience. Such a spirit is an expanse of water drenched by a sunlight of which the illumination of our visible sun is but the reflection.[1]

This Platonic vision of a hierarchy of being determined by form—for there must surely be spirits superior to ours, bodies cast shadows and the world of phantasy is not wholly non-existent—is expressed, in imagery largely derived from Canaanite mythology, by the passages in the Old Testament which speak of a primordial chaos, a waste of waters on which God's creative fiat has imposed the order of forms which constitutes the universe. Reality is multi-dimensional and can be known in more than one dimension. Modern positivism however confines it, or at best knowledge of it, to the dimension investigated by science. 'Faith' on the other hand, it has been well said, 'attributes to reality a dimension of depth inaccessible to the eyes of the profane'.[2]

The limitation of created being, that, if it is this, it cannot be an incompatible that, if A, then not all and every other letter of the existential alphabet, is its radical defect. Owing to this limitation good and therefore

[1] The impressionists therefore who devoted themselves to recording effects of light, in particular on or in water, whatever they may have intended, were not solely recorders of sense data. Like all genuine artists they penetrated, even if unconsciously, to the underlying idea, in this instance the spiritual illumination of which the sensible is a symbol.

[2] J. Lienhardt.

desirable objects are too often unattainable together. A choice must be made between them. According to a newspaper article a member of the cabinet has *as yet* failed to solve the problem of reconciling social justice which can be imposed only by a government sufficiently powerful, and individual freedom. The writer assumes that as both aims, social justice and individual liberty, are good, they *must* therefore be wholly compatible. Such an *a priori* assumption ignores the fundamental fact of the order of limited being in which we live. The evils which, as Plato observes, 'necessarily haunt this lower world' are the inevitable consequence of this limitation. For A's good often conflicts with B's. One value can be achieved only at the expense of another. Micro-organisms for example are indispensable to biological life. Nevertheless they are a source of disease in higher organisms, from plants to man. The weather that benefits the farmer may be disastrous to holiday makers and those whose livelihood depends upon them. Man's power of free choice, his noblest prerogative, involves not indeed the inevitability of any particular free choice but that immoral choices will inevitably be made. His control of natural process, consequent upon his amazing advance in scientific knowledge, though in so many respects beneficial, is ruining the beauty of coast and countryside, cumbering our streets with traffic, straining our nerves with pressure and noise, has exposed human happiness, even existence, to perils hitherto inconceivable. Pesticides destroy birds and butterflies, provision of homes spreads suburbia. Medical death control produces a population explosion. An individual group or society aware of the depth of human experience is likely to be insufficiently aware of its breadth; if open to its breadth, to be unaware of its depth. Quantity and quality are too often at war. The speaker or writer is faced with the fact that the qualification required by truth diminishes, may even destroy, impact. An orator and to a lesser degree a writer who qualified his statements to the utmost commanded by a meticulous regard for accuracy would make little or no impression and fail in his primary purpose, communication. He can but strike the best balance he may between these conflicting demands. Should he, moreover, attempt a statement so exact that it could be true without qualification, he must digress indefinitely and lose the thread of his argument. He must needs therefore content himself with substantial truth and trust his hearer's or reader's good sense to supply the necessary qualification or exception. In this also he must submit to the inevitable restrictions of limited being and knowledge.

Man's deification and transformation, to be complete only after death, by imparting to him God's own life and consciousness can alone free him wholly from frustration, error, suffering and sin. The mystic, however, even in this present life, penetrates or ascends to a reality where all is good, nothing evil, because here God is All in all.

The world, that is to say, is the product of two principles, a positive principle, the Good Source of positive being, and a negative principle, the limitation inherent in created beings as such and its necessary consequence, their mutual interference and conflict.[1] In its positive aspect, creation arises from God's Being as overflowing good. In its negative aspect, the source and cause of evil, it is diminished being, *comparative* unreality. The product of these two principles, the positive and the nega-

[1] The conviction that limitation is the cause and ultimate explanation of evil I owe to my old friend Fr Joseph Rickaby, S.J. (See his *In an Indian Abbey*, 'Omnipotence no Arbitrary Rule'.)

tive, the 'psycho-physical' world in which we live has been designated by a Russian philosopher[1] 'the Kingdom of enmity'. The universe is God's shadow and, like other shadows, reveals and conceals, even distorts, the figure that casts it.

The Platonic doctrine, accepted by Scholastic philosophy, that evil is defect of being, not positive being does not overlook its extent, intensity or power as experienced throughout human history. Starvation which is negative, the absence of necessary food, is more painful than many positive forms of death, shooting for example, or a painless poison.[2] It does however enable us to understand the mystic's insight of being as good, entirely good. Not only the Divine Superbeing, the Source of Being but also the positive being of His creatures. For 'He [God] declares the Epistle of Privy Counsel[3] 'is being both to Himself and to all. And in that only is He separated from all, that He is being both of Himself and of all. . . . He is the being of all.'

Though this Divine Reality is strictly nameless, the Platonist speaks of it pre-eminently as the One and the Good. It is the One because completely undifferentiated and the source of that unity of creation which prevents sheer chaos and is the reason why it is a universe not a multiverse. This One is the One at the summit of Plotinus' ladder of being, to an experienced union with which he was, though rarely, raised. It is the Godhead which for Eckhardt is higher than God. 'The Godhead and God are as distinct as heaven and earth. . . . God

[1] N. O. Lossky, *The World as an Organic Whole*, Ch. VII. Lossky's work combines penetrating and convincing thought with sheer fantasy.

[2] That such thinkers as Von Hügel and the Christian Platonist Dean Inge found these two qualities of evil incompatible is surprising.

[3] Epistle of Privy Counsel Ch. I.

manifests Himself only when He is proclaimed by all His creatures.' 'All creatures speak of God. Why do they not speak of the Godhead? Because in the Godhead all is One and we cannot speak of it.' 'When I reach the Foundation . . . and the source which is the Godhead . . . God vanishes.'[1] It is the Unity from which Ruysbroeck saw the persons of the Trinity proceed and to which they return. 'The Superessential Unity is above the distinction of the Persons. . . . In this unfathomable abyss of the Simplicity all things are wrapped in fruitive bliss. . . . To this the Persons and all that lives in God must give place: for here there is nought but an eternal rest in the fruitive embrace of an outpouring love.'[2] The One is the Good because it is Perfect Being and the positive being of creatures and positive being is good. As their being, so their value is God's communication of Himself. Did not Jesus say, God alone is good? This is Christian mysticism and Platonism.

In consequence of creatures' intrinsic limitation, the evil it effects and must effect, God cannot produce the good to be derived from His creation without evil, nor even without the degree of evil that actually has existed, exists or will exist. Because the Creator is utterly wise and good, wiser indeed than wise and better than good, the world He has created must be as free of evil as possible, though experience proves the possibility on this plane of material embodiment extremely restricted. If we call the good produced by creation X, the evil Y, Divine goodness could not have permitted Y, could X have been produced without Y or even with Y minus. That this is the best of all possible worlds its Creator is

[1] Sermon. Nolite Timere. French translation. Maitre Eckhardt, pp. 245–6.

[2] *Adornment of the Spiritual Marriage*, III. 3, 4. Trs. C. A. Wynschenk Dom.

guarantee, though such a best that it is a vale of tears. We are assured however by faith that God can and will, if we serve Him, render the evil He cannot prevent the means of our participation in His own bliss, make evil, though remaining such, the Cross which leads to Resurrection and Ascension, our entrance into the Lord's eternal joy.

Have I denied God's omnipotence? Not in any meaningful sense. God no doubt can do whatever is intrinsically possible. Power to do what is intrinsically impossible is a meaningless pseudo-conception, because self-contradictory. The fact that evil exists, though God is wisdom and goodness proves its prevention an intrinsic impossibility.

It may be objected, that, since God is inconceivable, we cannot know that it is a moral impossibility that He should cause or permit evil, not indispensable for the production of the good intended from creation. To which I reply: Though God exceeds inconceivably any value within the scope of human knowledge, He cannot fall short of any. Otherwise we must subscribe to the agnosticism which eradicates religion. For it holds it possible that ultimate reality may be less spiritual, less rational, less worthy, than a human soul acknowledging and pursuing moral and spiritual values. Such an agnosticism however the religious believer or spiritualist philosopher, the Platonist in particular, has decisively rejected.

Meanwhile the mystic's experience that positive being is good throughout, wholly good, confirms the metaphysician's affirmation.[1]

Our experience of prayer discloses an apparent contradiction. Prayer has not availed to save mankind from catastrophes produced by nature or human wickedness,

[1] See W. T. Stace, *Mysticism and Philosophy*, pp. 249–50.

did not, for example, avert the Messina earthquake or Hitler's mass exterminations. On the other hand there is abundant testimony that in individual cases prayer is heard; and even in the material order. I would suggest that the Divine Superenergy can answer prayer, can operate in this fashion, only from the level of spirit, where alone man can make vital contact with It. It is as when a deep boring discovers oil not to be reached on a more superficial level. That Jesus effected so few cures at Nazareth was not, we are told, because He would not, but that owing to His townsmen's lack of faith He could not.

The cures recorded from mediaeval shrines can hardly have been illusory. However credulous about their agency or method, the sick must surely know whether or not they have recovered or improved in health. I should conclude that, if such cures were so much more numerous then than in the Church today, it was because faith and its prayer were far commoner and, above all, far stronger and more unquestioning.

This prayer is the cry which the Psalms mention so insistently, the cry which the liturgy entreats may *reach* God, make contact with Him. It is in fact the sole prayer which can do so. It is a cry of the heart, understood as spirit, a veritable *cri de coeur*. How effective this prayer might be, if practised more frequently, more fervently and with greater faith, its *modus operandi* are in our present state of knowledge unknown. Nor can we decide whether its most striking and extraordinary effects are strictly speaking miraculous. For we cannot determine the limits within which material energy is naturally obedient to spiritual. An act of God is not simply as such a miracle. Though it deflects, it need not violate the operation of natural agents. A cure may be God's answer to prayer, even if its mechanism is natural.

Nor, since the human spirit is so deep rooted in God, can we demarcate precisely their respective action. We can but accept what evidence we have. In this prayer also religion is the affirmation of spirit, the penetration and transformation of the human spirit by the Divine Superspirit, however rudimentary in most cases it may be and difficult to recognise.

As a Catholic Platonist I receive the sum total of spiritual truth made known by Christ and His apostles and communicated by the Church in the course of her historical development, a development which, whatever its conceptual and exterior tergiversations, has been a progressive exploitation of spiritual riches. There has been a spiritual continuity, though the letter of its conceptual formulation may have been changed, even reversed. For whether in the Gospels or later these formulations have inevitably been conditioned by views of man, history and the world refuted by modern knowledge.

Even, St John of the Cross insists, should a vision or utterance be in fact from God we must not rely on its literal significance which may prove false. God imparts something better, a spiritual value, nay more, communicates Himself. Only by condescension to human weakness has He not communicated Himself purely and directly.[1] This too is the sense of Patmore's aphorism: 'God's promises are commonly broken to the letter and fulfilled past all hope to the spirit'.[2] This principle is also applicable to Divine Communications recorded in Scripture. St John in fact points out, and in this he follows Origen, that Jesus did not fulfil but contradicted the letter of the Messianic prophecies which promised worldly triumph and sovereignty. He fulfilled their spirit.

[1] *Ascent of Mount Carmel*, Bk. II, Ch. 18, 19.

[2] *Rod, Root and Flower*, Aurea Dicta XVIII.

The Jews however rejected Him, precisely because they were attached to their letter rather than to their spirit.[1] Moreover the principle enunciated by St John is applicable to doctrinal formulations. 'It is a fact of experience' writes a reviewer in the Downside Review[2] 'that Christianity does not supply us with an intellectual answer. ... It is the revelation of the great mystery of reality which it is surely our task, whether or no we are theologians, always to seek to penetrate and realise more deeply. We are not meant to cling to the static and ultimately illusory security which particular, limited dogmatic formulations of the inexpressible reality can give us.... Revealed truth experienced in faith does not give the "answers" ... it simply gives the certainty that there is a purpose and an answer which will be progressively realised in the life of the people of God.' Always we return to the same fundamental principle. The letter is not the spirit but its human and therefore fallible conceptualisation. The spirit is vital contact with incomprehensible truth. The principle after all is not new. It is the negative theology of St Gregory Nyssen and the pseudo-Denys, stated by Pope Gregory's dictum that the truest knowledge of God is to know that we cannot know Him.

In the same tradition of spiritual wisdom the French Oratorian contemplative De Condren warns us that God's communications inevitably condescend 'to the weakness of the human understanding'. He therefore

[1] *Ascent of Mount Carmel*, Bk. II, 19. 19. This rejection however was sincere. Guardians of the letter cannot accept its abrogation by the spirit. For they see themselves as the divinely appointed custodians of a sacred deposit of legal precepts or doctrinal formulas or an interpretation of a sacred scripture entrusted by God to their keeping which cannot therefore be superseded by a better expression of the spirit.

[2] January 1964.

'worshipped God and His mysteries as they are in themselves, not as he understood them'. The last words of his dying penitent Mlle de la Roche were in the same vein. 'I adore all that God is. I retreat from the being now present to me and withdraw into the unknown Being of God.'[1] This negative way to God was summed up most succinctly by the late Abbot Chapman: 'What do I mean by God? I have no idea.'[2] In the fourteenth century, we are told, the self-styled Areopagite's Mystical Theology ran through devout circles in England at 'deer rate'. The breathtaking close of this magnificent manifesto of mystical agnosticism, ultrapositive, not like the humanist's agnosticism negative, sums up this theology of the spirit. 'It,' the Divine Reality, 'is not anything such as we or any other being can have knowledge of.... Nor can the reason attain to it, to name it or to know it; nor is it darkness, nor is it light, or error, or truth; nor can any affirmation or negation apply to it.' For 'it transcends all affirmation'. 'It... does not live and is not life... nor can it be grasped by the understanding, since it is not knowledge or truth... nor is it one... nor Godhead or goodness: nor is it a spirit, as we understand the term... nor does it belong to the category of nonexistence or to that of existence.'[3]

How, it may well be asked, can we speak of such an unintelligible superbeing in personal terms, as though It were a superman? Negative theology, I answer, is one-way traffic. God is not less but infinitely more than man, infinitely more, not less, than human personality. We must therefore employ concerning Him personal

[1] Henri Brémond, *Histoire Littéraire du Sentiment Réligieux en France.* III, 383, 386–7.

[2] *Spiritual Letters*, Ed. 2, p. 59.

[3] *Mystical Theology*, Chapter V, trs. C. E. Rolt.

images and concepts as being the least unworthy at our disposal. But we should never forget that they are inconceivably short of the Truth and should keep this in mind by also using about God impersonal language, speaking of It as well as of Him. Personal and impersonal together express the superpersonal.

This negative theology, though the summit, is not of course the whole of theology. Experience of utterly incomprehensible Godhead, though God's supreme self-revelation is not his sole revelation. Mysteries concerning His Trinity, the relation of creatures to Himself, His operations, designs and decrees, His immanence in His creatures and incarnation, the redemption and deification of souls are objects of spiritual experience and its theological interpretation. Nevertheless God's complete transcendence, His immeasurable excess enters into all His communications to the human spirit imparting to them all a factor of unintelligibility, blending agnosticism with gnosis, ignorance with knowledge. As Faber well observed: 'all God's revelations of Himself are concealments also'. God 'makes himself known by hiding Himself'.[1] This principle, that all possible conceptualisation must be inadequate to the truth of Spirit and the utter Divine transcendence, is being applied throughout the field of a theology, in which recorded and transmitted experience is replacing today an external imposition of formulas, as themselves revealed truth, in short is reducing dogmatic to mystical theology.

To take an example: The doctrine of everlasting torment as stated by the letter of the Gospel and ecclesiastical doctrine translates in terms unacceptable to man's conscience today the truth that we can by our final and firm decision attain or lose God, either, at the close, it may be, of a purgatorial process, to enter fully

[1] *The Blessed Sacrament*, Bk. iii, Sections IV and II.

the Divine life or pass into the outer darkness of non-entity, annihilation, the most merciful doom possible upon a will fixed irrevocably in self-assertion. That a majority today accepts, even is content with this prospect, often welcomes it, does but measure their complete unawareness of the supreme issue or of their own spirit.

That so much in Scripture has been shown to be myth or legend does not disturb the Platonist who shares his master's valuation of myth as a vehicle for conveying truth beyond the grasp of reason. The withdrawal, enforced by the progress of science and historical research, to a theology of spiritual experience, though it must dismay and perplex, is withdrawal into that unfathomable depth which is the fertile womb of authentic theology and where the human spirit receives God's self-revelation. This withdrawal is the analogue and social counterpart of the withdrawal of the individual contemplative, described by the author of *The Cloud*, from imaginative and conceptual prayer to an adherence in the depths of spirit to the Godhead beyond image and concept.

When we study the letter of Scripture, the superficial meaning intended by the human writer, we are confronted by errors not only of factual statement but even of moral or theological teaching. For example the institution by the Old Law of the herem whereby all the living inhabitants of Jericho or the Amalekites, even their livestock, were consecrated to slaughter as a vast human sacrifice to Jahweh cannot be regarded as a decree of Divine Love. For the majority of Old Testament writers the sole life after death, if life it may be called, is the shrunken existence of a shade in a subterranean prison house, Sheol, an existence identical with that described in the Odyssey or the afterlife expected in pagan Mesopotamia, where good and bad share the same fate and are deprived for ever of communion with God: 'The dead praise thee not O Lord'. And as the Dominican archaeologist Roland De Vaux has told us,[1] rituals prescribed in the latest and most elaborate Code of Jewish law, the post-exilic Priestly Code, display features of primitive and magical superstition.

The law praised by the Psalmists as divine and everlasting was, as they understood it in the letter, the Jewish Torah which had in fact undergone a long process of development and for Christians has been superseded by the New Law. The spirit of the law, principles of moral choice, founded in the relation of man to God and in God to his fellows, the twofold ideal and norm of love persists and always will. Where the letter did not arise from the spirit and was irrelevant to it, it has been replaced by another letter, which, however, in so far as it has not derived from the spirit or has ceased to serve it, must in turn yield to a letter more flexible, because proceeding more immediately from the spirit and more directly determined by it. Those consequently who understand the Psalmists' praise of the Torah of its spirit rather than its letter, are truer to the meaning of God, though not to the meaning of the human writer. In this connection it is significant that the Jesuit Père Ribes detects in the present situation a striking analogy with the situation which confronted the Apostolic Church and in the responses to it made by the Second Vatican Council, an analogy, though not an exact parallel, with the response made by the Apostolic Council of Jerusalem, when it abolished for Gentile Converts—it

[1] *Ancient Israel. Its Life and Institutions*, trs. John McHugh, pp. 461–64.

would soon be for all Christians—the obligation to observe the Jewish law.[1]

If we turn to the New Testament is it credible that epilepsy is a diabolic possession, that the desert is devil haunted, that St Paul was caught up to a third heaven, that wives owe complete obedience to their husbands, that slavery, if humane, is morally permissible?

If however we turn from the letter to the spirit of Scripture, we become aware throughout of a profound and consistent orientation to God, a story of men finding God in experiences too deep for adequate enunciation, to be assimilated by prayer. What in the letter is incredible, at times even repulsive, yields to prayerful scrutiny, spiritual truths coming from God and leading us to Him. For the letter is the meaning of the human writer, the spirit God's meaning.

To this mystical or allegorical meaning of Scripture St Paul appeals.[2] It was the exegesis commonly practised by the primitive Church. Origen's preference of the spiritual to the literal sense is well known. For him the Old Testament signified only Christ and Christian doctrine. In general, whenever a command or statement of Scripture is unworthy of God, the literal sense must be rejected, the spiritual alone received. Indeed the incredibility or immorality of the letter forces the spiritual sense upon us.[3]

St Augustine's journey towards the Church, so he tells us in his Confessions, was assisted by St Ambrose's sermons, in which he would 'often times most diligently recommend this text for a rule. "The letter" (of Scrip-

[1] Article on 'True and False Novelty in the Church', *Etudes*, March 1965.

[2] I Corinthians x. 1–12. Galatians iv.

[3] Daniélou, *Origène et la Bible*, Ch. 11, esp. 149.

ture) "killeth but the Spirit giveth life"; whilst he drew aside the mystic veil laying open spiritually what according to the letter seemed to teach something unsound.'[1] In the two concluding books he himself exemplifies this exegesis by interpreting the account of creation in Genesis not literally but allegorically, according to the spirit not the letter. And he admits the possibility and profit of extracting from a passage of Scripture a variety of truths.[2] We may also cite St Jerome's words, quoted by the Catholic exegete Van Hoonacker:[3] 'It would take me too long,' wrote St Jerome, 'to explain the entire legend (fabula) of Samson' (his name means sun man) 'of the true sun, Jesus Christ', and he interprets other texts in the same fashion. No doubt, as mediaeval ignorance of history and lack of criticism would lead us to expect, the fundamentalism of a literal exegesis was also upheld. But at any rate as regards the Old Testament, it was the spiritual sense which Catholics prized and which fed their devotion.

Bede's valuation is typical. 'The literal' meaning of Scripture 'is a veil which has to be drawn aside to reveal the spiritual sense; it is the bark one must strip off to come to the pith; it is the shadow of the allegorical truth. When one translates the literal sense into the spiritual, it is the change of water into wine, like rolling the stone away from our uncomprehending hearts.'[4]

On the first page of every Bible I would have inscribed those lines of Dante:

[1] *Confessions of St Augustine*, Bk. VI, 4–6, trs. E. B. Pusey.

[2] Later Augustine became chary of this allegorical interpretation and preferred literal interpretations. In this, as in some other respects, his second thoughts do not improve upon his first.

[3] Van Hoonacker, *Les Douze Petits Prophètes*, Introduction to *Jonas*, pp. 322–23.

[4] *St Bede*, Donald Nicholl. With references to the passages cited. In *Pre-Reformation English Spirituality*, p. 5.

O voi ch'avete li'intelletti sani
Mirate la dottrina che s'asconde
Sotto il velame de li versi strani.

O ye of sound intelligence give heed to the teaching concealed beneath the veil of these strange lines.[1]

From Genesis to the Apocalypse we are spectators of a war waged in public and in private, socially and in the individual conscience between man seeking to deify himself by his knowledge and will and man being deified by humble reception of God's gift of Himself. A solidarity of evil, man from the beginning until now asserting himself in disregard of God, has confronted a solidarity of good, man admitting his entire lack of value apart from God and in process of transformation by loving obedience to Him, the total Adam at grips with the total Christ and overcome by the latter.

Since sin is essentially man's self-assertion against obedience to God, as he hears or believes himself to hear God's will in his conscience, every deliberate sin adheres to the solidarity of sinful mankind, because it adheres to the foundation of all human sin. Few, if any, who recite the Miserere psalm are, in peacetime at any rate, guilty of murder. Yet they pray: 'Deliver me from the guilt of bloodshed'. This prayer can be sincere, only in as much as by their sin they have affirmed the principle of which murder is a product and expression, self-will defying the will of God. This truth is strikingly expressed if, as has been most plausibly suggested[2] a source of Genesis attached a legend of murder, originally related in an entirely different context, to the sacred myth of the fall

[1] *Inferno*, IX, 61–63.
[2] *Bible de Jérusalem*, Note to Genesis, iv.

as its immediate consequence, making the first murderer the son of the first sinners.

The sin of the earliest men must have been in itself slight. For their conscious reason can have little exceeded that of their sub-human forbears. Nevertheless it was the first trickle, welling up from the ground of human self-assertion, of what would become a wide river of sin, a persistent pretence to autonomy, man's claim to be his own master, an attempted self-deification, more deliberate and arrogant today than at any time in the past. This collective sin is opposed, both socially and in the disintegrated individual by the communion which is the total Christ, Head and members engaged, both socially and in the individual soul in the crucifixion of self-will and the resurrection of the new man, being deified by God to whom he submits.

This entire obedience to God, this complete theocentrism, was, as Fr Baker points out in the most forceful terms, exemplified supremely by Jesus. 'Our blessed Lord as Man, having a most perfect knowledge, perception and feeling of the nothingness of creatures and the absolute totality of God, did . . . most profoundly humble Himself before the Divine Majesty of His Father, remaining continually plunged in the abyss of His own nothing. . . . As a creature He saw nothing in Himself but the nothing of a creature and in all other creatures He saw nothing but God.'[1]

Sartre has spoken of man's craving for deification, his desire to become God, which however, since God does not exist, is doomed to frustration. 'Man is the being who proposes to be God. . . . The notion of God is self-

[1] *Holy Wisdom.* The Second Treatise, Sect. II, Ch. xiii, 13. My attention was drawn to this passage by Sidney Spencer, *Mysticism in World Religion*, p. 248.

contradictory and we spend our endeavours in vain. Man is a fruitless passion.'[1] God, however, does exist. Indeed this desire itself witnesses to His existence, as, despite Russell, hunger to the existence of food. If man will but abandon all attempts, however indirect or camouflaged, at self-deification, he can be deified by God's free gift of Himself. Self-consciousness, which as *The Cloud of Unknowing* teaches[2] is the root of self-assertion and therefore of sin, will be replaced by God-consciousness, God's own consciousness imparted to a created spirit. And in the process, for most but a beginning for no mortal completed, man can achieve and secure all the values of a worthy humanism.

Creatures which, as substitutes for God, are idols (for this reason Scripture, spiritually understood, accounts idolatry so foolish but so fatal a sin)[3] are now images fittingly venerated as manifestations of God, not substitutes for Him.

Idolatry may also be committed more subtly by accepting as final or sufficient an unworthy conception of God, for example when He is envisaged as the celestial chairman of a watch committee to prevent or punish

[1] Quoted in *Etudes*, November 1963.

[2] Ch. 43, 44.

[3] The literal protest against the veneration of images, justified only until the exclusive worship of Yahweh had been firmly established, though continued throughout the early centuries of the Catholic Church, was later abandoned, and its reintroduction by the Reformers' biblical literalism was a disaster fatal to visual religious art, wherever it established itself. The deplorable iconoclasm of the Church when she destroyed the artistic treasure of pagan temples and images was at least compensated by Catholic art from the erection of Sancta Sophia to the baroque art of the seventeenth and eighteenth centuries. For the *volte face* on this matter, see Professor Hilary Armstrong's article 'Human Religion', *The Month*, December 1964.

sexual misdemeanours,[1] or more generally as the guardian of a political, social or even ecclesiastical establishment. Both forms of idolatry are combined, when in wartime the state is accorded, as consistently by Catholic and other Christian ecclesiastics, a sovereign power over its subjects' lives and conscience which belongs to God alone and God is proclaimed and worshipped as its Divine champion. The outbreak of war, like a draught from Circe's poisoned chalice, can transform a clergy, otherwise devoted to God's service, into fanatical idolaters zealously enslaving their flocks body and soul to the national idol, however evil its intention or unjust its cause, to be obeyed, even should it command the massacre of civilian populations. Most subtle however is the idolatry which in the individual's spiritual life clings to image and concept or is ignorant of any purer prayer, though the Divine Mystery invites the soul to find Him without image or concept in the depths of spirit.[2]

The redemptive process by which the solidarity of sin is vanquished is not the *exclusive* work of the historic Jesus. To be effective it must be continuous, as continuous as the process of sinful human self-assertion and self-deification which it conquers by apparent defeat. It must be continued in the individual spirit which can ascend into the glory of completed deification only by sharing, here or hereafter, Jesus' birth and death, resurrection and ascension. It must be continued socially in the redemptive process of Christ's entire mystical body, continuing and completing the redemption accomplished by

[1] Even Dante could believe that God punished Florence by a bloody defeat because the dresses of the Florentine women were too *décolletées* (*Purgatorio* XXIII, 97–112). The theology of a Victorian maiden aunt.

[2] St John of the Cross denounces this ultimate idolatry in the lengthy digression he inserted into his *Living Flame of Love*, III, 14–21.

its Head. For Head and body are one total Christ. Apart from the head the members of a body are powerless, apart from the members, the head. If Jesus is truly the Head of His mystical body, surely He cannot act otherwise than in accordance with the nature of a head, that is to say, not without the members' co-operation. If He is the vine, His members the branches, a vine *cannot* grow and be fruitful, without branches and the fruit they bear. Though no particular member or branch may be indispensable for the accomplishment of Jesus' work, man's redemption and transformation, members, branches are. The total Christ is God's human incarnation, the total Christ dies and rises from the dead, the total Christ ascends into God. In Dame Julian's 'Shewing'[1] the servant who falls, rises and fulfils his Lord's behest is at once Adam, the total Adam and Christ, the total Christ. The liturgy speaks of the redemption effected by the tears of Mary, by extension the Church. 'May the tears of God's mother, sufficient to cleanse a sinful world, obtain our salvation.'[2] My disobedience, that is to say, is redeemed, not alone by Jesus' obedience unto death, but in union with that obedience by the sacrificial deaths of martyrs, the sacrificial lives and sorrows of saints who without bodily martyrdom died to self and in God are alive.

Devotion has been wont to dwell compassionately on the passion of Jesus. If the historical passion is its object, is not this compassion as unreal as grief for the suffering of a friend whose agonising cancer has been completely and finally cured, and who is assured of perfect health henceforward? If however we contemplate, as we should, Christ's continued passion in His members, whereby, as Pascal remarked, He is in agony until the end of the

[1] *Revelations of Divine Love*, Ch. 51.

[2] *Feast of the Seven Sorrows.* Office hymn at Lauds.

world, this compassion, whether in liturgical celebration, private prayer or in the contemplation of works of sacred art is not only valuable but necessary. To this compassion Belsen and Hiroshima are Calvaries where it may stand at the foot of the Cross. For it is not, or should not be, a sterile emotion, but the genuine compassion which enters into this continuous redemption.

Man's deification has been well stated in terms of the Platonic-Aristotelian philosophy by a Jesuit Pole, De Letter.[1] Though God cannot enter into composition with 'anything created', not even, one might add, the humanity of Christ, 'by grace "God" is . . . the Act of our souls. . . . The Divine form or perfection is imparted to the divinised soul. The uncreated Act gives himself to the soul, the soul is truly made divine. It is not however made God or turned into God; it in no way fuses with the Divine Act. God is not the form but only the quasi-form', I would suggest rather the superform, 'of the soul. . . . He allows and causes the soul to be united to Him, and, as it were, to draw Divinity from Him without in any way being affected by this union'. That is to say, though God identifies creatures with Himself, He does not, indeed He cannot, identify Himself with them. There is 'a communication to the soul of the "form" of God, so as to divinise the soul: the Union is transforming'. 'The union of the soul' with God 'is its actuation by the Uncreated Act.' 'The Divine Object . . . transforms into Itself or assimilates and unites with Itself the subject or principle of Activity.' Mystics, and with particular clarity and detail St John of the Cross, have described this 'transforming union' as experienced in this life by a few privileged spirits, experience of the union in which the spirit has been transformed by the 'form' of God.

[1] *Irish Theological Quarterly*, July 1960.

What more, it may be asked, is or could be the hypostatic union? I must confess I have found little meaning in the explanations of traditional theology. Moreover, a tendency is visible among certain contemporary theologians—of its extent and scope I am uninformed, call it Nestorian, if you will—to admit that Jesus possessed a human centre or source of psychic acts, an 'Aktcentrum'[1] which surely is what is normally meant by a person. The distinction, I would suggest, between Jesus' union with God and that of His members when their deification is complete is that His humanity, unlike theirs, was created in this state of deification 'in the form of God'. That is to say He is and always has been deified by nature, but His members by God's subsequent gift, by grace. Do we not pray that 'we may be found in His form',[2] transformed, as He was formed, by God's super-formation? In this connection it is noteworthy that the simile of material[3] transformed by the fire which inflames it, then of course regarded as an external element, was employed by Origen and other theologians of the early Church to illustrate the hypostatic union, before it became the mystics' stock illustration of the transforming union. The writer of Second Peter affirms that God has promised us a share in the Divine Nature.[4] Accordingly the Divine Voice which at the Transfiguration proclaimed Jesus 'my beloved son' is understood by the Collect for the Feast to foretell His members' adoptive sonship. The Preface for the Ascension declares that Jesus 'was raised up to heaven to grant us a share in His Godhead'. And a

[1] So Michael Schmaus, *Katholische Dogmatik*, Vol. II, reviewed in *Theologische und Praktische Quartalschrift*, 1964, Vol. 3.

[2] Secret of the Christmas Midnight Mass.

[3] Iron, later wood. See G. L. Prestige, *Fathers and Heretics* (Bampton Lectures) pp. 221–22.

[4] II Peter i. 4.

secret prays: 'O God ... who dost make us to share the One Supreme Godhead'.[1]

Such also is the language of saints. 'My Me' (myself), exclaimed St Catherine of Genoa, 'is God. Nor do I recognise any other Me' (self) 'except God Himself. My Being is God ... by a true transformation of my Being. God is my Being, my Me.'[2] And recently Sister Elizabeth of the Trinity, in my judgment a more instructive mystical theologian than her canonised fellow Carmelite, writing to her sister, makes her own an apostrophe addressed by Lacordaire to Mary Magdalen at the Sepulchre: 'No longer ask for Jesus from anyone on earth or in heaven. For He is your soul and your soul is He.'[3] Biographers of St Catharine of Siena and St Catharine Ricci relate visual hallucinations in which the saint's face was changed into the bearded countenance of Jesus.[4] Were they not symbolic representations of the transforming union which these saints had received, the superformation of their spirit by the Divine Form which had superformed Jesus' spirit from the first instant of His existence?

Neither forming nor transforming union however can exempt any man from the need to conceptualise and imagine the spiritual truths he perceives in terms of his environment, cannot therefore render him immune from its limitations. A man exempt from ignorance would not be truly human. Nor has the emotional presentation and sentimental image of Jesus current in popular Catholic and Protestant devotion, done anything to counter-

[1] 18th Sunday after Pentecost.

[2] *Vita* quoted by Von Hügel, *The Mystical Element of Religion*, Vol. I (Ed. 1) Ch. 6, pp. 265–66.

[3] *Souvenirs*, pp. 155–56.

[4] St Catharine of Siena's earliest biographer, Bl. Raymond of Capua, witnessed this symbolic transfiguration.

balance a psychological Docetism. Jesus' human ignorance is evident from the Gospels. The truth, for example, of everlasting loss is conceived as endless suffering, the assurance that the Kingdom of God is being established is distorted by contemporary apocalyptic expectations into the conviction that the second coming and the end of the world are imminent, must happen before that generation had passed away.[1] The wisdom conveyed by the parable of 'the empty house swept and garnished' is stated in the language of popular demonology. Certainly we must commit our needs in trustful prayer to our Heavenly Father. Not however because He feeds the birds in hard winters, when in fact multitudes perish, because 'they do not gather into barns'. Presumably this was less evident in Palestine than in colder climates.

Exegetes are agreed that the book of Jonah is a didactic fiction. Jesus therefore was mistaken in regarding it as a historical fact. The Ninevites did not, as He believed, repent at the prophet's warning. And He was amazed at the centurion's faith, something, evidently, He had neither known nor expected.

Jesus' assurance moreover of perfect union with God was accompanied by liability to temptations, agony at the prospect of His passion. At every turn the contrast between letter and spirit recurs, between a letter of fallible mortality, a spirit divine.

The solidarity of the total Christ is spiritual, a communion of spirits united in their union with God. Its nature would seem to have been misconceived by many

[1] This belief is not incompatible with Jesus' institution of a Church and sacraments. The Catholic Apostolic Church was founded by Irving's disciples and equipped with an elaborate hierarchy and ritual, precisely to prepare for the Second Advent confidently expected at latest before the death of their last surviving Apostle. (cf. John xxi. 22–24).

of our Catholic liturgical reformers. For they look for Christian solidarity in a middle distance, where it is to find expression in a hearty fellowship of Christians gathered together to partake in a common meal, the Eucharistic altar viewed as primarily the supper table of God's people. The contemplative, if they give him a thought, is selfish and self-indulgent, engrossed in his personal sanctification. In fact *The Cloud of Unknowing*, a classic of mystical theology, insists that the contemplative *cannot* pray as an isolated individual. His prayer must necessarily be with and for his fellow men. 'A soul that is perfectly disposed to this work', the prayer of infused aspirations 'and thus oned with God in spirit doth what in it is to make all men as perfect in this work as itself is . . . Christ is our Head and we be His limbs, if we be in charity, and who so will be a perfect disciple of Our Lord's must strain up his spirit in this ghostly work for the salvation of all his brethren and sisters in nature as Our Lord did His body on the Cross . . . generally for all mankind.'[1] Dame Julian's *Revelations of Divine Love* are addressed to the entire body of her fellow Christians, nothing to herself in particular. 'That which I say of me, I say in the person of all mine even Christians. For I am taught in the ghostly shewing of our Lord God that He meaneth so. . . . If I look singularly to myself, I am right nought, but in general I am . . . in oneness of charity with all mine even Christians.'[2] 'Let no one,' says Baker in his Commentary on the Cloud, his *Secretum*, 'blame contemplatives . . . because they do not expressly pray for others dead or alive. In and by such exercises those offices towards others are performed in the best manner. For loving God' contemplatives 'love all creatures. . . . And in the exercise of love towards God nothing is

[1] *The Cloud of Unknowing*, Ch. 25.

[2] *Revelations of Divine Love*, Ch. 8 and 9.

neglected, but all things are in it performed and satisfied.' 'Those inexpressible devotions which' contemplatives 'exercise and in which they *tacitly* involve the needs of the whole Church are far more prevalent with God than the busy endeavours of ten thousand others. A few such secret and unknown servants of God are . . . the strength and bulwarks of the kingdoms and churches where they live.'[1]

This community however is a communion of spirits, a communion of prayer. Whether or not it is expressed by a vocal unison is comparatively of slight importance. The Mass itself, however privately celebrated, is the supreme external expression of the solidarity of Christian prayer. In the depths of prayer the individual's communion with God is one with the same communion of his fellows in God, is the deepest experience and most powerful operation of this community. In their campaign against a discredited letter Catholic reformers often seem too ready to jettison the spirit it expressed. It is impossible to read their manifestos attentively without becoming aware of a tendency to exalt love of our fellow men above the *first and greatest* commandment or more strictly, ideal on which alone it can rightly be based, the love of God.[2]

Outside a Congregational chapel I read recently:

[1] *Secretum.* Commentary on Ch. 3 of *The Cloud of Unknowing.* McCann's arrangement (Orchard Edition of *Cloud*) and McCann, *The Confessions of Father Baker*, Ch. 1.

[2] I have long been disquieted by a *commandment* to love God with our entire heart and our neighbour as ourself. To command the impossible must surely produce discouragement, self-deception or lack of serious endeavour. The fulfilment of this twofold love must however be the goal finally reached by transformed and deified souls and meanwhile is the norm by which the morality of our conduct must be judged good or bad, better or worse in the measure it approaches or departs from it.

Christianity 1965
Not so much a religion
More a way of life.

This path leads to religion's doom. To subordinate religion to ethics is to misconceive its nature and deal it a mortal blow. Our wayside pulpiteer betrays in fact an awareness of this when he exalts 'a way of life' above '*religion*'.

Our Catholic reformers, I fear, are too frequently setting their feet on this fatal road. Worship, above all Eucharistic, is no longer adoration of the Divine Mystery and entrance into it but rather the sacrament of a human community, a table fellowship. There seems little realisation that man has no value save as related to God and capable of receiving Him. Though his application of the principle may have been in some respects faulty, St Augustine whose genius lay in his powerful grasp and imposing presentation of fundamental religious insights, spoke truly when he said that man has nothing *of his own* but lies and sin. For everything he is or has in any respect good proceeds from God, is His communication, His reflection on a lower plane of being. Even could I be convinced of atheism, to make the supposition for argument's sake, I should not therefore worship man, man whose follies and crimes are writ so large on the pages of history. Without God the centre of his being is a void. The only justifiable humanism is theist, the most satisfactory Christian.

In his important book *The Holy* Otto has shown that the core, indeed essence of religion, is experience of the 'numinous', awareness of a Mystery at once awe-inspiring and fascinating, *mysterium tremendum et fascinans.* He admitted that precisely this numinous quality is absent from Protestant worship, present in Catholic. Indeed he makes suggestions for introducing it into Lutheran worship. Today it is Catholics who would deprive Catholic worship of its numinous character. The features which foster it, the hierarchic Latin, the incense, lights, vestments, bells, the solemn Elevation are attacked or disparaged, because they render the Mass less intelligible to the contemporary man in the pew. Only a liturgical language stylised and archaic is fitted to suggest the numinous. The numinous however, the heart of religion, cannot be replaced by the good fellowship of a common meal. Human fellowship, no doubt, is an excellent thing. But its place is the pub, the club, the ballroom, the church hall, not the church. The union of worshippers is on a far deeper level, is their common yet individual experience and adoration of the numinous Mystery, the Eucharistic communion, by which they enter it. Though the Mass when sown was enclosed in a supper, an Agape, when the seed had germinated the growing plant soon shed an envelope no longer protecting it but restricting its growth.

The spiritual realities with which religion is concerned are of their nature incomprehensible, to be experienced, not understood. An all too vulgar tongue, a congregation of hearty and benevolent Christians gathered round a supper table must destroy the numinous character, the sense of mystery hitherto the life of Catholic worship. The letter of traditional Catholicism, when it conflicts with modern knowledge, cannot be made credible by debasing the traditional liturgy to the standards of contemporary bad taste. It is a painful reflection that throughout the debates of the recent Vatican Council little, if anything, has been said of ceremonial beauty, of the liturgy's historical growth or of contemplative prayer, matters integral and indispensable to a satisfying religion.

Since Luther turned away from the mysticism of the

'German Theology' he published, mystical theology has been less regarded in Protestant Christianity than in any other variety of higher religion. Protestant mystics have been far fewer and far less appreciated than Catholic, have belonged mainly to a left wing on the fringe of the established Churches, disparaged, sometimes persecuted, by their representatives. Mystics such for example as Boehme, Frankenberg, Tersteegen, Rous or the Platonists Sterry and Smith, the ecumenical mystic Poiret, many Quakers especially in the Friends' earlier years, Boehme's English exponent Law or the ecstatic Teresa of Welsh Nonconformity, Anne Griffiths, were by no means representative of Protestant spirituality. Indeed Frankenberg's disciple Scheffler, 'Angelus Silesius' was converted to the Catholic Church by Protestant hostility to mysticism.

An overflow of Catholic mysticism into English religion in the seventeenth century was a backwash against the current of established Protestant religion. For when Protestant dogmatic theology was most hostile to Catholic, Catholic devotional and mystical literature fed the spiritual life of many Protestants. When for example Sir Thomas Browne in the conclusion of his *Hydriotaphia* speaks of 'Christian annihilation, exstasis, exolution, liquefaction, transformation, the kiss of the Spouse, gustation of God' he evidently has in mind works of the Counter Reformation mystics. And Ritschl's monumental *History of Pietism* (*Geschichte des Pietismus*) is dominated by his conviction that not only mysticism but even the emotional and experiential devotion of Pietism are Catholicising deviations from pure Protestant religion. Similarly baroque art, the art of the Counter Reformation, overflowed into Protestant countries, as in the Frauenkirche in Dresden, London's St Paul's, churches by Wren, Gibbs and Hawksmoor, and later Frederick the Great's rococo architecture at Berlin and Potsdam.

Luther's withdrawal from the contemplative and mystical background of religion to its middle distance has been in general continued by Protestantism. By and large it has indeed been a religion of middle distance, its foreground trim and tidy, carefully weeded of the rank growth of the Catholic foreground, popular superstitions, but lacking religion's mystical background. This withdrawal to the spirit's middle distance has been most obviously and most massively expressed by Protestant rejection of the religious life, the life dedicated to prayer.[1] The theology and worship of institutional Protestantism have been cemented to a Biblical fundamentalism, severed from its spiritual and contemplative background and today no longer tenable. The withdrawal, that is to say, has been twofold, from the background of Catholic religion to this fundamentalist middle distance, from its foreground of ceremony, symbolism, folklore, colourful, if extravagant, hagiography.

The entire works of Luther and Calvin weigh light in the balance against such pre-reformation mystical masterpieces as *The Cloud of Unknowing*, Dame Julian's *Revelations*, the Spiritual Writings of Bernard, Hugh and Richard of St Victor, William of St Thierry, Bonaventure, Tauler, Ruysbroek, Nicholas of Cusa. And their mystical tradition attained new summits in the Church of the Counter Reformation with St Teresa, St John of the Cross, and what Brémond has termed the mystical invasion of France. To the religious foreground

[1] Many Catholic reformers unfortunately are pursuing the same goal indirectly. Following the ecclesiastical policy of that 'enlightened' despot, Joseph II who suppressed the contemplative orders in his dominions, they are seeking to transform them into active.

and background alike the Church held fast. Baroque art and this splendid array of mystics are sufficient justification of Trent's refusal to compromise with the Reformation.

Is such a judgment ecumenical? I appeal to mystical theology. What more ecumenical than a world-wide experience of the human spirit? But it is an ecumenism of the depths, not the surface, of the background, not the middle distance. Ecumenism should be founded on mysticism, Christian unity arise from the insights of a contemplative prayer shared by men and women of diverse ecclesiastical allegiance.

In the same vein Luther, followed by his official successors, rejected the spiritual or 'mystical' understanding of Scripture, particularly of the Old Testament, which as its fuller sense, *sensus plenior*, had fed the devotion of Catholics. A striking illustration is the mediaeval sequence which delights to accumulate allegorical meanings of Old Testament episodes. Unfortunately the Protestant distaste for this 'mystical' interpretation of Scripture is shared by modern Catholic exegetes. Unfortunately; for the spirit of Scripture rather than its letter, not the external meaning intended by the human writer but the inner meaning in which the Holy Spirit speaks to the Christian reader is its true meaning and the only meaning indestructible by the conclusions of critical scholarship.[1]

For ceremonial beauty only the Catholicising school of Anglicanism and the Catholic Apostolic Church have been concerned. Are we in the name of ecumenism to take the Protestant road? We should rather adopt for

[1] The spiritual sense of Scripture however may be better discerned by looking deeper than the often fanciful play of patristic and mediaeval allegorists.

our motto the words of Psalm 117:[1] '*Ordinate pompam cum frondibus densis*'. 'Set the procession in array' lavishing the resources of liturgical art on the beauty of divine worship, but, otherwise this would be no more than aestheticism, 'with the dense foliage' of contemplative prayer. Such was in fact the ideal of post Tridentine Catholicism splendid alike in its art and its mysticism. Can we believe that the contrary tendencies, prevalent at the Council, a liturgy simplified and superficially intelligible and a middle distance view of religion are a manifestation of the same spirit? Or can we hope for results equally valuable? Hardly.

Since religion is concerned with that which we cannot understand, to attempt this intelligibility is to pursue a will-o'-the-wisp. Liturgical formulas should evoke from the depths of spirit what is beyond and above reason. If the language of worship is too comprehensible superficially, its superficial incredibility becomes obvious. Like other poems liturgical poetry and ceremonial drama defy translation. The purpose of liturgy, as on the kindred, though lower, level of poetry is to make present the ultimate Mystery, not to explain it away. The object of religion is the Eternal. It should therefore find expression in unchanging rituals. Where these are immoral or false to the truth of spirit they must indeed be changed. Not however for merely factual or conceptual error. For, when they speak of what lies beyond the domain of legalist moral decrees or conceptualisations of spiritual insights, they fix the worshipper's spirit on immutable truths comprised in God's self-revelation to man. And their fixity frees us from a distracting and confusing flux of novelties. That the Introit sung this Epiphany greeted Henry II, when in 1154 he landed at Southampton with the proclamation of a ruler's advent:

[1] New Latin Translation.

Ecce advenit Dominator, that the Litany chanted at Rogationtide is substantially the litany sung by Augustine and his fellow missionaries in 597 invites my spirit to attach itself to God's immutable Majesty or to the communion of saints as the total Christ abiding above the ever-flowing stream of time. Contemplation is of the abiding and unchanging; therefore it should not be hindered by frequent and needless change.

Religious aggiornamento is with the truth as such unchanging, though progressively discovered, but in the first place with eternity. Not however with fashions or facts of feeling or thought, valuation or interest. Nor should we prefer language more immediately intelligible to more expressive or richer significance. Of this our reformers seem unaware.

It may be replied that the present changes are restoring the worship of the primitive Church. Surely the flower should not be surrendered for the budding plant, the full grown tree replaced by the sapling. Liturgical flowering and mature growth have been reached long since, many centuries more than a millennium. Though the doctrine and hierarchy of the early Church were Catholic, its lack of ritual was Protestant. Beauty is the sign manual of truth.[1] When the bare worship of the primitive Church blossomed into the loveliness of a fully developed ceremonial, the truth of Catholic Christianity was made manifest.

The prospect for Catholic liturgy is dark. Already the chain of the canonical hours of prayer has been wantonly broken. No longer is the Psalter, compendium of

[1] To produce an adequate artistic expression however, insights of religious truth must be integrated with insights of truth in other spheres of knowledge, e.g. philosophy, science and history. For want of such integration, Lourdes lacks the beauty of Chartres.

Old Testament Scripture and the common prayer of Christians and Jews, recited in its entirety every week by the Church's liturgical ministers. Prime was wont to bless the beginning of daily work, a blessing invoked with the force of a triple repetition unique in the liturgical office. The Church prayed that the splendour of the Divine Daylight might enlighten us and guide our daily task. And the office concluded on the note that the sum of all the blessings is God Himself. All this is no more. Prime has been discarded on the plea that it duplicates Lauds which in fact it supplements. Nor are the clergy any longer summoned three times between morning and evening to withdraw a few minutes from the press of their occupations into the presence of God, to renew their strength at its source. Because the pressure is greater today, though the greater therefore the need of this retreat, once is now reckoned enough. And these things are but the beginning of liturgical revolution.

'In Christianity what exquisite beauty lies in the movement of the Mass.' These are the words of an expert critic of the ballet, Arnold Haskell.[1] Havelock Ellis also saw the Mass as a work of art and moreover saw in it not merely an aesthetic spectacle but the presentation of a spiritual mystery and a means of communion with it.[2] Unlike secular ballet this sacred dance is not the product of deliberate craftsmanship. It has developed over the centuries, no artefact but a natural growth, product of the interaction between a cultural environment and a profound awareness of the mystery it expresses. Unhappily a masterpiece of subtle and intricate rhythm is all too easily destroyed.

[1] *The Dance.* His Contribution, No. 15, to the Downside Symposium 'Arts, Artists and Thinkers'.

[2] See my quotations from Ellis in *Men and Tendencies*, 'Havelock Ellis', p. 122 et. sqq.

The traditional liturgy however with its wealth of spiritual significance remains on record and available to us, to be appreciated, pondered and prayed. Even a novel liturgy, however wanton may be its breach with historical tradition, whatever its failure to convey the numinous value of solemn ritual and hieratic speech, may surely be expected to strike like its predecessor four notes, persistent prayer for light, for life, for peace and for health. Light of reason but still more light of spirit, life activating a man on every level of his being but in his spirit God's eternal life, profound peace arising from the spirit's contemplative union with God, the balanced health of mind and body which enables spiritual light and peace to permeate its possessor and exercise their psychiatry unimpeded: for these the liturgy importunes. Whosoever is richly endowed with these is at once deep and broad, responsive to all human values but detached from all. In the hymn for Sext, composed to be sure where noons are hotter than ours, we pray: 'Quench the flames of strife; Banish harmful heat; Bestow a healthy body and peace of spirit'. The recipe for happiness.

Admittedly this liturgical ideal has not been altogether that of traditional Catholic holiness. Even a Saint Ignatius could forget the content of his sacerdotal prayer when he forbade us to prefer health to disease. But this treasure is open to all to be duly prized and to integrate man's life.

Above all, the supreme and inexhaustible treasure of Catholic mystical theology remains for us untouched and untouchable by fluctuations of human taste or interest, of ecclesiastical policy or theological opinion. Mystical experience is not indeed confined to Catholicism or Christianity. I do not question that in all the oriental religions contemplatives can attain and have attained a supernatural mystical prayer, the experienced union with God possessed by Christian mystics.[1] But it is, I believe, better stated and understood by Catholic mystical tradition, stated and understood more comprehensively, because enriched by distinctive insights of spiritual truth and better related to the sum total of human experience. At the very least we of the Christian tradition would be better advised to seek a spiritual wisdom at home rather than in a context wholly alien and for us most difficult to interpret.

There is a Buddhist image of the jewel in the lotus. If by the lotus we understand the traditional theological conceptualisations of Christian wisdom as it has been experienced, we must admit that its petals are wilting. But the jewel, the wisdom of the spirit, *sapientia cordis*, abides in its pristine and imperishable brilliance.

There may well be times when the persistent pressure of a secularist environment, the humanists' conceited self-assurance, the impossibility with our present knowledge of harmonising all the truths discovered by the sciences with the truths of which the spirit is dimly but powerfully aware oppress the mind, overcloud its certainties and make the spiritual experience recorded and taught from the New Testament onward by Catholic contemplatives seem illusory. This will be the test of faith, and its opportunity. But a void at the heart of men's life, a final insignificance, the inevitable collapse of all attempts at human self-deification will sooner or later reward this faith by evoking a religion as deep as

[1] Whether the Satori of Zen Buddhism is, as Professor Zaehner would appear to hold, a natural mystical experience of God *exclusively* as immanent or is identical with the experienced union which Baker describes in his *Remains* in which the Divine Nothing, God apprehended without image or concept identifies with Himself a human Nothing, a spirit emptied of image or concept, I am uncertain.

in the past but richer, because more comprehensive. The letter of former doctrine, the inevitable conceptual formulation of contemplative insight will be transfigured by the glory of its spiritual understanding. We are faced with an inexorable alternative. Go in from the letter of Catholic Christianity to the spirit or go out into the desert of scepticism and frustration. For the former this essay has been a heartfelt plea.

A spiritual understanding, reserved hitherto for a minority of contemplatives, will be extended widely to all who without it would lose hold of religion altogether.

Such I believe, unless man's criminal lunacy should destroy human civilisation, possibly the human race, will be the Third Kingdom of the Spirit fulfilling the promise and partial achievement of the Second. As the Catholic Church succeeded the Synagogue, the Church of the Third Kingdom will succeed the Church of the Second.[1] I do not expect a revelation of new doctrines but a spiritual rather than a literal understanding of the old. At the advent of the Second dispensation, the dispensation of the Risen Lord and the Catholic Church, there was a withdrawal that was also an ascent from the letter to the spirit. Speaking of this St Paul observed: 'The Lord is the Spirit and where the Spirit of the Lord is there is freedom'. 'For freedom Christ has set us free; . . . do not submit again to a yoke of slavery.'[2] The time however was not in fact ripe for a wholly spiritual dispensation, a dispensation in which the letter is admitted to be the spirit's human and fallible expression. In its stead there has been a dispensation in which the letter, though enclosing and sheltering a spiritual dispensation, the wis-

[1] This expectation founded on an attempt to read 'the signs of the times' I have entertained for some fifty years past. It is stated in a book of verse published in 1917.

[2] II Corinthians iii. 17. Galatians v. 1.

THE AUTHORS

MICHAEL DE LA BEDOYERE, formerly Editor of the *Catholic Herald*, founded the independent privately circulated newsletter, *Search*, four years ago. Today, *Search*, available only by annual subscription from 59 West Cromwell Road, London S.W.5, England or P.O. Box 102, Garden City, Michigan, U.S.A., is read in nearly all countries of the world.

YVONNE LUBBOCK, author of *Return to Belief*, is a housewife and lives in Hildenborough, Kent.

BERNARDINE BISHOP, herself a novelist, is the wife of the pianist Stephen Bishop, and daughter of Bernard Wall and Barbara Wall, both of them writers and journalists.

MAGDALEN GOFFIN contributed a much discussed essay in *Objections to Roman Catholicism*. She is the daughter of the writer E. I. Watkin.

JOHN M. TODD, author of many books, is a director of Darton, Longman & Todd, the Publishers.

T. L. WESTOW, who lives in the West country, is a writer with particular interests in European Catholicity.

ANDREW BOYLE has written lives of Group-Captain Cheshire, V.C. and Field-Marshal Trenchard and is on the staff of the B.B.C.

RONALD BRECH was on *The Economist* and is an economics business adviser.

DANIEL CALLAHAN, author of *Honesty in the Church* is on the staff of the *Commonweal* (U.S.A.).

ARCHBISHOP ROBERTS, S. J. has written *Black Popes* and his life has been written and is being published by Darton, Longman & Todd at the same time as this volume.

E. I. WATKIN, the father of Magdalen Goffin, has written a great number of books on religion, spirituality and history.

dom of men and women of prayer, has become increasingly predominant in the constitution and government of the Church. A new legalism took shape binding men's minds as strictly as the Jewish code their bodies. Today the destruction of this letter, an externally imposed fundamentalism and legalism, is opening the way to a dispensation of the spirit.[1] In the same passage St Paul pointed out that the glory investing the inauguration of the new dispensation exceeded the glory which invested the inauguration of the old. 'If the dispensation of death ... carved with letters on stones came with such splendour ... will not the dispensation of the Spirit be attended with greater splendour.'[2] Surely the splendour investing the third dispensation, a dispensation of the Spirit in its fullness, a further withdrawal—ascent from letter to spirit, must be far more splendid. For its splendour will arise from the profoundest depth where the human spirit is invaded and possessed, transfigured and deified by the Divine and extend to its external and bodily expression a numinous worship, a worship more beautiful and more numinous than the most splendid liturgical worship hitherto.

[1] A future Kingdom of the Spirit is the theme of Ibsen's *Emperor and Galilean* and surely is foretold by a Russian poet Mayakovsky in revolt against Marxist orthodoxy and oppression: 'From the depths of time a ... third revolution rises, the revolution of the Spirit'. (Quoted in *Observer*, May 2, 1965.)

[2] II Corinthians ii. 17.